INFORMAL READING DIAGNOSIS

A Practical Guide for the Classroom Teacher Second Edition

GWENNETH RAE · THOMAS C. POTTER

What of the research that suggests that the child's self-image, which is interpreted as feelings and attitudes concerning one's own abilities, is the most genuine indication of probable school success? And how can children feel successful if the way their parents and/or teachers evaluate them is not positive?

As the authors suggest, "These questions and many others require creative and cooperative solutions. They also require an investment in time and energy by all concerned." The answers illustrate the topics discussed in **Informal Reading Diagnosis: A Practical Guide for the Classroom Teacher, Second Edition.** The up-to-date material challenges parent and teacher regarding the controversial issues of teaching reading methods and evaluation.

This book offers many stimulating and practical ideas. Part I: Diagnosis and Nature of Reading; Part II: Early Reading Skills; Part III: Reading Skill Assessment; and Part IV: Reading: Function and Fun. An abundance of informal reading tests cover memory, oral language, oral reading, silent reading, study skills, attitude and interest, and literary interpretation.

GWENNETH RAE

University of Rhode Island

THOMAS C. POTTER

California State University, Northridge

INFORMAL READING DIAGNOSIS

A Practical Guide for the Classroom Teacher

Second Edition

PRENTICE-HALL, INC., ENGLEWOOD CLIFFS, NEW JERSEY 07632

Library of Congress Cataloging in Publication Data

Rae, Gwenneth.
    Informal reading diagnosis.

      Authors' names in reverse order in the 1973 ed.
      Bibliography: p.
      Includes index.
      1. Reading—Ability testing.   2. Educational tests
and measurements.   3. Education, Bilingual.   I. Potter,
Thomas C., joint author.   II. Title.
LB1050.P67 1981   372.4   80-16912
ISBN 0-13-464628-2
ISBN 0-13-464610-X (pbk.)

To my chosen family, who sustain and enrich my life
GWENNETH RAE

To my children, Linda and Eric
THOMAS C. POTTER

Editorial supervision and interior design: Serena Hoffman
Cover design: Rita Kaye Schwartz
Manufacturing buyer: Edmund W. Leone

Printed in the United States of America

10 9 8 7 6 5 4 3 2 1

PRENTICE-HALL INTERNATIONAL, INC., *London*
PRENTICE-HALL OF AUSTRALIA PTY. LIMITED, *Sydney*
PRENTICE-HALL OF CANADA, LTD., *Toronto*
PRENTICE-HALL OF INDIA PRIVATE LIMITED, *New Delhi*
PRENTICE-HALL OF JAPAN, INC., *Tokyo*
PRENTICE-HALL OF SOUTHEAST ASIA PTE. LTD., *Singapore*
WHITEHALL BOOKS LIMITED, *Wellington, New Zealand*

Contents

Reading Tests

Preface

The teaching of reading has remained controversial in the years since the first edition of this book appeared. Demands for teacher accountability have escalated, and the multiple pressures of a complex society have produced confusing and occasionally conflicting messages.

Quality education is the common goal, but whose concepts of quality? The school board's? The parents'? The principal's? The teacher's? The cry "Back to Basics" is countered by "We need to take them where they are." The desire to maximize individualized instruction is often in conflict with the reality of inflation-bound budgets.

And what of the research that suggests that the child's self-image, which is interpreted as feelings and attitudes concerning one's own abilities, is the most genuine indicator of probable school success? And how can children feel successful if the way their parents and/or their teachers evaluate them is not positive? These questions and many others require creative and cooperative solutions. They also require an investment of time and energy by all concerned.

For teachers to be accountable in teaching reading, they need adequate information to effectively justify curriculum decisions. For teachers to maximize individualized instruction within a limited budget, they must use teaching time efficiently. If teachers can recognize specific pupil needs, they can avoid redundancy by use of grouping. Knowing the strengths of each child and teaching to enhance self-image demands a high level of expertise from the teacher. Successful learning rests on the teacher's willingness to seek this information and use it to make the programs meaningful and exciting. Accountable, efficient, successful teaching is a worthwhile and attainable goal. We hope this volume will prove helpful in achieving such a goal.

The present edition of this text is designed to provide inservice and preservice teachers and appropriate paraprofessionals with background information in the theory and practice of diagnosis, along with specific instruments in the major skill areas of reading.

The book has been updated to include material appropriate for culturally divergent classrooms and has been reorganized to be more directly useful in the classroom. The appendix has been greatly expanded to provide copies of all the tests, so that the teacher does not have to retype them for the children's use. Permission for readers to copy this material for classroom use is hereby granted and remains an important facet of this material.

This volume cannot be all things to all people. Decisions to include some materials and delete others were necessary to maintain a workable size and still provide as many alternative testing formats as possible. Posttests, additional bilingual tests, and in-depth discussions of many topics were deliberately omitted in most cases for the sake of practicality. It is assumed that those using this text will expand, change, and replicate the material to suit their individual needs and interests. For example, the sample record sheets at the end of the chapters can be adapted to the various blank forms in Appendix I to meet the specific needs of each class. Naturally, it is our hope that most of the text will be directly usable as presented, but we recognize our limitations and trust to the common sense of the user.

The work could have never been completed without the assistance of many people whose advice and encouragement were of great value. The authors particularly wish to thank C. Ray Graham of California State University, Northridge, Thomas Bean of California State University, Fullerton, and Nelida Lopez Lucas and Nancy Feldman, whose love and knowledge of the Spanish language improved the manuscript in most significant ways. Evelyn Bautista Lum provided critical advice and much relevant information of this work; her inspiration helped to see us through. And finally, thanks to Irene Nichols and Alexis Langford, who undertook and completed the monumental job of cut-and-paste typing. Thank you all.

Gwenneth Rae
Thomas C. Potter

DIAGNOSIS
AND
THE NATURE OF
READING

1

Overview of Testing
and
the Diagnostic Process

Life in a complex and fast-paced society such as ours is often hectic and exasperating. Life within the classroom usually reflects the same complexity and demands much of both the teacher and pupils. Classes are large. Children are varied in interests, needs, and abilities. And teachers are pressed to seek better ways to guide children in the learning process. These demands have led many educators to advocate increased individualization of instruction.

A variety of factors has contributed to this need for individualization. Dissatisfaction with the isolation of children who have special needs has led to the concept of *mainstreaming,* incorporating these children into the regular classroom. Teachers can increasingly expect to work with children with a variety of physical and/or emotional handicaps who were previously in special classrooms.

Decisions of state and federal courts have integrated large numbers of schools through busing of children to other areas of the city or suburban community. These shifts in the school population create classrooms in which widely diverse language and cultural backgrounds co-exist.

Even when children stay within their own community, the demand for bilingual bidialectal programs requires the teacher to use more diverse skills and educational strategies to develop an effective program.

Many educators believe that the degree to which teachers meet the needs of the individual child will usually determine the effectiveness of instruction in any subject area. This factor not only affects the learning of elementary school subjects, but lays the foundation for learning experiences in the secondary schools. The only meaningful classroom setting is that which reflects the interests and the works of the children who spend six or more hours each day within its walls.

It comes as no surprise that the larger number of children within the classroom, the smaller the gains in skill and attitude development. As children are grouped into larger and larger sections, the range of interests and abilities increases geometrically. This inevitably results in lessening the immediacy and the continuity of instruction for the individual child in even the best instructional setting.

It is evident that not all children in a classroom need or can benefit from instruction in all phases of a skill or subject area at the same point in time. In fact, some children learn a substantial amount of material incidentally, while other children need carefully structured experiences to acquire the same skills. One study showed that a large proportion of beginning third graders knew half the words they were to be taught in the basic readers of both the third and fourth grades. The child who develops many basic skills early in his or her academic career may find that much of what is subsequently taught is highly repetitive. Boredom is a deadly enemy in the classroom. While individualization of instruction cannot guarantee maximum progress for every child, it can provide more of an opportunity for the teacher to assist the child by establishing more efficient learning through appropriate instructional sequences.

Every child needs time and attention from the teacher. The more specific and direct the contact, the more learning is likely to take place. But this does not imply that group instruction should be banned from the classroom. Grouping certainly has a significant and proper place. When a group is formed for a specific purpose, and when it has been determined that the children do in fact need the skills and attitudes for which the group was formed, then group instruction becomes an effective and efficient means of teaching. Flexible grouping to meet specific needs is the key concept here.

Whether we are teaching on an individual or a group basis, we still must deal with two fundamental questions: What can the child already do in relation to a particular learning objective? What gaps in skills and attitudes does the child have that may prevent him or her from learning the task? The development of effective teaching strategies must be based on sound answers to those questions.

Diagnostic teaching is a direct attempt to address these fundamental issues. A teacher who attempts to be a diagnostician is sensitive to the development of the entire child. Effective diagnosis requires the gathering of information from all available sources, including school records, previous teachers, direct observation (both in the school setting and in the home environment, if possible), and assessment through appropriate formal and informal tests. Information is then recorded in a usable way and meaningful teaching can begin.

PRINCIPLES OF DIAGNOSIS

Diagnosing a child's past learning and present capabilities is a demanding task for any teacher. Yet it is a task that promises great rewards in increased teacher effectiveness and the best possible utilization of resources.

Some general principles of diagnosis are:

1. *Diagnostic testing is the basis for making curriculum decisions.* Detailed information is necessary for making decisions regarding each child as an individual.

2. *No assumptions should be made about the effectiveness of previous instruction or the child's retention of those lessons.* For example, just because a child is in the third grade, we cannot assume that he or she has mastered the tasks traditionally taught in the first and second grades.

3. *Diagnosis must start with measurement of the more general abilities.* With this information, specific areas of difficulty can be selected for further testing. As more information is gathered in these specific areas, the teacher will be able to develop a suitable plan of instruction.

4. *Diagnosis is an ongoing process.* In areas where weaknesses are found, it is best to use diagnostic tests frequently to verify original test results and to determine changes in student abilities.

5. *Tests must be built from samples of the actual behavior being studied.* A teacher cannot know how well a child comprehends silent reading from a test of oral reading comprehension. There is little evidence for transfer of knowledge or skill from one type of performance to another. Information gathered in an inaccurate manner will not lead to appropriate teaching strategies.

6. *Children must be informed of the nature of their strengths and weaknesses.* Then they should be told why they should work in a certain way. This will encourage them to continue with a difficult task.

7. *Children should be rewarded for the effort they put forth.* The teacher should not dwell on incorrect responses. A child deserves to be rewarded if he or she is trying to accomplish an assigned task, regardless of the correctness of the responses. Children's efforts may be more closely related to their real abilities if they feel that they will receive approval or recognition for their efforts. This approach often reduces anxieties that many children show in a test situation. A feeling of defeat frequently accompanies repeated failure in any endeavor. This is particularly true of reading difficulty.

8. *Diagnostic procedures should be as short as feasible in order to obtain reliable information.* In most skill areas it is more

important to determine an individual's ability to perform a given task than to determine stamina or fatigue rate. The short test is best for ensuring maximum attention to the problem at hand.

9. *Instructions should be clear.* Concise language ensures the child's understanding. If an individual's score on a test is low, it may be impossible to determine whether the result arises from a weakness in the skill tested or a misunderstanding of the instructions.

With these concepts in mind, we can explore the diagnostic process in more detail. The principal means of gathering specific information is a test of some kind. In a clinical setting, an entire battery of intelligence and personality tests can be administered by trained people. In the classroom, however, a combination of informal diagnostic tests and standardized achievement tests is appropriate.

TYPES OF TESTS

Informal Diagnostic Tests

A wide variety of informal techniques is used by all teachers. *Informal tests* are defined as nonstandardized procedures for gathering information about a child. In order to obtain data on the relative skill development level of the children at the time that the test is given, teachers generally use specific *criterion-referenced tests.* These tests give information on immediate learning objectives selected by the teacher. Their use provides specific information on each child in relation to explicit criteria, for example, whether the child can recognize primary colors. The criterion is the actual task of identifying particular colors. The child either can or cannot perform the task; therefore the information gained is specific and directly related to classroom goals.[1] Informal tests are usually flexible and can be modified to meet a particular instructional need. They can be easy to administer and check.

The purposes of informal tests include:

1. Establishing base level skills in a given subject.

2. Determining progress in a particular activity.
3. Screening to determine which children may best profit from particular instructional plans.
4. Indicating an instructional sequence for a particular child.
5. Determining the nature of oral English competencies for speakers of divergent languages and dialects.

Standardized Tests

Most standardized instruments can be defined as those seeking information concerning overall functioning in relation to a broad skill area, such as the reading level of the child. This type of test is initially given to a large number of people whose scores are then used as the standard by which later groups are compared. For example, if in a particular reading test most third graders originally received a score of 50, that would become the "norm" for all future third graders taking the test. Also standardized are the explicit directions and format of the tests; these should be followed exactly each time the test is given. In this way the results will be most comparable to the original group tested.

Standardized tests have been used to accomplish some or all of the same purposes as informal tests. In addition, they are especially well suited to the following purposes:

1. Evaluating new programs.
2. Allowing comparisons of various groups to determine teaching or material effectiveness.
3. Developing an Individual Education Program (IEP) for children with special needs, such as extensive learning disabilities, emotional problems, or a physical handicap that interferes with regular classroom learning.

The strengths of standardized instruments are their general validity and reliability, their large group norms, their carefully developed administration procedures, and their efficient scoring procedures.

But these very strengths also contribute to the weaknesses of standardized instruments for classroom diagnosis. Frequently the group used to establish the norms for a particular test may not be comparable to the group to

[1]Not all informal tests are criterion-referenced, however. A wide variety of formats is possible. For more information on the criterion-referenced format, see Popham and Husek, 1969, or Popham and Baker, 1970.

be tested; for example, the groups could be from different socioeconomic or ethnic backgrounds. If the mean (or average) score of a group being tested is at either end of the original norming curve, the accuracy of the resulting standardized scores should particularly be questioned. A test's power of discrimination is often crude and inaccurate if the scores are at the extremes of the test. For example, if a group of children perform poorly on a particular test, it may be because there were not enough questions or items at their level to assess performance accurately.

A standardized test frequently depends less on specific criterion referenced tasks matched to classroom performance than on the ability to transfer learnings to new situations, for example, the ability to reason out a general problem. Thus low scores may indicate poor ability in the skill being tested, or poor transfer skills, or both. This means that the teacher has little data on which to plan curriculum.

On occasion teachers are given only total scores from a particular test. For example, they may be told a child reads at a fourth grade, 5-month level. While a number of children may attain the same result, they may have missed entirely different questions for entirely different reasons. Global scores give little information on which to base specific skills instruction.

The necessity for rigid adherence to specific procedures and time limits with standardized tests may cause confusion, particularly among young and inexperienced test takers. This lack of flexibility can cause children to fail a task on which, under more relaxed circumstances, they might have been able to succeed.

Reading achievement and intelligence tests are the most common standardized tests used in the school setting. Whether they are administered in the classroom, in a group situation, or individually by the appropriate school personnel, they can be especially misleading if the child's primary language is not standard English. No matter what the child's ability, a test given in an inappropriate language will produce a poor score. Unfortunately, current research suggests that a teacher who encounters such scores on a child's records adjusts his or her expectations for that child accordingly. The expectation that the child will perform below average is communi-

cated in a variety of ways to the child, who incorporates that assumption into his own self-image. This circular path creates a self-fulfilling prophecy that becomes harder to break with each succeeding experience.

This constellation of weaknesses limits the usefulness of standardized tests in the day-to-day diagnostic procedures of the classroom teacher and makes a file of specific informal tests a highly valuable adjunct to teaching. Although informal tests can also be administered inappropriately, their flexibility allows for a language shift more easily than with standardized instruments.

Ideally, information from standardized instruments can be used in conjunction with results from informal tests, thereby making the teacher's curriculum choices more comprehensive and meaningful. For example, a child with a learning disability who is mainstreamed in the regular classroom needs an in-depth evaluation by a team of specialists (school psychologist, speech teacher, social worker, etc.). This evaluation is used to develop an IEP (Individual Education Program), as mandated by federal law. The teacher's use of informal tests can provide information that supplements the specialists and possibly alerts them to *program* concerns they might overlook. Thus the individual child can be helped to learn better, and the teacher's program for that child and for the entire class can be enhanced.

USING INFORMAL TESTS

Generally speaking, informal tests fall into two broad categories: individual tests, which are given on a one-to-one basis, and group tests, which are administered to more than one child at a time. Each type of test offers strengths and weaknesses for the classroom teacher.

Individual Tests

When we work with a child on a one-to-one basis, we can gather more information than when he is "lost" in the crowd. This is especially true when we are looking at reading behavior. During an oral reading test, for example, we can not only determine the reading level of the child, but also record the kinds of reading error he makes. Is he guessing at words? Does he reverse words and say "ton" for "not"? Does he use only the initial consonant as his clue to the whole word? In addition, we can gather information about his attitudes and general level of performance. Is he tense? Does he act as if he were upset or afraid?

Information of this type can help us to select not only appropriate materials but also appropriate techniques, such as the pacing of the child's lessons, the kinds of reassurance he needs, and the amount of pressure he can accommodate in order to do his best. When carefully recorded and analyzed, this kind of information can lead to many new insights for the teacher.

While some informal tests are designed to be given individually, many are group tests. Any group test can be administered individually, however, when more specific observations of the child's behavior during testing are desired.

Individual testing gives the teacher one important advantage when working with the linguistically unique child: an opportunity to observe individual language differences that the instrument being used is not specifically designed to test. For example, a Spanish-speaking child may be reading orally in English and seem to mispronounce medial vowels by omitting or substituting sounds such as "bat" for "but." The alert teacher realizes that these are not errors in basic decoding but rather pronunciation problems which may stem from a variety of sources, including specific conflicts in the two language systems. Mispronunciation requires a different teaching strategy than a decoding error.

The principal drawback to individual testing is the amount of teacher time it requires. Rarely will the rest of the class consent to disappear while a teacher works with one child. Thus the teacher finds it necessary to do a great deal of planning for independent activities when he or she wishes to do individual testing. Whether the additional information is worth the extra time and effort will depend on the needs of the child and the energy of the teacher.

Group Tests

Group testing can make it possible to gather great quantities of data in a relatively short period of time. Efficient scoring procedures can minimize correcting time, thereby making these tests both easy and economical to give.

Basically, the child can respond to visual or oral information. These inputs or some combination of the two can be used in both group and individual testing procedures. The types of responses will vary considerably with the kinds of abilities being tested. For example, the child's ability to comprehend spoken language can be measured by her written response; her demonstrational response, such as pointing to an object or holding up a card; or, in case of individual testing, her oral response. It is inadvisable to gather group test data from oral responses. Children will be influenced by other children's responses and will be distracted by the presence of the others.

ADMINISTERING INFORMAL TESTS

A child's responses in a test situation basically fall into two categories: recognition and production. In the first, the child is asked to identify the picture, letter, word, or word combination called for. In the latter, the child must generate the answer either orally or in writing. While the recognition response is in many respects an adequate means of identifying a child's strengths and weaknesses, the process of generating an answer will give considerably more information about the child's productive ability. If the child can produce the correct answer at the recognition level but not the productive level, different teaching strategies will be needed; thus the teacher can identify the most effective methods as well as content for a particular individual.

A teacher can administer the same basic material in different ways. A phonics test can be given with pictures at one time, administered orally at another, and read and written silently at a third. These techniques allow individuals to demonstrate competence in a particular skill even though they may have a limited capacity to express ideas or communicate interests.

Varying the method of administration seems especially appropriate in light of some of the more recent research on individual learning styles. It seems probable that some children learn or respond better to visual stimuli than to oral stimuli while others learn in the opposite manner.

When the dialect or language spoken by the child is not that spoken by the regular teacher, classroom aides or teachers who speak the child's home language may be most useful in test administration. If an aide who has been well trained to administer tests can explain directions, the test results are more likely to reflect the ability of the child than if the test is given using only standard English.

For any test, whether individual or group, the purposes of the test should be clear in the minds of both teacher and pupil. To yield the most accurate information possible, the student should feel a commitment to doing a good job. He will usually cooperate more fully if he understands that the test's purpose is to find the best ways to help him learn, not to assign him a particular grade on his report card.

DEVELOPMENT OF TESTING PROGRAMS

Initial Testing

At the beginning of each school year the teacher usually receives an inadequate profile of the individual's skills. In most instances data are at least three months old, and even this information may be inadequate for a sound diagnosis. Certainly all new children who have not been a part of a curriculum familiar to the teacher will need to be carefully examined. Initial tests may assess both oral and silent reading with the aim of establishing a general level of reading competence for each child. It must be emphasized, however, that this is by no means the end of the diagnostic process.

As with standardized testing, two children may score at the same level in reading and yet have very different sets of skills contributing to that result. For example, two children may reach a score that indicates a third grade reading level. But one may be very strong in word attack skills and relatively lacking in comprehension skills, perhaps because of deficiencies in background language experiences and the accompanying vocabulary development. The other child, apparently at the same grade level, may have highly devel-

oped comprehension skills but poor decoding skills. Because of this diversity of skills, additional testing may be desirable to ascertain particular strengths and weaknesses in relation to each skill needed for the task. Inventories that check various decoding skills, such as recognition of long and short vowel sounds, or tests for the degree of standard English oral fluency in a speaker of nonstandard English, may be used depending on the functioning level and the needs of that particular group of children.

When testing young children or those who are entering a regular classroom for the first time at any age level, it will also prove useful to assess social and emotional maturity. If the child's attentional skills are poor, for example, native ability and good teaching may still not provide enough input to compensate for this difficulty. Special teaching techniques will be needed, as well as a large dose of patience. Children who are being mainstreamed from smaller special classes may find it especially difficult to interact with the large numbers and active pace of the normal classroom. Informal assessment of attention span, ability to follow directions, cooperation, and other related areas will be useful during initial testing.

As data are collected, they must be recorded in a meaningful and usable way. Class record sheets, group and individual check sheets, and individual reading profile sheets are highly useful for this purpose. Group records allow the teacher to get an overview of the skills and abilities of the class and make grouping for specific skills easier. Check sheets and individual profile sheets can then be made listing only those skills that need to be taught. These devices allow the teacher to plan meaningful and appropriate learning for the class. The teacher may also use this sheet to keep track of progress for the group and the individual. Examples of record-keeping devices are shown in Chapter 2.

The initial testing period, then, provides the teacher with base line data for designing curriculum and for measuring the effectiveness of the teaching as the year progresses. The retesting of the skills that are essential to satisfactory completion of the program will give the teacher information on the growth of each child at key junctures.

Ongoing Testing

Teachers take for granted testing for retention of new material. Diagnosis is a continual process, however, and the teacher will find many times during the semester when retesting is appropriate. It is too often assumed that the child will remember a skill and be able to utilize it two or three months after learning it. As teachers recheck periodically, they may find that they need to reteach certain skills. Learning gaps are not unusual for any of us. Sometimes our attention wanders or we are absent on the wrong days. Children often feel frustrated when they recognize they are slipping behind and aren't quite certain where the problem lies.

New students naturally require the same type of testing that was used at the beginning of the semester. In areas of highly transient population, inventories can be put on tapes so that a youngster can be assessed with a minimum of disruption of the regular class schedule.

Testing may be necessary at other points because the child develops or the teacher recognizes a problem that was not evident before. If a particular child's performance takes a sudden dip the teacher will want to spend some time to discover the source of the problem. Often this process requires more specialized individual testing than the procedures used earlier.

Tests given at the end of the semester permit an assessment of group and individual gains. They also provide information on the general effectiveness of the teacher's program. An objective look at the year's accomplishments and failures can greatly aid the teacher in planning for personal growth.

Finally, from an ongoing testing program the teacher will be able to provide data to administrators, supervisors, and others interested in the development of programs. These data are vitally necessary to the continued modification and evaluation of materials and techniques for effective teaching. Teacher accountability, a watchword in many school districts these days, can rest on data which show clearly where each child began and what steps were taken to bring the child to his or her present performance level. This approach provides the best base for efficient, successful teaching.

All these factors make diagnostic teaching an important tool for the classroom teacher.

The following chapters discuss the particular instruments in the repertory of informal diagnostic testing and give more detailed information on the testing process and on meeting special needs.

2

A Model of Reading and Assessment Management

This chapter will provide a convenient sequence of reading skills, outlining the reading process and then discussing various aspects of managing the assessment procedure.

Experts in the reading field have developed elaborate models to explain the reading process. While these models have many implications for educational research, a simple view of the reading process is all we require.

We will assume that the reading process starts with the reader seeing print. This neurophysiological process includes the reader's perception that this image is, in fact, something to be read, that the print has a purpose. The transformation of this image into meaning, either expressed or internalized, is the process of *decoding*. Whether the child recognizes the words "by sight"—that is, as a whole word she has memorized—or as separate sounds blended into a word, she is still utilizing a decoding process. The reader then attaches meanings to these words from both past experience and the context in which the words appear. The child modifies the initial meanings she has grasped as she perceives surrounding meanings within the passage. Any particular reading act can thus be seen as the total process leading from the neurophysiological assimilation of print to the reader's thought processes and potential reactions to what has been read.

SEQUENCE OF READING SKILLS

It is well to remember, however, that the reading act, like any other process, comprises preexisting skills and internal components that affect and even extend the act itself. Just as a child must scrawl in large strokes before he can develop the skill and dexterity to write his name, so must he master certain prereading skills before he can successfully become an independent reader. And just as the child prints before she can write her name in our more elaborate cursive style, so she masters some reading skills before others.

Below is an outline suggesting a possible sequence of these skills. While no research has shown conclusively that one sequence is superior to all others, it will be easier for us to look at specific skills from this frame of reference.

A. Prerequisite skills
   1. Extensive listening background
   2. Rich oral language development
   3. Auditory discrimination
   4. Visual discrimination
   5. Varied experiential background
   6. Sufficient social and emotional development to attend and cooperate within the classroom setting.

B. Beginning reading skills
   1. Perception of the word as a semantic unit
   2. Letter recognition and naming
   3. Ordering skills
      a. Left-right
      b. Top-bottom
   4. Phonics skills
      a. Sound-symbol relationships (phoneme-grapheme)
      b. Blending
   5. Syllabic analysis
   6. Structural analysis
      a. Inflectional parts
      b. Root meanings
C. Reading comprehension skills (both oral and silent)
   1. Word comprehension
      a. Multiple meanings
      b. Denotative and connotative meanings
   2. Sentence and paragraph comprehension
      a. Literal meaning
      b. Interpretive meaning
   3. Levels of comprehension: Bloom taxonomy
      a. Memory ⎫
      b. Translation ⎬ Literal meaning
      c. Inference ⎫
      d. Application ⎪
      e. Analysis ⎬ Interpretive meaning
      f. Synthesis ⎪
      g. Evaluation ⎭
D. Study skills
   1. Locating information
   2. Organizing information
   3. Adjusting reading rate
   4. Summarizing and abstracting
   5. Utilizing verbal-visual material (charts, maps and diagrams)
E. Analysis and appreciation
   1. Pitch, stress, and juncture patterns in relation to meaning
   2. Similes, metaphors, and analogies
   3. Inferential language
   4. Styles and modes of expression

THE READING PROCESS

With this sequence in mind we can discuss the reading process in more detail. Recent research shows that the infant has highly developed perceptions from the time of birth.

Within a few days, a baby is able to distinguish the mother's voice from other voices and from less meaningful sounds such as a door being slammed. Thus the receptive faculty, the ability to distinguish and understand what is heard, develops before oral language skill.

Naturally the child's earliest oral expression is merely the babbling, crying, gurgling noises of the infant. Toward the end of the first year these sounds become words the parent can recognize. Labels for objects, people, and acts ("mommy," "car," "bye-bye") grow into sentences of increasing complexity as the child matures.

Reception and expression of the oral language are the child's first and, for several years, only means of communication; they are considered most critical in the development of reading skills. The basis for the child's processes of skill development are laid during these early years of language acquisition. We now have evidence that the variety and frequency of exposure to oral language, together with the development of auditory discrimination skills and the opportunity to use expressive language, is the main consideration in the development of language process.

When the child enters school and turns to the task of reading, the visual discrimination task becomes of key importance. This skill must already be highly developed before letter recognition and the ability to identify the relatively small differences between one letter and another will be possible. The child's experiential background influences this beginning reading process, both through attitude (Are books and reading a part of the home life?) and through the vocabulary and knowledge brought to the printed page.

In addition, the social and emotional development of the child will prove vital to all school experiences. The ability to function in a group setting, to cooperate with others and take "turns," and to attend to the tasks presented by the teacher is essential. Without these prerequisite skills, the child may begin reading with a high probability of failure.

Naturally, these prerequisite skills flow into and influence the acquisition of the beginning reading skills. Children possess varying degrees of all of these experiential components as they begin the task of associating meaning and print.

At this juncture, the child has been using words for years. Yet his understanding of words as discrete semantic units may be vague, if, in fact, it exists at all. If the child has been exposed, for example, to bedtime stories in which the reader points to the printed words as the child sees and hears them, he develops an association between the words in print and the sounds of words he hears or generates himself. Understanding that a word functions as the basic building block of printed as well as oral communication is a major beginning step in the reading process.

Naming the letters of the alphabet is also an important part of the process toward the learned association of a particular letter (grapheme) with a given sound (phoneme). The child who does not know the alphabet letters and their sounds is handicapped in acquiring methods for recognizing new words.

Also of major importance in beginning reading are ordering skills, or skills of directionality. Left-to-right or top-to-bottom move-movements of the eye are quite significant in the development of reading patterns.

Acquisition of phonics skills, the relationships between specific sounds and specific symbols, must now be mastered. In languages in which there is only one sound for each letter, this step is relatively easy. In Spanish or Hebrew, for example, reading instruction is considered to be a one- or two-year process by many elementary school teachers because most necessary decoding skills can be taught by the end of the first or at most the second grade. This is followed, of course, by many years of "language" instruction, that is, grammar, composition, and study skills, particularly through the use of dictation exercises. In such instructional planning, reading and decoding are usually excluded as unnecessary after this initial learning period. But in languages like English the association of various different sounds with a particular letter and various different letters with a particular sound makes mastery of the sound-symbol relationship more difficult. English has over 2,000 spellings for its approximately 44 sounds.

Learning the sound-symbol association alone, however, is not sufficient to enable the child to decipher unfamiliar words. The student must also be able to blend these sounds together into a recognizable word. Knowing common letter blends and regular sound patterns (*blue, black, blend* or *pat, cat, hat*) aids this process. Additional aids to independent word attack include the ability to divide words into syllables and the use of structural word analysis to distinguish prefixes, suffixes, and root meanings.

Simultaneous with the acquisition of phonics skills is the assignment of meaning to words encountered in print. Much of the initial meaning of these words is drawn from the children's background experiences in their environment. Virtually all the words that the children use in their initial reading experiences are a part of their regular oral vocabulary and do not require them to master or even consider new meanings. Significant exceptions to this generalization are found among children whose primary language is not English or is nonstandard English. For those children, the mastery of printed English becomes a process of oral language acquisition, and they must acquire such language skill well before they are taught reading skills. Such children therefore need many enriching oral language experiences in a wide variety of circumstances.

Comprehension skills develop and mature as the child encounters words in print that appear in a new context. In the traditional reading circle, a child is asked to pronounce words aloud and discuss their meaning. The child learns that words have multiple meanings and that some words have implied or connotative meaning according to the culture, for example, what does it mean to be "an old bat"? Sound teaching methodology calls for the reading of these passages silently before reading aloud. But whether first contact is silent or oral, in the actual reading process the child finds the words or the word order unfamiliar. While most children find this novel encounter both stimulating and growth producing, it can also be a threatening experience. When children become too anxious, alternative techniques such as choral reading or impress reading (teacher reading while child follows print) can reduce anxieties and facilitate learning.

As sentences combine into paragraphs and paragraphs into stories, the meanings of words and ideas become more complicated. Both literal and interpretive skills become increasingly important. To aid children in their use of these skills, it is important for teachers to understand and use all levels of comprehension questions. A discussion of levels of comprehension will provide a background for understanding and use in assessment.

LEVELS OF COMPREHENSION

In recent studies of levels of comprehension, the earlier teacher's guides in various reading series were found to tap only the lowest or direct recall levels of comprehension skills (Bloom, B. S., et al, 1956; Bloom, B. S., 1968). Children without experience at using higher levels of thinking find it difficult to both "crack the code" and *think* about what they are reading. It has also been shown that if the teacher asks questions exclusively at any one level, it is difficult for the child to transfer to another level when the question type is varied. Benjamin Bloom (1956, 1968) identified seven levels which are applicable to the questions asked before and after the reading of portions of a story. Following is an overview of these levels.

Level I.   *Memory,* or simple recall of information given.
            Question: "Read and find out where Jimmy goes." "What were the five things Sally took with her on her journey?"

Level II.   *Translation,* or changing material into another form with words, art, or other media.
            Question: "Find a word as you are reading that means the same thing as thin." "Make a picture of your favorite part."

Level III. *Inference,* or drawing a conclusion from given fact.
            Question: "What does Juan's dog do that makes you think he is happy?"

Level IV.   *Application,* or using information or ideas toward solving a real-life problem.
            Question: "If you were lost in the store like Peter, what would you do?"

Level V.   *Analysis,* or using information given to draw conclusions and analyze *possible* results.
            Question: "The police officer in our story had been trained

before he could work on his job. What kinds of training were you able to tell this police officer had? What other kinds of training might he need?"

Level VI.   *Synthesis,* or going beyond the information or story in a creative way.
            Question: "If Ping hadn't found his own boat, how else could we have ended the story?"

Level VII. *Evaluation,* or making a judgment, right or wrong, good or bad, based on logical thinking.
            Question: "Was Hud wrong to steal the ham to feed his family?"

Notice that only at the first level is only one answer required or possible. At higher levels the teacher must be able to accept divergent answers and help the children evaluate whether the thinking and logic of the answer are appropriate to the material. Varying the questions and helping children learn to think about their reading material both before and after silent reading can be tremendous aids in improving comprehension skills. A child's reading of a self-selected passage orally to "prove" an answer has much more meaning and vitality than a "round-robin" or "line-a-round" system (each child taking a turn).

In this manner, the child's comprehension skills can keep pace with the increased demand to read and make use of what is read in other subject areas.

ADDITIONAL SPECIAL SKILLS

The need to use reading as a tool makes instruction in study skills a highly important adjunct to the reading process itself. The young reader must learn how to use books for a variety of purposes—to gather information, to generate ideas, to develop problem-solving skills, to experience the literature of mankind. This instruction can begin soon after the child learns to read his or her first words. For example, locating information begins with the child's earliest choices of what passage to read aloud to answer a question from the teacher. Later, locating information in early attempts to "study" a favorite topic will require searching in more than one source. When several sources are utilized, organizing the information becomes a logical necessity. Although direct teaching for such skills as outlining and summarizing will be necessary, the simple procedure of providing a variety of reading resources, such as newspapers, magazines, and filmstrips, aids the student in searching out information.

Skills that flow from a real need or interest are easiest to teach and remember. For example, pointing out the difference in ease and speed of reading in one source versus another as the reader goes from an encyclopedia to a sports magazine can provide a natural understanding of reading rate. Use of charts, maps, and diagrams, while often a late acquired skill that has to be directly taught, can excite and involve the students if the teacher is alert to the interests of the class and the variety of reading material available. These skills will prove of crucial importance as the child moves through upper elementary school and into high school, college, and the adult world.

Finally, the appreciation of literature as language becomes a part of the child's reading skills. Most children have the opportunity to learn about themselves and the world around them vicariously through print. Some children make inferences and gain insights into the subtler shades of meaning in which the printed word becomes much more than written speech and carries the reader far beyond the direct meanings of the words themselves.

This growth in the understanding of inferential meaning and the recognition of styles and approaches in literature is directly related to the amount of reading the child does. The teacher who provides an opportunity for choral verse, dramatic readings, plays, and reading aloud will have fine models for pointing out how pitch of voice, stressed words, and juncture (pauses between words and sentences) change meaning and provide interest and excitement.

Awareness of colorful language such as similes and metaphors is part of any expressive reading program and will become part of the child's written work as well. Frequent exposure to beautiful and imaginative language leads to the development of one's own style and an appreciation of a variety of modes of expression. Just as success breeds success, so does constant and enthusiastic exposure to literature increase the child's desire to read

and understand. Programs that include oral reading by the teacher and discussion and imitation of literary devices greatly increase the child's ability to understand reading and writing.

It is obvious that many elements of this continuum of reading skills overlap and complement one another. The continuum's separate strands are tightly woven together. Some strands begin early, others later, but all contribute to the strength of the whole fabric. Their full development enables the child to reach optimal level as a reader.

MANAGING READING ASSESSMENT

All of the skills in the reading process can be tested by appropriate types of criterion-reference tests. The choosing of tests is only the first step in the process, however. The testing procedures themselves, the way the children are grouped for testing, and the way the results are analyzed and interpreted all have an impact on the usefulness of the assessment process. The rest of the chapter will deal with these management areas.

CATEGORIES OF READING TESTS

There are three categories of tests that can be utilized in the reading area—general assessments, specific inventories, and individual skill tests. Each type of testing is appropriate for particular needs in the classroom. A general assessment is commonly used at the beginning of the year or with a late-entering child. When more information of a specific nature is desired, or where areas of weakness are noted, an inventory is utilized. When an area needs to be pinpointed, a skill test of just the one dimension is administered.

The *general assessment* asks certain broad questions about the child. For example, the ability to respond to written language is a relatively general skill. A child's response to a paragraph that gives specific information or directions can give the teacher some insight into his general reading skills. But if he has some difficulty, the general assessment does not tell the teacher the nature of the child's problem. Does he not know the basic sight vocabulary? Are his decoding skills weak? To find this out we turn to an inventory.

The *specific inventory* lets a teacher pursue hunches as to what the child's particular problem might be. For example, if the child is able to pronounce a large number of words but does not appear to understand them, a comprehension inventory may be called for. This inventory may narrow the problem down to one or two areas of specific difficulty.

Now a *skill test* would be appropriate. For example, if synonyms and antonyms appeared to give a child difficulty during the comprehension inventory, she can be tested in more depth in this area to explore the degree of the difficulty. If she does not understand synonyms or antonyms, she could be taught that concept and given appropriate practice. If she understands simple synonyms and antonyms but has problems with more advanced concepts or shows gaps in understanding, her instruction can be directed to those needs. This process of testing from the general to the specific can save time and energy in the classroom, since only the areas of particular weakness need to be pursued in depth for any particular child.

RECORDING METHODS

Whatever kinds of tests are administered, they will prove of little value unless the information they provide can be recorded in some usable fashion. Recording procedures are critical to the success of a diagnostic approach.

These methods can be divided into three categories: case studies, profile sheets, and check sheets. *Case studies* are in-depth recording for one child and are usually the province of psychological or reading specialist clinics. The Individual Education Program (I.E.P.) that the school compiles for special needs children is one form of case study. They inquire into the child's background; the specifics of medical, psychological, and educational history; and specific data from various tests, including individually administered intelligence tests and personality tests as well as various standardized and nonstandardized reading tests. Such studies are compiled in order to suggest the optimal use of instructional time and resources; however, the classroom teacher generally lacks both the training and the time to conduct them. For this reason we do not recommend a case study unless a teacher wishes to explore in depth a particular concern about a child.

Profile and check sheets, however, can be a great aid in recording informal testing information for both the individual child and the entire class. A cross-sectional *profile sheet* can be constructed for a single individual or a large reading group. Using a profile sheet, the teacher can look at a number of skills for one child or one skill for a number of children to note particular areas of strength or weakness. Two examples follow:

Individual Profile Sheet

Name __John Jones__   Age _____   Grade _____   School _____

	Auditory Perception			Visual Perception		
	Level I	Level II	Level III	Level I	Level II	Level III
High	15	20	20	35	25	20
	(14)	19	19	(34)	(24)	(19)
	13	18	18	33	23	18
	12	(17)	17	32	22	17
Average	11	16	16	31	21	16
	10	15	(15)	30	20	15
	9	14	14	29	19	14
	8	13	13	28	18	13
	7	12	12	27	17	12
Low	6	11	11	26	16	11
	5	10	10	25	15	10
	4	9	9	24	14	9
		8	8	23	13	
		7		22	12	
		6		21	11	
				20		
				19		
				18		
				17		
				16		
				15		

The numbers listed in the Individual Profile Sheet represent all possible scores in each of the tests named at the top of the columns. The circled numbers are those scores attained by a hypothetical child and can be connected to indicate a very general relationship between the various skills. It should be noted that the possible scores do not represent stanines, percentiles, or other directly comparable scores.

	Group Profile Sheet																	
Children's Grade _____ Teacher _____ School _____																		
	Auditory Perception									Visual Perception								
Name	Level I			Level II			Level III			Level I			Level II			Level III		
	H	A	L	H	A	L	H	A	L	H	A	L	H	A	L	H	A	L
John J.	✔			✔				✔		✔			✔			✔		
Sue M.	✔			✔			✔			✔			✔			✔		
Ann B.		✔		✔					✔	✔				✔				✔

Note that on the Individual Profile Sheet different scores on different levels of the tests can indicate equally high performance. This feature is related to both the difficulty of the items and the number of items at each level. On the Group Check Sheet only the high, average, or low position is indicated. Such comparisons enable the teacher to give specific help only to those with a low rating.

Individual and group *check sheets* are used in much the same way as the profile sheets, but they relate to more specific skill needs. For example:

	Group Initial Consonant Check Sheet																				
	✔ Knows item								O Needs work												
	b	c	d	f	g	h	j	k	l	m	n	p	q	u	r	s	t	v	w	y	z
Barbara L.	✔	✔	✔	✔	O	✔	O	✔	✔	✔	✔	✔		O	✔	✔	✔	✔	O	O	✔
Sally J.	✔	✔	✔	✔	✔	✔	✔	✔	✔	✔	✔	✔		✔		✔	✔	✔			
Bobby K.	✔	O	O	O	O	✔	O	O	O	✔											

This type of sheet gives the teacher an overview of the needs of the group. At this point, groups can be formed to teach the specific skills needed without repeating the instruction for those who have already learned it. An individual check sheet for a particular child would indicate a number of different phonics skill areas in much the same way.

Utilization of these kinds of recording devices make the teacher's job easier and more efficient. Examples in this section are hypothetical. However, blank profile and check sheets are included for the tests in the Appendix. The choice of recording instruments will depend largely on the area being tested and the use to which the data will be put. At the end of each chapter tests and skills from the chapter are shown on a sample record sheet.

CONCEPT OF LEVELS

It should be obvious from the discussion of the sequence of reading skills and the nature of the testing and recording process that probably no two children will possess exactly the same skills at the same point in time. Because of this problem, it seems most appropriate to look at the functioning level of the child in relation to the total sequence of necessary reading skills.

Grade levels are customarily assigned to a particular degree of performance in a certain skill. This system provides a convenient if somewhat arbitrary method of communicating with another professional or of measuring growth over time in a given competency. However, grade designations may obscure the functioning level of the child in a given skill. "Third grade level" can mean quite different profiles for two different children, though both may be able to read a given text with a particular comprehension level.

Tests in this book are constructed on the basis of levels corresponding roughly to grades or developmental norms, or on the basis of the components within a skill. In using them to evaluate a child, therefore, caution must be used to specify as thoroughly as possible what skill is being measured and how.

A particular test may have more than one level to indicate the hierarchy of competence in a skill. To illustrate, one of the tests described later in this text, the oral reading paragraphs, comprises seven competence levels. Each successive level represents more difficult vocabulary, longer sentences, and more advanced ideational concepts. Furthermore, some children may operate on level III or IV in a particular skill while others, who are in higher grades and whose overall reading level is higher, may operate only on level II. Thus level scores can hide real differences in performance.

To facilitate cross-referencing and communication, grade level designations will be given for some tests. However, for most skills the levels will indicate a hierarchical relationship within the skill. For example, in the structural analysis test, level I deals with plurals and tenses, which most primary children will be including in their reading repertoire; by level III the test is assessing knowledge of root words, which are generally not studied

until the later grades (fourth to sixth). The teacher need use only those levels which are appropriate to the class.

Some instruments in the book have different subtests for the component parts of a skill. In Chapter 10 the shades of meaning test consists of two parts. One test is for alliteration and word inference and another for synonyms and antonyms. A student may have mastered one of these components but not the other. However, both of these subtests are tapping relatively high-level skills which would not be expected before fourth grade. Difficulty in some part would merely point to areas which should be included or stressed in the reading curriculum of the child.

If the purpose of our testing is to enable us to teach the child what he or she needs to know, beginning at that child's own level, with the skills the child already possesses, grade designations will be meaningless. With a functioning level concept we can concentrate on skills rather than grades.

Also, various programs will vary in the order in which they teach various aspects of a skill. It is expected that the teacher will use judgment as to which levels or parts of tests will be appropriate to the particular class. Therefore we urge that in your assessment profiles you incorporate level designations with caution and that you concentrate on skills as much as is feasible.

INITIATING THE READING TESTING PROGRAM

At the start of every year the teacher is faced with a new challenge and perhaps a new threat: "Where do I begin?" This is a common feeling and most appropriate to the season. The old answer "Begin at the beginning" doesn't quite fit, since we don't always know what the "beginning" is for a particular student. And that, of course, is our cue. We can start by finding out what that beginning point is for each student. To determine that point, we must use a comprehensive testing program. At the beginning of the year relaxed, get-acquainted activities can be interspersed with specific informal tests, including tests for children who may have particular needs related to dialect or foreign language backgrounds. Such a program can prove a valuable and effective start for the teacher and students. This is especially so if it is made clear to the students that the purpose of the testing is to help the teacher discover what each student needs to learn.

Testing should not be approached as a threat or punishment for the student, as is too often the case with both testing and grading. Instead it is a means of getting help. Tests can help the teacher select material that is appropriate, and they can help the student by revealing strengths and weaknesses. In many cases an open, accurate accounting to children of the results of the tests can help them to gain insight into their specific problems and develop increased awareness of the purposes of instruction in the areas in which they have difficulty. To discover these difficulties, however, we need to employ a careful sequence of tests.

In initiating a test sequence, it is important to identify the *general* capabilities of the individual before starting to develop a profile on the *specific* skills that the child possesses. It is especially important to get a general idea of the child's broad reading skills and potential reading levels so that the level of difficulty of the tests that will be given can be adjusted to the student's present capabilities. For example, a child who is already doing some reading generally needs to receive both oral and silent reading tests so that she can be given specific skills tests at a level that will neither frustrate her unduly nor waste time and resources. As a general rule, it is advisable to initiate a specific skills testing program at a level that is well within the child's independent reading level. For some children, this may be as much as two or three levels below the instructional reading level.

The specific skills tests to be used following the general testing battery should be suggested by weaknesses indicated in the general tests. It may even be wise to give some children a few items from each of the specific skills tests to provide a check on the information gathered in the general testing sessions regarding their strengths in different areas. For example, an upper elementary pupil occasionally fails to master some basic skill such as identifying the names of the letters of the alphabet. If each teacher assumes that the child has already learned the skill, this

weakness can slip by undetected year after year.

Tests should be administered in increasingly difficult stages until the child reaches a level of performance that allows a careful analysis of the test results and clearly suggests instructional needs. In other words, we don't know what to teach until the child misses something. Correct responses may tell us what we don't have to teach that child, but mistakes and an analysis of their types tell us how to plan our instructional time more effectively.

Still, it is well to remember that one bit of data on a child is insufficient for constructing an instructional plan. Plans should be based on repeated measures of a given skill with different types of tests to ensure that the information being gathered is, in fact, a reflection of the child's ability in the specific skill rather than a function of his emotional responses to a particular test-taking situation.

SUGGESTED GROUPS OF TESTS

Each of the tests that have been described in this volume are cross-level inventories—that is, they are designed for a variety of competence levels. Since not only do the various students in a class differ in skill level, but also a particular student may vary greatly from one subject or skill to another, the usefulness of a particular inventory with a given individual is best determined by the teacher. The guide that follows is only an approximate indicator of the tests that may be appropriate for various levels of functioning. If the reading process is viewed as a whole consisting of increasingly complex skills that develop both independently and in interaction with each other, the concept of levels of functioning becomes more meaningful than that of specific grades or years in school.

Tests should be selected from the following groupings or from other available tests as they seem appropriate to the particular class or child being tested.

Prereading and Beginning Level Reading Tests

1. Auditory and visual discrimination and memory

2. Entering language skills, where indicated, with particular emphasis placed on oral competency
3. Generative language, including echoics (ability to repeat oral stimuli)
4. Listening comprehension
5. Following directions
6. Alphabet recognition and generation
7. Letter-sound correspondence

Primary Level Reading Tests

1. Oral and silent reading paragraphs
2. Letter-sound correspondence
3. Listening comprehension
4. Blending
5. Syllabication
6. Following directions
7. Alphabetizing skills

Intermediate Level Reading Tests

1. Oral and silent reading paragraphs
2. Blending
3. Syllabication
4. Structural analysis
5. Alphabetizing skills
6. Dictionary skills, including phonetics and definitions
7. Following directions
8. Attitude and interest inventory

Upper Level Reading Tests

1. Oral and silent reading paragraphs
2. Following directions
3. Structural analysis
4. Dictionary skills: phonetics and definitions
5. Study skills, including information location and scanning
6. Literary inference and multiple meanings
7. Attitude and interest

Again it must be emphasized that the general test pattern at the beginning of the year will vary greatly from child to child and from group to group. Some children may need to "hurry backwards," especially if their oral reading paragraphs indicate needs in many skill areas. The least complex level in which the child needs instruction is most important. For example, if the child seems to be having trouble with letter names, his auditory discrimination should be tested be-fore his knowledge of letter-sound correspondence. He must learn to hear differences in sounds before he can hope to learn to associate a particular sound with a particular letter. Since children with reading problems often have multiple difficulties, we must be sure to test at a level that will get back to the basic components of a particular skill.

A teacher will often want to retest an area later in the school year in order to gather data on the effectiveness of the instruction pattern. If a weakness was originally discovered in the area of basic vocabulary development and it now seems to be corrected, it is important to determine whether it really is. In most instances this determination requires an alternate form of the test that was given at the outset of the school year.

An alternate form usually consists of the same type of test with the items modified or rearranged slightly. This is often referred to as a *pretest-posttest pattern*. It is important that both tests be similar in format to provide an equivalence in the testing situation. Alternate forms also guard against the memory effect that appears when the same form is repeated. A child may remember the specific items he missed and choose the right answers on an identical retest not because he has learned them but because he can remember the isolated example from the pretest.

Retesting before the end of the school year on specific curriculum areas not only can assist the teacher in determining the effectiveness of the program, but may also suggest procedural changes to improve instructional efficiency. However, a caution related to retesting must be mentioned. Tests can cause a child anxiety that may be harmful in later learning situations. This is particularly true if the child knows he has numerous difficulties that prevent his achieving at the level of his expectations. If given too frequently, tests can create such tension that they will not measure performance accurately nor permit an atmosphere in which the child can grow at an optimum rate.

FLEXIBILITY OF TESTING PROCEDURES

Increasing the number of items in the sample tests will benefit teachers who want more information on an individual's strengths or weaknesses in a particular skill area. For instance, a particular inventory may contain eight or ten items related to medial vowels but may not identify to the teacher's satisfaction the particular vowels with which the child needs help. Five or ten more items in the same format may pinpoint the problem. This addition could include specific items in the area where the child's class performance has indicated weakness. Language experience stories, for example, can be one source which will give the teacher clues to the child's vocabulary problems. It may be well to consider the problem words as the basis of the additional inventory items. Partial testing is suggested for teachers who wish only to survey the skill areas where more complete inventories are provided. By carefully selecting items from each of the appropriate inventories, the teacher can increase the number of skills tested and decrease the time necessary for testing.

GROUPING FOR TEST ADMINISTRATION

Obviously, the larger the group to be tested and the fewer the number of tests administered, the more efficiently the relevant data can be gathered.

Administration must be carefully planned to ensure that the children clearly understand the directions of the test and are following them properly. A group that is too large for the type of test being given does not provide true efficiency. Many of the informal inventories suggested here can be administered to an entire class of normal children at one sitting. Caution is advised, however, since many classes include children whose under-

standing of oral and written directions and whose ability to work independently for an extended period of time are not as great as those of their peers. Testing in large groups may not be valid for such individuals, and adjustments in procedures will be required. The teacher may find it necessary to place these children in a smaller group and test them under close supervision while the rest of the class works on a test that can be completed independently. The tape recorder with sets of earphones also offers numerous possibilities in testing. Many simple group tests can be administered with it, especially if the teacher checks to see that sample items are done correctly. The machine is also helpful for the inevitable student who enters the class after the beginning-of-the-year testing program is completed.

Some informal inventories in this volume must be individually administered. These naturally include all tests that require an oral response from the child. Such tests can best be given during a recess period, after school hours, or during times when others in the class are working on different projects. A quiet corner reserved for the purpose will help these tests go smoothly.

Considerations in Grouping for Testing

The following concepts are useful in planning for testing:

1. Number of children to be given a particular test
2. Format of test (individual, group, etc.)
3. Number of minutes necessary to give test
4. Alternative activities during small group or individual testing

Sample Block Plan

A possible block plan might look like this:

Third grade, 90-minute reading period

Small group	*Individual testing*	*Small group centers*
Alphabetizing test on tape recorder— 15 minutes Followed by independent skill sheet— 20 minutes	Oral reading paragraphs with teacher— 7 minutes per child— 5 children	Independent work Art Free reading Science table etc.

Whole class: Interest Inventory—20 minutes

Repeat first block by switching groups. *Other hints:* Use other adults and older children to administer some simple tests. Help children in class to understand purposes and work with each other in a manner similar to peer tutoring.

ANALYZING AND INTERPRETING TEST RESULTS

Test results should be recorded on group check sheets and profile sheets such as the ones suggested earlier in the chapter. The individual profile will also be useful in determining a child's specific skill needs at a glance.

The analysis of the results of tests and informal inventories requires skill. If the teacher observes that a child performs a given reading task effectively in class, the teacher should expect the child's performance on a valid test of this skill to reflect this ability. In the same way a child with a day-to-day problem in a particular area should perform similarly on informal inventories. Discrepancies between test results and ongoing performance should be followed up by the teacher.

If the test results support the teacher's initial guesses, then this information should be shared with the child. Children need to become aware of what skills they need. They also need opportunities to work in the skill areas indicated by the inventories, and they need information regarding their progress. The reinforcement and motivation that arise from the analysis of the skill profile become an important part of a child's sense of progress. Seeing for themselves where they stand at different points in time helps children set goals for themselves and increase their feelings of success. Success is the teacher's most powerful ally. The focus should always be on what a child *can* do and what the child needs to learn next.

Another word of caution is in order. Test results are highly personal information. Making them public through such devices as posting a class profile on a bulletin board may be devastating for one child who has a low score. Confidentiality is particularly important for grades and the evaluation of the results of end-of-the-year tests. Positive attitudes and feelings of self-confidence that have been carefully developed during the entire year can be destroyed if this sensitive area is overlooked.

CONSTRUCTION OF INFORMAL READING INVENTORIES

Since every class and every child are unique, there will probably come a time when the teacher requires a new test to meet special needs. The construction of informal inventories is relatively easy if a few general principles are followed.

Format

Each test item should have a format that is simple and easily understood. If the children can see clearly and intuitively the nature of the task, then they are free to concentrate their energies on the test items themselves without being unduly concerned with the mechanics of taking the test. For instance, a child who is asked to use a separate answer sheet before he really understands the correspondence of the test item and the number on the answer sheet may record many answers incorrectly or spend too much time figuring out where the answer goes.

In the primary levels, it is generally preferable to have the kind of test in which the answers are placed on the same sheet as the test item. Intermediate level children generally can be expected to respond to the tests on separate answer sheets without getting test item numbers or other administrative features confused.

The number of steps and the degree of abstraction required of the test taker should gradually increase. Each test should start with items the child can answer easily and quickly so she can establish a solid base in a particular skill area.

We must also consider the child's emotional reaction to the test itself. If children feel that they can succeed in the testing situation, that they can answer some of the items correctly, they are more likely to have a positive attitude toward the entire procedure and are more likely to try to do their best.

It cannot be denied, however, that from a diagnostic point of view, items of appropriate difficulty, that is, at the level where some errors are made, are of more value to the teacher and the reading specialist, since they give us a more accurate picture of the child's problem-solving strategies. A balance between difficult items and "emotional support" items must be found.

Directions

It is important in the development of informal inventories to consider the role of the directions to the student. They should always be behaviorally oriented. This means that each step should require an action that can be monitored by the teacher or another person. Thus the test administrator gains immediate feedback regarding the effectiveness of the directions, since the child must demonstrate that he or she understands the instructions by doing what the instructions ask. Instead of telling the primary grade child to look at the word "directions," for example, the teacher can ask the child to point to or underline the word. The directions should be clear and simply stated. There should be a minimum of words, and each word should clearly state what is to be done. Instructions should use simple words and avoid words the children may not know. An example of clear directions, behaviorly oriented, is: "Put your pencil on the number 1. Now put your pencil on the picture of the cat beside the number 1. Now put your pencil on the word 'cat.' Underline it. Now find the word 'cat' in the box. Underline it. Do not underline any other word in the box."

Test administrators should keep in mind that many children may not know left from right. It is better to label a column with something clearly recognizable to the child, such as a picture of an animal or a star, than to ask the child to look at the left-hand side of the page.

Finally, the directions should contain performance samples. They give the child an opportunity to perform the required task in a practice situation and let the test administrator make sure that the child clearly understands the task by observing him perform it correctly.

Administration

From the point of view of the test administrator, it is important that a test be easy to give. Testing can be unnecessarily time-consuming, both in administration and scoring, unless careful thought is given to the form of the test items and answer sheets and to the steps necessary to arrive at a valid score for each student. A child in the upper grades may express ideas best in an essay format. Yet scoring techniques for essay material are not as efficient as a true-false or multiple-choice format, even though the latter techniques do not yield the amount of information in a reading comprehension test that essays do. This is not to say that essay tests are not appropriate, but rather that other types of tests often will serve the purpose and will save a substantial time in administration and scoring.

Expense is also a factor to be considered. The limited resources at the command of most teachers require that time and materials for tests be used in the most efficient manner possible. An example of low-cost test techniques is utilization of separate answer sheets for intermediate and upper level students wherever possible. This is true in informal inventories as well as standardized tests. The reuse of the test forms with long paragraphs or other involved items may save the teacher many hours of retyping and mimeographing.

Following these simple guidelines in format, directions, and administration should make it possible to create or rework tests as needed to get specific and appropriate information regarding student needs.

3

Cultural Diversity within the Classroom

OVERVIEW

Through many generations, America has been a melting pot in which many divergent cultures have attempted to form a homogeneous milieu. The school has often been the means by which people have acquired an understanding of those who are culturally and linguistically different from themselves. Recently we have acquired new insights and new tools which recognize the value of cultural divergence in the classroom. Assisting pupils to validate and use their own language or dialect while learning is a significant new concept in many classrooms. In short, it is becoming feasible to use different dialects and languages within the instructional setting. Accepting the cultural and linguistic identity of the individual is a necessary component in the development of language skills and attitudes toward language learning.

Modern linguistic studies suggest that most languages include a variety of dialects. These dialects are all valid and appropriate reflections of the various groups within a primary language system.

Dialect is defined as the pattern of pronunciation and word arrangement characteristic of a group; as such, a dialect cannot be judged "good" or "bad." Our society tends to place value judgment on particular dialects, and *standard English*—the language that matches the textbook—is generally regarded as the preferred speech pattern. Textbooks, school learning materials, and the teacher's oral language are usually in standard dialect. This fact usually penalizes the child whose language/dialect pattern does not coincide with one referent. Standard English is a pattern which the child will probably eventually need in order to participate fully in our cultural system. However, this one pattern must not be presented as the "right" or "correct" dialect. Problems in self-esteem and school-family conflict may be the natural results of this limited view of language. The concept of valid language difference is a more appropriate and realistic model for both teacher and child.

This concept of valid language differences can be fostered through the use of reading materials available in a variety of languages and dialects. In this way it is implied that the teacher's language and culture is considered as one of the numerous systems of communication.

THE TEACHER'S ROLE

The skills necessary for learning a dialect or a second language can be more readily appreciated by a teacher who has first-hand knowledge of the difficulties and rewards of learning such a dialect or language. It is suggested that the teacher have an oral command of some of the basics of those languages or dialects used by the children he or she teaches. A sympathetic understanding of the children's language will help the teacher plan an appropriate curriculum which builds on the children's linguistic competence.

When a child feels that she is understood, a sense of trust and mutual respect can grow between herself and the teacher. Only in this atmosphere will genuine learning take place.

Two-way learning should be utilized by the teacher so that the child and teacher have a joint responsibility for the curriculum. The following factors are necessary for the implementation of this two-way learning process.

1. The teacher's willingness to acknowledge the value of the child's language.
2. A class and school environment stressing the importance of integrating the child's culture and language as well as the school's.
3. Frequent and specific feedback to the child on his progress in acquiring new skills in both his primary language and standard English.

In addition teachers should attend inservice classes which focus on the cultural background of the children, including the cultural practices and the historical contributions of the child's culture to our society. Then, in teaching specific items in the curriculum, the teacher can, for example, point out related or parallel events in the history of Hispanics, Chinese, blacks or other groups. An effective way to develop an understanding of the child's home and community is through frequent interaction within the child's culture. That can be accomplished in part through participation in community events, home visits, and school-sponsored open houses and parent-teacher meetings.

A LEARNING MODEL

Whatever the child's primary language/dialect, he or she should acquire language habits through an ordered set of learning experiences that include these characteristics:

1. Intensive practice in listening and speaking in the primary language.
2. Development of oral fluency in this primary language prior to reading in this language.

3. Development of oral fluency in a secondary language or dialect prior to reading in the secondary language.

Once the oral skills in the primary language are well established, the child can begin developing reading skills in that language, a context designed to give early success. The rules that are learned and the competencies that are acquired in the basic reading process can eventually be transferred from one language context to another.

The significance of this method lies in the child's understanding of the "speech to print" process. It must be emphasized that the child's primary language is the vehicle for developing this understanding.

Once the child has sufficient base skills in the primary language, learning to speak and read standard English can become part of a natural progression. As the child matures, he or she will be able to "choose" from several viable options the language/dialect that is appropriate in a particular situation.

APPROACHES TO BILINGUAL EDUCATION

Numerous programs have been used to teach the child who brings to school a primary language other than standard English. The traditional ESL program (English as a Second Language) takes the child from the regular classroom for one or more periods during the day to "learn" English. In this approach, the regular program usually continues in English and there is little or no attempt to integrate the child's language.

Another approach is based on monolingual instruction in standard English utilizing materials in standard English. It employs aides and paraprofessionals in the classroom who can clarify and explain in the child's primary language any concepts and ideas being learned.

The "transition" approach acknowledges the child's primary language through the use of abbreviated materials in that language. However, the elaborated presentation and most printed materials are in standard English. An abbreviated oral program including tapes and records is presented in the child's primary language.

The goal of this type of program is to transfer the child into standard English as quickly as possible. These methods are consid-

ered by some to be appropriate stopgap measures in classrooms where a small minority of the children speak a similar tongue on entering that classroom. However, such programs are usually less effective than a bilingual approach for the classroom in which a large percentage of the children are non-English-speaking. In these classrooms a multilingual aide or teacher is necessary to assist the non-English speakers.

Bilingual programs were mandated by the *Lau* v. *Nichols* 1976 Supreme Court decision. These programs require a more complete approach to language instruction. The decision states that each child has the *right* to instruction in his or her primary language. Most school districts interpret this mandate by instituting programs if 50 percent or more children speak one language other than English. Multilingual classrooms usually use partial approaches.

There are two basic approaches to bilingual instruction. The *dual approach* divides the day or week into English and alternate language segments. Thus the child learns concepts and subject matter in the primary language and spends part of the time learning English. The *concurrent approach* uses both languages in the classroom, with instruction being given in each language simultaneously. The teacher presents a concept in one language and then in the other. Materials for the classroom are written in multiple languages.

The ideal goal of both of these methods is *full literacy* for both the English-speaking and the non-English-speaking child, an approach to language learning that includes culture and history as well as all regular skills in reading and writing.

The celebration of cultural differences is a valuable technique for helping children develop the cultural pride and sense of history that are the rightful heritage of all pupils.

DIALECT DIVERGENCE IN THE CLASSROOM

Since the 1954 Supreme Court decision declaring racial segregation in public schools unconstitutional, cultural and racial heterogeneity has been increasingly evident in classrooms across the country. Busing, whether voluntary or mandatory, is a reality in many school districts, and the new "school community" created by busing presents a challenge to

teachers. Their skills and techniques have to be modified to meet the needs of all their pupils. These facts affect the teaching of reading and the language arts most profoundly. In order for teachers and curriculum planners to use new materials and teaching techniques, and to accept new language patterns, they need to have a thorough working knowledge of the oral language competency of each child in the classroom. When standard English is used as the only instructional language, it is obviously important for a child to know the syntactic and semantic patterns being required. In this case, teachers should test all children to establish the entry skills each child possesses. If a child does not possess these patterns, techniques similar to ESL methods are often used. A game format with repeated sentences (*Susie* will *skip* to the front, *John* will *hop* to the front, etc.), songs, rhymes, and choral verse are all fun as well as instructive.

Another option is to integrate the child's dialect pattern into the classroom instruction. Black English, for example, may be legitimately used as the instructional language, especially when reading is initially taught and when students' language skills do not "match" standard English. For example, there are now reading materials in black dialect for use in the elementary, junior high and high school reading programs. This approach employs teachers or aides who speak the dialect fluently; no attempt to "fake" a dialect will be believed or trusted.

The child's success in reading as well as in other subject areas is directly related to the child's feelings of competence and acceptance in the school setting. Nonacceptance of the child's language is felt as rejection both of the child personally and of his or her home and community environment. It is extremely important to meet with integrity and on equal terms each language and dialect used.

A knowledgeable and understanding teacher and a program that accepts the child "where he is" are the most important ingredients for developing self-esteem.

IMPLEMENTATION TECHNIQUES

The language experience approach to teaching reading lends itself well to the use of dialects and multiple languages in the classroom. Of course, this method requires that the teacher be conversant with the foreign language or the dialect; the child should understand the teacher and the teacher should also be able to speak and write in the language correctly enough to reproduce the child's own stories. It is generally possible for a classroom teacher who is not proficient in the dialect to locate someone in the community, perhaps a parent or a paid paraprofessional, to assist in the development of language experience stories for children.

Ideally, group and individual stories are developed around the common experiences that children have in the school setting. In this way the reading and language process is more meaningful and there is the necessary match between the language of the child and what he or she is expected to read. Phonics and skill lessons use the child's own language to build understanding of the reading process.

Peer tutoring is an effective means by which a dialect or other language can be utilized in the reading process. Frequently, a more able reader who speaks Spanish, for example, may assist another child with less-developed reading skills to learn to read in Spanish. The tutor might first read a story in Spanish to the child and progress to shared reading and finally to having the student read independently.

Research suggests that it is helpful to instruct the tutor in how to work with a younger or less able child in order to make maximum use of time and resources. Some tutors will be able to write a language experience story for a younger or less experienced reader. The tutor/tutee relationship is of course crucial to the success of this process. Care in matching tutors and tutees must be taken. Regular classroom time set aside for peer tutoring can achieve remarkable results both with younger and older children.

Because of the positive relationship that can develop between the tutor and tutee, affective objectives may be attained in the peer tutoring situation which can greatly enhance self-esteem for both children. Of course, it is not suggested that a peer tutoring program should replace an entire reading program, but rather that it is a valuable adjunct to a program initiated by a teacher.

A similar process uses role modeling as a reading aid. Younger or less experienced readers observe and participate with older and more experienced children in the language acquisition or reading process. The *impress*

method, for example, with colorful and interesting reading materials, lends itself to a role-model style. In this type of instruction a child seated next to a more able reader imitates him or her while participating in choral reading of the material. The younger child follows with his eyes and hears and speaks the words at the same time. The several senses "impress" the language pattern.

Bidialectical books and materials are also available and can be used with the above method. Of particular note is a series for upper elementary and secondary children (Simpkins et al., 1977) entitled *Bridge, A Cross-Culture Reading Program.* Similar materials for younger elementary children are also available.

Books for instruction in appropriate languages and dialects should be available in the classroom. These books can be read by all children in a classroom and will assist immeasurably in developing positive attitudes toward cultural differences.

Photography and oral history can be of great assistance to the teacher in helping children develop positive cultural values and self-esteem. Lending an inexpensive camera to a child will help him to become more aware of the community in which he lives and allow him to photograph those things that are meaningful to him in his culture. Filmstrips and tapes by those who are knowledgeable about a culture in which language differences exist will provide information and personal relevance for the individual learner.

The participation of all the children in the classroom in these projects will build mutual understanding. And as the children come to understand each other in the classroom, they learn how a culturally diverse group can develop a working value system. The classroom can become a microcosm for the larger world.

ASSESSING ENTRY LEVEL LANGUAGE SKILLS

Since the primary language is for the most part one's "thinking language," it is not surprising that mental translation is necessary whenever one is learning a secondary language or dialect. This thinking process slows down a child's ability to respond in proportion to the number and complexity of the concepts that are being translated. Time and practice can lead to commensurate skill in both languages but only if care is given to begin at the appropriate level and pace.

This situation suggests a process for evaluating the language skills of the child. For a child whose primary language is not standard English, is there a substantially longer time required to read or to comprehend oral passages in standard English than in comparably difficult material in the primary language? If there is substantial "translation time," then skills specific to the transition process may need to be taught.

Assessing the child's auditory discrimination for English sounds, her understanding of spoken English, and her speech patterns in her primary language or dialect as well as English are all practical and necessary steps in planning instructional strategies.

This text includes tests that will help to identify those skills the child can best learn in the primary language as well as the transition skills required for comprehending and reading standard English. These special tests are in the chapters appropriate to the particular reading skills, as listed below.

Auditory Discrimination Test, Level I, Chapter 4 (conflict points between English and Spanish)

Test of Listening and Repeating: Echoics, Chapter 5 (Spanish and black English conflict points)

Grammatic Understanding Test, Part B, Chapter 5 (black English word and sentence patterns)

Spanish Word List, Chapter 7

Spanish Oral Reading Paragraphs, Preprimer through third grade, Chapter 7

part

II

EARLY
READING
SKILLS

4

Perceptual Discrimination Skills

The child's acquisition of language is a marvelous and complicated process. Every normal infant is born with the capacity to learn any language. Yet within the first year of life, the child learns to match random vocalizations (cooing and babbling) to the speech sounds of the language environment.

In addition to exploring his language, the young child is busy exploring his physical environment. In this *sensory-motor period,* concepts are built and expanded based on the child's active interaction with his world. As the child listens, looks, touches, and tastes, he steadily learns to refine and extend his perceptual discrimination abilities.

As the time for entering school and beginning formal learning approaches, this ability to discriminate fine differences in auditory and visual stimuli will become a vital part of the reading and writing process.

AUDITORY DISCRIMINATION

Auditory discrimination, the ability to differentiate sounds, is one of the most important factors in the acquisition of spoken language. In initial experiences with any language, the listener becomes sensitive to almost imperceptible differences in sounds. *Minimal pairs,* those sounds or patterns that differ in only one way, contribute greatly to the meaning

of speech. Hearing the subtle difference between "big" and "bug" or "stop" and "top" is essential to both the effectiveness of communication and the ability to use phonics as a decoding device in reading.

Phonics instruction depends on the sound-symbol relationships of our language and the child's ability to associate a sound with its corresponding graphic symbol. The child's ability to hear and discriminate the 44 sounds of English is a prerequisite to any such instruction.

Auditory discrimination and phonics skills become more complicated if at home the child speaks a language other than English or if his dialect pattern—the pattern of pronunciation and word arrangement usually associated with a geographical or socio-economic group—differs markedly from that of the teacher or of the reading texts.

In addition, conflict points exist between some dialect patterns within one language system as well as between different language systems. A conflict point is a set of sounds or grammatical patterns which differ in such a way as to be mutually exclusive. Examples include:

1. *Conflicting sound units.*
   The *r* sound in an initial position does not occur in Japanese; therefore a native speaker will substitute the closest Japanese

sound, which becomes *l*: "loof" instead of "roof."

The initial *ch* sound does not occur in Spanish, so the speaker will substitute *sh*: "share" for "chair."

2. *Conflicting grammatical patterns.*

Speakers of black English often do not use a plural *s* if there is a number word in front of the noun, so "see the two boy" is substituted for "see the two boys."

This often means the child must learn additional or alternate sounds orally before she can associate a written symbol with them. For example, the Spanish-speaking child who does not hear the *ch* sound at the beginning of "chair" and says "share" is unaware of the difference and may be confused if the teacher insists she is "saying it wrong." The child must learn to *hear* the sound as being different. Experiences such as pretending to be trains and chugging around the room, or learning a song about Charlie Chipmunk, begin to give the sound meaning in an oral context.

Once the child can hear the sounds and use them reliably in a variety of patterns, a phonics program can be implemented. Therefore assessing the child's auditory discrimination is an important step in the initial phases of learning to read.

VISUAL DISCRIMINATION

Similarly, visual discrimination aids the child in the acquisition of language meanings. Relatively minor differences in the child's environment have great impact on his life. The visual discrimination skills of relatively young children may make the difference between safety and peril, for example, if the child is crossing a busy intersection. The discrimination of a mother's face from that of a stranger, or the correct association of a word label with an object, helps the young child associate meaning and appropriate language with what is seen.

Noting which way the arrow points on a one-way street is a rather obvious discrimination for the adult driver. However, for the young child, shape discrimination is much more global than the subtle discrimination of individual graphic symbols. The difference in configuration or figural outline of a square

and a circle, for example, is relatively clear. However, the configuration of printed words is more complex. For example:

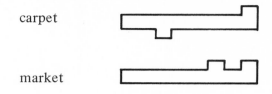

carpet

market

And the differences in the configuration of individual letters can be extremely fine:

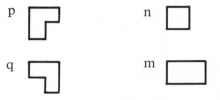

p

q

n

m

Visual discrimination can be further complicated by physical immaturity. The muscles and nerves that control visual perception are often not fully developed until about seven years of age. It is not uncommon for young children to perceive individual letters (*static reversals*) and whole words (*kinetic reversals*) in a right to left direction. Parents and teachers should expect this phenomenon and not be unduly concerned.

Occasionally what is diagnosed as a reversal problem is really more related to the amount of exposure the child has had to printed symbols. Also orientation in space as well as configuration serves to affect conceptualization. Our convention of print from left to right and from top to the bottom of a page is an arbitrary reflection of our own culture. This type of patterning is usually developed quite naturally as the child is read to at home or school and as he views television, billboards, market labels, and so on. However, if a child's exposure to print has been limited or if he has some type of visual impairment, he may need to have these skills directly taught.

AUDITORY AND VISUAL MEMORY

The child's ability to remember auditory and visual sequences taps both her perceptual discrimination skills and her level of cognition or intellectual development. The young child cannot retain and use some concepts until she has had sufficient experience and interaction to be ready to understand and recognize them.

For example, the child will not "remember" that a group of sticks was placed in graduated order (ₗ₁₁₁) until he has developed the ability to place the items in that order himself. Thus, the child who can remember only three or four items in a visual or auditory pattern could not be expected to repeat a phone number readily or spell a four- or five-syllable word.

Memory training itself suggests its own developmental sequence. Maria Montessori developed tasks for children at three levels, appropriate to three steps in learning. The first level is *matching*. At this level a child can put together a group of circles or squares or pick out all of the letter "a's" from a group without needing to know the names or description. At the second level, *identification,* the child can pick out the square or "a" from a varied group when asked, "Which is the square?" or "Point out the A." The label is being provided and the child associates the label with the object. At the third and most difficult level, *recall,* the child is asked, "What is this?" and must be able to supply the label that goes with the object. New material can tap these levels at any age. A college exam with multiple choice questions is operating at the identification level, whereas an essay exam will require recall and other memory skills. Some caution must be exercised that the correct level of memory is being assessed when one is evaluating the child's knowledge and abilities.

TACTILE DISCRIMINATION

Tactile discrimination, the ability to differentiate stimuli that are perceived through the sense of touch, is perhaps the least developed of the senses that may be useful in acquiring language facility. Children with various types of physical handicaps may need to use touch as a primary basis for learning. Blind children using Braille would be the most obvious example. However, techniques for children with other difficulties, including palsied, neurologically impaired, and deaf, have been developed. Some methods use body movement (kinesthetics) as well as the tactile sense. As more children with

special needs, including various physical handicaps, are *mainstreamed* into regular classrooms (as required by federal law 94-162) the need for teaching activities that include all the senses will become increasingly important.

Children with only minor difficulties or with no real reading problems can also find the tactile and kinesthetic senses useful as an adjunct to the more usual visual and auditory approaches. Grace Fernald developed a word-tracing technique in which the child traces the letters of a word with the finger while repeating them. After several repetitions, the child turns the paper over and writes the word from memory, thus getting an additional type of experience to aid the memory process. Other techniques, such as tracing letters in trays of sand or clay, rolling clay strips to form letters, using sandpaper or felt word cards, or playing hopscotch and jump rope to a letter rhyme, are all useful and novel enough to be fun for the learner.

Both listening and reading, the receptive skills, and speaking and writing, the generative language skills, are affected by the child's perception. Testing of perceptual discrimination is a useful starting point in assessing the child's readiness for more formal reading instruction.

AUDITORY DISCRIMINATION TEST

The auditory discrimination test, like all tests described in this volume, begins with items considered easy and appropriate for beginning elementary school children. Level I is most useful if given individually and should be administered before any phonics program is begun. Level II requires more sophisticated responses since some nonsense words and multiple syllables are included. This level is appropriate for children who have some reading skill and are beginning to decode by syllables.

Each level of this test contains 30 word pairs; 21 of the pairs are dissimilar, 7 varying in the beginning, 7 in the ending, and 7 in the medial sounds. The other 9 are identical pairs, to ensure that the child is not responding by rote. In Level I three sets, 2, 22, and 25, are words which contain conflict points between English and Spanish. Having 7 pairs vary in each position makes it possible to analyze the child's particular type of auditory problem. Initial position differences *(allitera-tive)* are the easiest for young children to discern. Ending positions are slightly more difficult since words in regular speech may be run together or pronounced indistinctly. Work with rhyming is appropriate for children who have difficulty in this area. The varying sounds in medial positions are usually vowels and are the hardest to distinguish. If a child under seven has difficulty with medial sounds this problem should not cause too much concern; it may be developmental and not related to beginning phonics teaching. More than four errors, especially if scattered throughout the positions, is an indication of possible difficulty and should be followed up with additional testing including a possible hearing test.

It is important to make sure the child understands the concept of "same," "not same" before beginning. Some children respond to the idea of "twins—being just alike." It may be helpful to practice with several word pairs with obvious differences before starting the test: "I'm going to say two words and you tell me if they are just exactly the same, like twins, or if they are not the same. 'jump—run.' Are they the same or not the same? What about 'dog—Dog'?" and so on. Be careful to speak naturally without dropping your voice on the second of paired words or overarticulating.

In Level II the test may be administered to a group if the teacher desires. Sample answer sheets are shown at the end of this section

AUDITORY DISCRIMINATION TEST: LEVEL I

Directions to the teacher:

Turn the child away from speaker to avoid lip reading. Have a printed copy for marking errors. More than four errors indicates difficulty. Give the child several examples before beginning. In the list below, the position of the sound is indicated by E for ending, M for medial, and B for beginning.

Directions to the child:

Tell me "Same" if the two words that I say are the same. Tell me "Not the same" if the two words that I say are not the same.

E	1.	pat - pad	M	11.	cut - cat	M	21.	jet - jut
E	2.	sun - sum		12.	(good - good)	B	22.	chair - share
B	3.	cat - hat	E	13.	ben - bed	M	23.	seal - sail
	4.	(but - but)	B	14.	fare - tear		24.	(forgot - forgot)
E	5.	mean - meal		15.	(more - more)	M	25.	heat - hit
M	6.	pet - pat	B	16.	got - hot	B	26.	Jim - Tim
E	7.	rod - rot	E	17.	big - bit		27.	(feel - feel)
M	8.	dig - dug		18.	(some - some)	M	28.	bat - bet
	9.	(sat - sat)	B	19.	sum - dumb	E	29.	read - real
B	10.	jug - rug		20.	(come - come)		30.	(from - from)

AUDITORY DISCRIMINATION TEST: LEVEL II

Directions to the teacher:

Children's answer sheet is in Appendix I. Samples follow this test.

Directions to the children:

Today we're going to play a listening game. Listen very carefully to the words I say. If they are the same you will circle the word "yes." If they are different you will circle the word "no." Let's try sample A. "gar - gar." Are they the same? Yes they are the same. So circle the word "yes" beside the A.

If the words I say are not the same, then you will circle "no" beside the number. Let's try another one, sample B: "rick - glick." Are they the same? No. Circle the word "no" beside letter B. (Circulate and check that all children have followed directions.)

Samples

    A. gar - gar
    B. rĭck - glĭck

	1. (lўm - lўm)	M	11. consōnant - continant	M	21. wĕckcōe - wĕllcōe
B	2. thăm - shăm		12. (līre - līre)	B	22. grēepŭm - crēepŭm
E	3. gōpīle - gōpeēl	E	13. quicksăn - quicksăm		23. (wātion - wātion)
	4. (rĭf - rĭf)		14. (happenstance - happenstance)	M	24. sĭbbălĕnt - sĭbbĭlĕnt
M	5. dĭs - dŏd	E	15. different - difference		25. (chimney - chimney)
E	6. wăbmăl - wăbmăw		16. (săbcō - săbcō)	B	26. blend - trend
B	7. Quĕpsŏd - kĕpsŏd	E	17. lēēgō - lēēhō	B	27. fīnal - vīnal
E	8. mōime - mōine	M	18. mĭshbĕr - mĭshtbĕr		28. (recapitulate - recapitulate)
B	9. chōut - prōut		19. (dălbāin - dălbāin)	E	29. roughening - roughener
M	10. brŭd - brĭd	B	20. interest - imterest	M	30. discrimināted - discrimānated

SAMPLE ANSWER SHEETS:

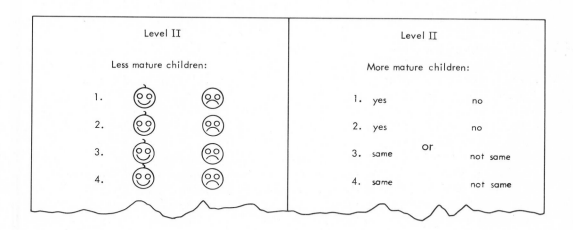

VISUAL DISCRIMINATION TEST

Good visual discrimination is essential in the reading process, and the sample tests in this section deal with this important area. The visual discrimination tests begin with items that are dramatically different from one another. As in the auditory discrimination tests, there are both letters and geometric forms (corresponding to the words and nonsense syllables of that test).

All parts of the visual discrimination test consist of matching to sample items. In each problem, a figure, letter, or letter group is given first and a series of similar items appears to its right. Variables include size, shape, internal and external parts, rotation, and static and kinetic reversals.

In Level I the child is asked to mark the items on each line that are the same as the sample at the beginning of the line. The initial items of the test, as shown in the examples below, are easily discriminable. Triangles are clearly different from circles or parallelograms, and N is different from a capital R or M.

Sample:

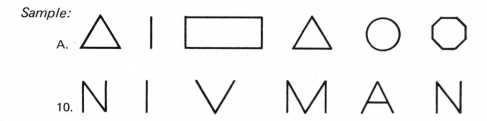

Gradually discriminations become finer and finer and letters and numbers are included. Following is an example of items in Level II.

Sample:

A. bp	bq	pd	bd	bp
B. mnn	mnm	nmm	mnn	nnm
1. gh	gn	ph	bh	gh

Following are directions for both levels of visual discrimination tests. The tests will be found in Appendix II.

VISUAL DISCRIMINATION TEST

Directions to the teacher:

In these tests the child's task is to circle the item in each row that is exactly the same as the first item. Directions to the child are minimal, but you will want to complete the samples with the children to make sure that they all understand the directions. Items are designed to discover difficulties in recognition of external configuration, size constancy, rotation, reversal, and order. Each child will need an answer sheet, which can be found in Appendix II.

LEVEL I

Directions to the children:

Today we are going to do a task in which you have to have sharp eyes. In each row you are to circle the picture that is the same as the one in front. Everyone look at *A* on your paper. Look at the shape in the front. Put your finger on it (check to see if children point correctly). Now find another one just like it in this row and circle it. (Check papers.) Good. Now try *B* by yourself. Now do the rest of the page.

LEVEL II

Directions to the children:

In each row you are to circle the letters that are the same as those at the beginning. Try samples *A* and *B* and I will check them. (Teacher checks samples) Now do the whole page.

TESTS OF VISUAL AND AUDITORY MEMORY

The rationale for use of the visual discrimination tests is that they relate as closely as possible to the actual task the child faces in the reading process. In all tests described so far the child sees or hears the sample and the instances of "same" or "different" that follow. He may compare both and then check his initial responses. Thus the factor of memory is involved little or not at all. But to read, especially at an independent level, and to utilize phonics teaching, he must be able to remember a visual and/or auditory pattern. The child who just can't seem to remember "that word" has a difficult time acquiring basic sight vocabulary or attacking new words in a decoding process. In addition, auditory memory is essential for such school tasks as following directions and retaining facts and concepts presented orally in any subject. Some simple tests of auditory and visual memory can help the teacher find those youngsters who need additional training in these areas.

The visual memory test has two levels. The first level is given individually and is for young children and those older children who show difficulty in the second level of the test. Some children need to manipulate real objects before they move into a paper and pencil mode. The test is designed also to tap the memory levels of matching, identification, and recall at Level I and identification and recall at Level II.

VISUAL MEMORY TESTS: LEVEL I

Directions to the teacher:

You will need two sets of identical cards (4 by 6 or 5 by 8 inch index cards are appropriate) plus one card marked with an X. Each card has a simple geometric figure 3 inches high. Five cards in each set are adequate.

A screen can be constructed from a 12 by 30 inch sheet of oak tag. Fold the two narrow edges back 3 inches on each side so it can stand without being held.

Spread the two sets of cards in two horizontal rows on a table in front of the child, with cards in random order. Have the screen ready at the side to place in front of the cards. Cards will be shown for approximately 3 seconds and then recovered.

Directions to the child:

Part A (Matching)

We're going to play a memory game today. See all these cards? In a minute I'm going to hold this paper in front of my cards and take one away. Then I'll let you take a quick look at my cards. When I put the screen back and say "Now," you'll point to the card you have that is the same as the one I took away. Let's try it.

Steps:

1. Put screen in place in front of teacher cards.
2. Remove a card.
3. Remove screen for 3 seconds for child to look.
4. Replace screen and replace card.
5. Say "Now" and have child point to card in his set.
6. Do this for three or four cards.

Part B (Identification)

Directions to the child:

Now I'm going to make it a little harder. What are the names of these shapes? (Use any names child gives.) Okay. I'm going to take your set of cards and put them in a row over here (place at side of table). Then I'm going to put *some* of my cards together in front of you. Then when I hide them and take one away, you'll have to tell me which one is missing. Here we go.

Steps:

1. Put one set of cards in a row at the side.
2. Put two of teacher set in a horizontal row behind screen:

3. Show cards to child for 3 seconds.
4. Replace screen and remove one card.
5. Show child cards and have child tell you which is missing.
6. Move on to a three-card pattern and repeat steps 3-5.
7. Do a four-card pattern. Stop at four.
8. If child does especially well, you could go on to remove two items. Do not remove more than two.

Part C (Recall)

Directions to the child:

Now you will use your set of cards to make the same group I show you. Start with the shape that is under the X (put out X card) and put the cards in the right order when I say "Now."

Steps:

1. Put up screen.
2. Put two cards in a horizontal row with first card under the X. This will allow you to check for left-right orientation. But remember the child is facing you.

3. Remove screen for 3 seconds.
4. Replace screen and say "Now." Allow child up to 5 seconds to put appropriate cards in correct order.
5. If they are backwards, remind child to start with the one under the X; remove screen so the cards can be compared.
6. Do another two-card pattern.
7. Do several three-card patterns, with the X always over the first card.
8. Go on to four- and five-card patterns if the child does not miss more than one out of three patterns.

Stop at any part of the test when the child makes three errors in a row. Any number of errors in a pattern is counted as one error. Note both the level of memory and the number of items retained if appropriate, e.g., Recall level, 3, or Identification level, 1.

VISUAL MEMORY TEST: LEVEL II

This test can be administered in groups. For Part A an answer sheet is required; it can be found in Appendix II. For Part B paper and pencils will be needed. For both parts the teacher will need a set of 15 cards with geometric figures and letters as shown in the illustration. (Size will vary with the number of children taking the test at one time and their distance from the image. Four to eight children at a table could see 3-inch figures on a 5 by 8 inch index card.) A child who had difficulty with visual discrimination may have difficulty with this test.

Part A (Identification)

Directions to the teacher:

Hold up a card for 3 seconds. Then put card face down and wait 2 seconds. Then say "Go" and have children circle the appropriate shape on their answer sheets. The most difficult point will be when three shapes or letters are presented on the teacher card and the child's row has five options.

Directions to the children:

I'm going to show you a card and you look at it carefully. Then I'll put it down and when I say "Go," circle the shape that was *not* on my card. Sometimes, there will be more than one missing shape. We'll try the first two just to see how you do.

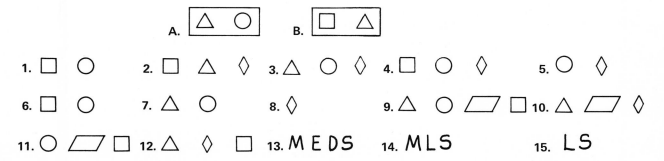

Part B (Recall)

In this part of the visual memory test the children will draw from memory the grouping they see. A sheet of paper 12 by 18 inches is a good size. A thick crayon is better for primary age children. Have the children fold paper in half three times to get eight rows.

Directions to the teacher:

Use the following seven cards from Part A:
#1, 2, 3, 4, 9, 13, 14.
To these, add the following three cards:
8. Alcm 9. Leorh 10. counts.
Show card for 3 seconds, put card face down for 2 seconds, and then say "Go."
If you are unsure whether the children can copy figures and letters, be sure to check in advance or do not administer this level. When correcting tests, note reversals, rotations, and so on.

Directions to the children:

Today we're going to see if you can remember a group of figures or letters and then copy them on your paper. You are *not* to pick up your pencil/crayon until I say "Go."

AUDITORY MEMORY TEST: LEVEL I

Directions to the teacher:

Level I is to be given individually. The teacher will need a small box (approximately 3 by 5 inches) with a lid, a small ball, a nail, a paper clip, and a pencil with an eraser. (These same items will be used in Level II of the Listening Vocabulary Test in the next chapter). An index card with a X on it is also needed. Spread items on a table in front of the child and place the index card to the child's left as a starting point.

You may repeat once if the child hesitates on the first three combinations below. Do not repeat for numbers 4 to 7.

Directions to the child:

Can you tell me the names of the things I've put on the table? Good. Now I'm going to say the names of some of the things. When I do, I want you to put them in a row on the table. I'll say only some of them and you are to put them in the same order I say them. The first one goes right under this X. (Point to card.) Be sure to wait until I say "Go" before you pick anything up. Let's try it.
1. Ball, nail. Go. (Have child return them each time)
2. Box, pencil. Go.
3. Clip, box, nail. Go.
4. Ball, clip, box. Go.
5. Nail, box, clip, pencil. Go.
6. Box, nail, ball, clip. Go.
7. Pencil, ball, box, nail, clip. Go.

AUDITORY MEMORY TEST: LEVEL II

Directions to the teacher:

The various parts of this test may be given to individuals or groups. Children will have an answer sheet to mark (see Appendix II). It is sometimes necessary to practice reading the material in advance to avoid mispronunciations and to avoid stressing a particular answer. You may repeat once.

Directions to the children:

Today you are going to have to be good listeners and remember what I read to you. After I read, I will ask you to put some numbers in front of pictures that tell the order in which you heard the words I said. Don't do any writing until I say "begin." Let's try sample A. Listen to the Words I say: "dog, bird, cloud." Now, put a one in front of the picture of the first word I said, and a two in front of the second word. (Pause.) Listen again: dog, bird, cloud. Did you put a one in front of the picture of the dog? What did you put the two in front of? What would you put in front of the picture of the cloud? Good! (Check answers to make sure they all understand.) Let's begin now.

Sample A _____ dog, bird, cloud.

1. _____ car, house.
2. _____ boy, rabbit, dog.
3. _____ The wall is by the fence.
4. _____ The girl and the cat sat in front of the tree.
5. _____ The horse and the dog ran over the hill to the house.
6. _____ The fountain by the house has birds and butterflies on it.
7. _____ The many-colored leaves are falling from the trees and the children are raking them.
8. _____ Put your comb and brush on the table and sit in the chair by the fireplace.
9. _____ The train passed two houses, a barn, and a tree as it sped along.
10. _____ The book is about a rabbit, a dog, and a boy who lived in the forest by the hills.

SUMMARY

All the tests in this chapter are designed to give the teacher as much information as possible concerning the children's maturity level in perceptual and memory skills. The tests are divided into levels for convenience in administering, and should be used and adapted in any way that seems appropriate for a particular group or individual. It is a good idea to organize the information you have gained by using a class or individual record sheet, such as those shown at the end of this chapter.

If a child is having difficulty at a particular level of auditory or visual discrimination, the teacher should give tasks that train to this area before continuing with more advanced skills. For example, children who are having problems with auditory discrimination will find rhyming activities and sound identification games useful. Memory tasks and games are helpful training for most children. The teacher will need to be sure that the directions and tasks given are not beyond the number the students can remember, thus matching the task to the learner.

SAMPLE CHECK SHEETS

Child's Name _____   Age _____

Date Tested

Test

Auditory Discrimination						
Level I						
Level II						
Visual Discrimination						
Level I						
Level II						
Visual Memory						
Level I Part A						
Part B						
Part C						
Level II Part A						
Part B						
Auditory Memory						
Level I						
Level II						

AUDITORY DISCRIMINATION CHECK SHEET

✓ = has sufficient discrimination at this level

O = needs additional work

	Level I			Level II			
CHILD'S NAME	B	E	M	B	E	M	
							B = Beginning Sounds
							E = Ending Sounds
							M= Medial

5

Receptive and Generative Language Skills

The human being is born with a capacity to acquire language; barring some type of impairment, language will develop in a predictable, genetically determined sequence. At the same time, language becomes a direct reflection of the child's language environment. Understanding both the natural development and the nature of environmental influences is crucial to planning an appropriate program in the language arts.

The infant cries, coos, gurgles, and squeals from the moment of birth. The first step toward meaningful language, however, is babbling, which may begin as early as the second or third month of life. Since even deaf infants babble, we know this is not the mere repetition of sounds. In fact, the infant uses virtually all the sounds of the different languages of the world. By the sixth to ninth month most of the sounds from other languages which are not a part of the environment are dropped and the babbling assumes a vowel and consonant pattern, complete with intonation (pitch and stress), which makes it sound "sentence-like."

By the ninth or tenth month the child begins to show evidence of understanding language. Appropriate actions will be elicited with words or phrases such as, "Wave bye-bye," "No!" "Where's the toy dog?" etc.

In this manner, the child in our culture acquires the first of the four vocabularies he will need to function in society. This *listening vocabulary* will be the largest one that the child possesses for many years and is the basis for the *speaking vocabulary*. This second vocabulary, the one used regularly in speech, consists only of words and sounds that the child has heard and is capable of understanding. Listening and speaking form the child's *oracy* and are at the core of all future language learnings.

Oracy is a natural developmental process and some cultures still use only this form of expression. However, our culture, like many others, requires *literacy*, which is possession of reading and writing vocabularies. Literacy is not a part of the developmental process and therefore it must be directly taught. This teaching is most often part of the function of the school. It is extremely important to keep in mind that literacy is based on oracy. The child cannot in initial stages read and write words that she has not heard and, preferably, used. Literacy is a learned set of arbitrary visual patterns which are associated with meaning but are not real or functional by themselves.

Language skills can also be divided on the basis of *receptive language,* in which we "decode" or "figure out" meaning (listening and reading), and *generative language,* in which we "encode" or "create" meaning (speaking and writing). These are often useful designations in the teaching process. The decoding process allows new input continually; however, before an item (sound, word, grammatical device) can move permanently into the material used for encoding, there must be repeated exposure and practice.

When one looks at language development, it should be quite clear why a child with an impairment might be slower at developing certain language skills. Deaf children, for example, have great difficulty learning to speak, and their reading and writing will also develop with some difficulty.

In the same vein, children who have a language environment different from that of the schools need a firm oracy base in any sounds, words, or grammatic patterns that are not present in their usual environment. The earlier the oracy base is broadened, the more extensive all of the vocabularies will be.

This chapter will assess the receptive and generative language skills in this oracy base. Listening and speaking vocabularies will be tapped in a number of ways. With this information the teacher can see what items need to be introduced to the curriculum both before and during early literacy efforts.

LISTENING VOCABULARY TESTS

The listening vocabulary tests assess the words and sentences a child may understand but does not necessarily use in regular speech. The assessments are made at three levels.

In kindergarten a child may possess from 3,000 to 10,000 words in the listening vocabulary and· yet will probably pronounce only about half of these. Because the words a child knows are specific to the child's environment, one can expect a high degree of "scatter." That is, a child may miss supposedly "easier" items and understand more "difficult" ones. For example, a child whose parent is a politician may know the word "senator" at three

years whereas we would normally expect that word to be understood at around the tenth year. Because the child's oracy base begins early, most of these tests will use developmental norms in terms of age rather than school grade.

Level I, Real and Nonsense Test, assesses word understanding using a simple nonsense question format. The format and norms are based on the Illinois Test of Psycholinguistic Abilities (Kirk et al., 1968).

Do dogs run?
Do rabbits fly?

The child may answer "yes" or "no" or mark an answer sheet.

In Level II, Riddles Test, words within sentences are assessed with a riddle: "This is round and you can play with it." This test is designed to be given individually using real objects; however, an answer sheet could be used with appropriate pictures except for the last item.

Level III, Following Directions Test, taps the understanding of the directional concepts so necessary in the classroom. There are two parts in this test, Part A for younger children or those with limited experience and Part B for older children. Auditory memory is also further tested incidentally as the tester notes the number of directions the child is able to follow and the word concepts the child understands.

Because we do depend on the children's listening skills so much of the time, it makes sense to have some idea of what they can understand and follow orally. In addition, the process of following written directions must begin with the appropriate application of oral ones. A test to ascertain the children's ability to follow oral directions can save the teacher time and temper. Therefore Part B addresses itself particularly to following directions similar to those frequently given in classroom work periods.

LISTENING VOCABULARY TEST: Level I (Real and Nonsense Test)

Directions to the teacher:

Child can respond either individually to the teacher or by indicating "yes" or "no" on an answer sheet. Children under seven usually do best when tested individually. If a child misses an item, it is a good idea to go back after the test is finished and ask why a particular answer was given. If the child's answer is logical and shows she understood the word, that is sufficient. For example, for number 14, "Do canoes paddle?" the usual answer is "yes," but occasionally a child will respond "no." The reasoning might be that *people* paddle canoes. If so, the item would be accepted. The child's knowledge, not the score, is our objective. You may need to practice reading items out loud so as not to telegraph the answer when the item seems funny. While items will generally be answered in progressive order, differences in language environment can cause additional scattered correct answers beyond the usual age. It is best to give all of the test and then count the answers to determine child's level.

Directions to the child:

I'm going to ask you some questions. Some of them may seem funny but you just let me know with a "yes" or "no" what the answer is.

1. Do dogs run? (Y)	15. Do scissors scream? (N)
2. Do cats meow? (Y)	16. Do bicycles spin? (Y)
3. Do rabbits fly? (N)	17. Do helmets swim? (N)
4. Do houses fly? (N)	18. Do refrigerators frown? (N)
5. Do boys eat? (Y)	19. Do horns blare? (Y)
6. Do toothbrushes jump? (N)	20. Do actors entertain? (Y)
7. Do people laugh? (Y)	21. Do students walk on the ceiling? (N)
8. Do oranges talk? (N)	22. Do motorcycles relax? (N)
9. Do spiders climb? (Y)	23. Do microscopes murder? (N)
10. Do clocks tick? (Y)	24. Do warriors sleep? (Y)
11. Do tables dance? (N)	25. Do camels dig? (N)
12. Do swans gallop? (N)	26. Do carpenters measure? (Y)
13. Do books close? (Y)	27. Do elephants stampede? (Y)
14. Do canoes paddle? (Y)	28. Do senators bloom? (N)

Age characteristics:

	No. correct
5 years	14
6 years	20
7 years	25
8 years	28

Note: Don't be surprised at some scatter.

LISTENING VOCABULARY TEST: Level II (Riddles Test)

Directions to the teacher:

You will need a nail, a small box, a ball, a pencil, and a paper clip, as described in the Auditory Memory Test in Chapter 4. Place items on a table in front of the child.

Directions to the child:

I'm going to give you a riddle about some of these items. You pick out the right one. I may do some things more than once.

1. This is round and you can play with it.
2. This has sides and you put things in it.
3. This is long and you write with it.
4. You use this with a hammer.
5. This holds things together in an office.
6. This has sides and a top and bottom that are flat.
7. You can erase with this.
8. This can bend.
9. This will be the heaviest.
10. This will be the lightest.
11. A carpenter needs this.
12. A secretary can use two of these.
13. Which ones would fit in the box?
14. Which one would be most useful for a clown? Why?

Age characteristics:

	No. correct
5 years	7
6 years	10
7 years	12
8 years	14

LISTENING VOCABULARY TEST: Level III (Following Directions)

In this test children are provided with a simple set of materials and are asked to perform tasks related to those materials. The ability to follow short and long directions to perform specific actions is tested. The first directions are simple statements. Later, the number and complexity of directions increase to include both lengthy sequences of words and words whose meanings may be inferred from the context but may not be specifically known by the listener.

Part A

Directions to the teacher:

Part A is given with an individual child and one prop—a pencil. The words in bold type indicate the directions being given. The number of directions the child is to follow is indicated in parentheses after the item. Give the items to children according to the age characteristics table: items 1-5 for five year olds, items 1-6 to six year olds, etc.

Directions to the child:

Simply listen carefully and *do* the following things:

1. Put your hands **over** your head. (1)
2. **Clap** your hands **three** times. (2)
3. **Clap** your hands **against my hands**. (face to face) (3)
4. Take **two steps forward** and **one** step **backward**. (4)
5. **Turn** to your **right**. (2)
6. **Turn right**, take **two steps backward** and **turn left**. (4)
7. Put this pencil **between us** and then **nearer to you**. (2)
8. **Turn around twice**, clap your hands **three times**, and then **jump backward** with **both feet**. (7)

Age characteristics:

5 years: Numbers 1 through 5
6 years: Numbers 1 through 6
7 years: Numbers 1 through 7
8 years: Numbers 1 through 8

PART B

Directions to the teacher:

This test can be administered individually or in small groups. A child scores one point for each item completed correctly. A tally sheet is one easy way to note each child's score. Analysis of the results is especially profitable in this test both for the number of directions that a child can follow and for key words which the child has difficulty following, such as first, second, half, over, under, and so on. However, if younger children become frustrated as the number of directions increases, stop after 10. Each child will need a pencil, three sheets of paper, five crayons—red, green, blue, yellow, and black—and a book. A sample tally sheet follows:

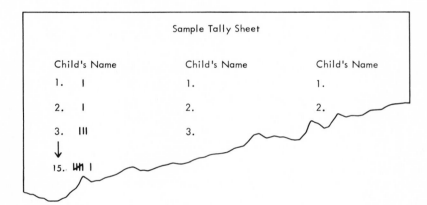

Directions to the children:

Today we're going to see how well you can listen and follow directions. Be sure you have these things on your desk. (Hold up each item and name it as children check.) Now I am going to give you some directions. Listen carefully, and when I finish and say "Begin," do exactly what I said. Do not start until I say "Begin."

Note: The words in bold type indicate the directions being given. The number in parentheses indicates how many directions are given in the item.

(1)   1.   **Hold up** your pencil. Begin.
(2)   2.   **Put** your pencil **on** your desk. Begin.
(3)   3.   **Open** the book and **put in the paper.** Then **close** the book. Begin.
(4)   4.   **Take** the paper out of the book, **fold** it in **half** and **make** a black dot on it. Begin.
(4)   5.   Take your **red crayon** and **make a square over** the black dot. **Color the square green.** Begin.
(5)   6.   **Make three triangles** with your **blue crayon.** Color the **first triangle red** and the **second triangle green.** Begin.
(5)   7.   **Copy every other letter** from the **title** of your book **on the top** of your paper with a **pencil.** Begin.
(6)   8.   Take your **second sheet** of paper and **fold** it in **half. Unfold it** and **draw a line** with your **yellow crayon on the crease.** Begin.

(6) 9. At the **top of** your paper make a **green circle** with a **red X** in the **center**. **Make a blue square under** the circle. Begin.

(6) 10. **Print your name with pencil** at the **bottom** of your paper. Now **cross out** the **third letter** with a **black crayon**. Begin.

(7) 11. **Put** your book **face down on the desk** and **trace** the edge of the book **on one piece** of paper **with a pencil. Draw lines diagonally** across the paper **from the corners.** Begin.

(7) 12. **Count** the windows on the **(choose direction)** side of the room and make a **green square** on one piece of paper to represent each window. **Color** each square a **different** color but make the **last square black.** Begin.

(8) 13. **Put your papers** in the **top right hand corner** of your desk. **Put the book on top of** the papers. Put your pencil **next to** your book and **put the crayons under** the book. Begin.

(8) 14. **Open** the book to **page 8. Write** the **second** word on the **first line** in **blue** on one piece of paper and **fold** in it **half.** Begin.

(11) 15. **Make four** lines each of a **different** color on **one side of** your **third** paper. Then **turn it** over and **print your** name in **pencil** on the other side. **Fold** it in **half** and **put it** in the book, **back of page 20.** Begin.

Age characteristics:

K to second grade: 4 directions
Third to fourth grade: 5 directions
Fifth to sixth grade: 6 directions

LISTENING COMPREHENSION TESTS

Following directions is very important in the school setting, but other types of listening comprehension have as much or more impact on children's learning level. At a more advanced level of listening skills, we can assess the ability to comprehend, interpret, and infer information. Here children's listening vocabulary and their thinking skills align in a manner which closely approximates the actual reading task.

In giving a listening comprehension test we ask the question, "If the child could read this material, would he actually be able to understand it?" If he cannot understand while listening, there is little reason to believe that he will be able to do so when he is reading similar material. In the same way, we may find particular skills the child lacks and thus be able to pinpoint problem areas in comprehension apart from the additional complications of the reading process itself.

Many times it is not possible to tell how much a child understands through a regular silent reading test. After all, if the words get in the way, the opportunity for understanding is greatly decreased. For example, if a child gets a low score on a social studies test, it is difficult to determine if the problem was the child's understanding of the subject matter or her inability to read the material offered.

The Listening Comprehension Test is divided into three levels: (1) the recall of general information, (2) the interpretation of oral language, and (3) the inferential analysis of oral language.

The first of the test explores the recall of setting and character. This test seeks to determine the child's ability to recall the nature of the people and animals in the story and the other features of the setting that are of particular importance in determining the author's purpose. The statements are arranged in order of increasing complexity. The listener is scored on the ability to determine the words that best describe the characters portrayed and to recall the words actually used by the author.

The next test, Interpretation of Oral Language, was developed to assess the ability to interpret the material at hand. Understanding the meaning *behind* stated information is closely related to understanding and using both oral and written language. Alternative interpretations are presented after each paragraph in this section, and the child is asked to choose one. The ability to use synonyms and to use phrases that summarize, generalize, and categorize the words and ideas presented constitute interpretive listening comprehension.

The last test in the listening series, Inferential Analysis of Oral Language, asks the child to draw inferences from statements and to judge what are the most likely ways to conclude incomplete statements. The ability to make judgments and to determine the author's "next step" is the subject of the test.

The tests are progressively more difficult and tap more and varied oral linguistic skills. The teacher is expected to give those levels appropriate to the maturity of the class. High, medium, and low scores should be determined by the teacher with regard to his or her own curriculum goals.

LISTENING COMPREHENSION TEST: Level I
(Direct Recall of Information)

Directions to the teacher:

The story material, the questions, and the possible answers must be read to the children. Even if a child can read them himself, he should hear the material. Each child will need a copy of the test. (See Appendix II.)

Directions to the children:

Listen carefully. I am going to read a sentence and then I am going to read questions and answers and you will circle the answer to each question. Don't circle anything until I tell you to circle the answer. Let's try the sample. Listen: "The white cat caught the little gray mouse." On your answer sheet, question A states, "The cat was (1) little, (2) white, (3) gray." Circle one of the answers. Question B says, "The mouse was (1) white, (2) tiny, (3) gray." Circle one of the answers. Which was the correct answer about the cat? (Let the children answer.) Which was the correct answer about the mouse? Good! Be careful! Sometime there may be two right answers. Be sure to circle both of them. Now we'll do the rest.

Sample:

The white cat caught the little gray mouse.
A. The cat was (1) little (2) white (3) gray.
B. The mouse was (1) white (2) tiny (3) gray.

Read:

The sleepy dog sat watching the old cowhand.
1.   The dog was: (1) old (2) gray (3) sleepy (4) soft.
2.   The cowhand was: (1) young (2) sleepy (3) tall (4) old.

The soft gray light of morning woke me from my dreams.
3.   The person talking was: (1) eating (2) dreaming (3) yawning (4) hopping.
4.   The time of day is (1) morning (2) afternoon (3) night (4) summer.
5.   The morning light is (1) gray (2) white (3) hard (4) soft. (Note two possible answers.)

The tall man walked quickly up the brick stairs and into the dusty old house.
6.   The house was: (1) new (2) dirty (3) old (4) fancy.
7.   The man was: (1) young (2) tall (3) fast (4) jumpy.
8.   The stairs were: (1) steep (2) dusty (3) brick (4) stone.

The two children ran and jumped in the leaves, laughing happily. Their dogs chased their tails till they were exhausted.

9. The children were: (1) quick (2) exhausted (3) happy (4) sitting.
10. The dogs were: (1) running (2) chasing (3) jumping (4) exhausted. (Note two possible answers.)
11. The ground was covered with: (1) grass (2) leaves (3) flowers (4) dogs.

In those last solemn moments before they parted, the two men sat staring intensely at the half-empty glasses on the table in the now silent room.

12. The room was: (1) deserted (2) lonely (3) intense (4) silent.
13. The men were: (1) talking (2) staring (3) sitting (4) drinking. (Note two possible answers.)
14. The glasses were: (1) half size (2) half empty (3) completely full (4) completely empty.
15. The men are going to: (1) sing (2) drink (3) part (4) join.

LISTENING COMPREHENSION TEST: Level II
(Interpretation of Oral Language)

Directions to the teacher:

The test may be given to individuals or groups. Read the story material twice and the questions and answers only once. Each child needs an answer sheet. (See Appendix II.)

Directions to the children:

I'm going to read you some sentences. I will read each one twice. After I read them to you I will read the questions and the answers that are on your page once. When I finish, you will circle the answers that are correct. Let's try the sample. Listen. "Joe was mean, heartless, and less than a friend to the children." (Read the sentence twice.) The sample question on your page is: "How would you describe Joe? (1) lazy, (2) careful, (3) old, (4) cruel." Circle the correct answer. All right. What was the correct answer? Good! Now we'll do the rest.

The horses were sweating heavily as they strained and tugged at the heavy load.
1. The horses were: (1) resting (2) playing (3) working.
2. They felt: (1) cross (2) hot (3) tired.

The man shouted at the children who hurriedly ran away, trembling and shaking.
3. The children were: (1) noisy (2) frightened (3) angry (4) happy.
4. The man was: (1) angry (2) calm (3) hurried (4) gentle.

The soft light of dawn caused the rooster to crow noisily, waking the cowhand rudely.
5. The time was: (1) evening (2) summer (3) morning (4) afternoon.
6. The cowhand had been: (1) working (2) sleeping (3) eating (4) rude.

The young girl sighed deeply and a tear rolled down her cheek as she looked at the picture of the handsome young man in his gray uniform.
7. The girl is: (1) sick (2) happy (3) sad (4) crazy.
8. The girl is probably: (1) lonely (2) busy (3) an actress (4) his mother.
9. The young man is probably: (1) a soldier (2) a photographer (3) her father (4) with the girl.

"The book is too difficult for me," said Jane. "I will go to Jim and have him explain it to me."

10.   Jane thinks: (1) Jim can read (2) Jim is tall (3) Jim is kind (4) Jim is busy.
11.   Jane wants Jim to: (1) read to her (2) help her understand (3) return her book (4) go to the library.

Back and forth, back and forth swayed the mast of the ship as the waves beat the hull and tore at the decks. "Lower the life boats!" called the captain as the lashing continued.

12.   The ship is: (1) old and cracked (2) in a storm (3) on a cruise (4) falling apart.
13.   The captain is: (1) abandoning the ship (2) radioing for help (3) putting the sailors to work (4) going to sleep.

With coats gleaming in the bright sun, the mare and her colt raced across the green pasture seemingly for the sheer pleasure of being alive, while deep in the forest thousands of newly hatched insects scurried from beneath the damp moss-covered logs.

14.   The main message of this story is: (1) the coming of winter (2) how bugs are different from horses (3) how colorful the day was (4) the power and contrast in young life.
15.   Young animals live: (1) only in pasture and under logs (2) in large numbers (3) only if they can run fast (4) in many different conditions.

LISTENING COMPREHENSION TEST: Level III
(Inferential Analysis of Oral Language)

Directions to the teacher:

Read the story material and questions and answers to the children. Each child should have an answer sheet but should not read and answer questions independently. Check the answers they give for number 1 to make sure all the children understand the directions. Read only once.

Directions to the children:

I am going to read some sentences to you, each of which has a special meaning. Then I will read some questions and answers about the sentences. Do not mark your paper until after I have read the answers. Then put an X on the line in front of the most correct answer. Listen carefully.

1.   "A penny saved is a penny earned."

What does that sentence mean?

_____ If you save money you will only get pennies.
_____ If you save money you can be a coin collector.
__X__ If you save money it is as if you had earned it.

2.   "If you are careful, the life you save may be your own."

What should the reader do, according to that statement?

_____ Live a long time.
_____ Be careful and save the lives of others.
__X__ Realize that if he is careless he will endanger his life as well as other people's lives.

3. "A stitch in time saves nine."

    The statement means:

    _____ You should learn to sew.
    _X_ Fixing something right away will keep it from getting worse.
    _____ In time things will get better.

4. "Time heals all wounds."

    This probably means:

    _____ Your cuts and bruises will get better.
    _____ We need to learn first aid.
    _X_ We will forget about the things that have hurt us after awhile.

5. "The early bird gets the worms."

    This tells us:

    _X_ If we do something right away it will work out better for us.
    _____ Birds get up early.
    _____ Worms are good to eat.

6. The lumberjack stepped back from the tree as it started to fall and
    _____.

    What is likely to happen next?

    _____ ran away.
    _____ hit the tree again.
    _____ sharpened his ax.
    _X_ yelled "Timber."

7. The rain had been falling for hours when a cold north wind started to blow. The
    rain _____.

    What is likely to happen next?

    _____ stopped.
    _X_ turned to ice.
    _____ melted.
    _____ caused a flood.

8. Johnny walked through the thick brush to get to his house.

    Days later he discovered that:

    _X_ he had poison oak.
    _____ he had a snake bite.
    _____ he was lost.
    _____ he was hungry.

9. The children saw a jagged flash of lightning across the sky.

    They knew they would soon hear:

    _____ a horn.
    _____ yelling.
    __X__ thunder.
    _____ a policeman.

10. The Brown family was out on the lake in their boat.

    All was quiet until Johnny yelled:

    __X__ "I caught a fish."
    _____ "I'm sleepy."
    _____ "I want to go to school."
    _____ "I see a pretty cloud."

SPEAKING VOCABULARY TESTS

The second portion of the child's oracy base is the speaking vocabulary. This includes sounds, words, and grammatical patterns. It is useful to understand that grammatical sequences build slowly. Children assimilate regular patterns and internalize a "rule" which is eventually broadened and modified as the exposure to irregular patterns accumulate. Therefore, a three- or four-year-old may say, "See the mans" because the regular rule is to add an *s* sound to indicate more than one. The irregular plurals develop later. Similarly, a five-year-old may be confused by a sentence presented in the passive voice, "The cat was chased by the dog," and interpret the meaning as the cat chased the dog. Usually the child of five or six years has acquired our complex English grammatical system, but minor refinements and vocabulary increases continue. In addition, remember that conflict points can exist between grammars as well as between sounds of different languages or dialects. Lists of some of the grammatical conflict points between standard English and black English can be found in works by Baratz and Shuy (1969). Conflict points between English and Spanish are discussed in Zintz (1979) and Holquin (1975).

The first two tests of speaking vocabulary are the test of Listening and Repeating (Echoics) and the Grammatic Pattern Understanding Test. These will assess the child's ability to repeat words and sentences and to supply missing grammatical items in sentences. Items are chosen to reflect common speech and grammar problems for standard English. In the event a child has difficulty with these patterns and there is reason to believe the child uses black English, a test is included which uses words and patterns from this dialect.

Research suggests that if the child does not "know" the pattern, she will alter sentences and words; the *echoic* device has proven to be a useful tool for assessment in this area. Note that echoics is also based on auditory memory; thus the child is not likely to repeat sequences beyond her memory capacity.

The remaining tests of speaking vocabulary will assess the child's generative language skills.

TEST OF LISTENING AND REPEATING (ECHOICS)

Directions to the teacher:

This test must be given individually. It will be helpful if you practice the sentences aloud in advance. You will need one printed copy for each child, so that you can mark the errors each child makes.

Mark each error in a response according to the following directions:

omissions   two lines through ~~word~~

mispronunciations   one line through ~~word~~

insertions ∧ write in word

hesitations 〰〰under word

Directions to the child:

Listen carefully. I will say some words. You may not understand the words, but say them back to me just the way I say them to you. (Repeat once if necessary.)

1. Slowly.
2. Children.
3. Hung up.
4. Repeatedly.
5. Bears climb trees.
6. Two men chased sheep.
7. I am going to band the mice.
8. He has stolen the biggest soap.
9. With long strides, the three boys covered the frozen ground.
10. The bigger man threw his cloak over himself to hide.

GRAMMATIC PATTERN UNDERSTANDING TEST

Directions to the teacher:

This test is given to one child at a time. The picture cards shown are used with this test. Point to the first picture in each set and say the first sentence for that item. Then point to the second (and third and fourth if required) while beginning sentence (2). At the appropriate point, raise the voice as if asking a question and let the child supply the missing word. If the child does not respond, ask, "What would I say next?" You may repeat once.

Directions to the child:

I'm going to point to some pictures, and when I stop, I want you to tell me the word that comes next.

1. (1)   Here is a rabbit.
   (2)   Here are two_____.
          (rabbits)
          (Simple plural)

2. (1)   Here is a dress.
   (2)   Here are two_____.
          (dresses)
          ("z" plural)

3. (1) This dog likes to bark.
   (2) Here he is _____ .
       (barking)
       (Simple verb)

4. (1) I can write.
   (2) This is what I _____ .
       (wrote)
       (Irregular verb)

5. (1) This ball is *not* big.
   (2) This ball is big.
   (3) This ball is even bigger.
   (4) This ball is the very _____ .
       (biggest)
       (Comparison)

6. (1) Here is a man.
   (2) Here are two _____ .
       (men)
       (Irregular noun)

7. (1) Here is some soap.
   (2) And here is some more _____ .
       (soap)
       (Irregular noun)

8. (1) See this picture falling.
   (2) Now it has _____ .
       (fallen)
       (Irregular verb)

9. (1) These children are home alone.
   (2) They were left at home all
       by _____ .
       (themselves)
       (Irregular possessive)

10. (1) This dog likes to chase cats.
    (2) This cat was chased _____ .
        (by the dog)
        (Passive voice)

Age Characteristics

	No. correct
4 years	1 to 3
5 years	4 to 5
6 years	6 to 7
7 years	8 to 9
8 years	10

Black English Patterns Test

The next test is specifically for those children who use black English as their standard dialect.

The black English terms and patterns listed below are not intended to be a comprehensive list of black English words that differ in spelling or meaning from their standard English counterparts. Rather they are selected for their usefulness in helping the teacher determine a child's ability to read and define in his or her own words those terms that are used in a unique manner in black English.

As a general guide, if a child reads and can define orally 50 of the 71 words or phrases, the teacher has strong reason to believe that the child will benefit from black English instruction materials and from lessons based on transition skills for developing standard English. In cases where reading skills are very limited, the teacher may pronounce the words and the sentences orally and require the child to define them in his or her own words.

BLACK ENGLISH PATTERNS TEST

Directions to the teacher:

Older children *can* be asked to read the material to the teacher, but in many instances more accurate information will be gained if the teacher reads the columns. For younger children, it will be *necessary* to read columns one and two and then ask the child what the key word or phrase means. Select the number of items according to the child's age: for children ages five to six years, select items marked 1; for children ages seven to eight, add items marked 2; for children nine years old and up, use the entire list.

Directions to the child:

Say the key word(s) in the second column. Then read (or listen to) the sentence that follows it and say the key word(s) again. If you can, tell what the word(s) mean.

Age Range	Key Word/Phrase	Sentence	Definition
3	aloose	He took that string *aloose.*	(to take) out of, loose
2	bad mouth	He *bad mouth* the man.	to refer adversely to a person
2	blood	That *blood* cut out.	a member of the black race
2	blow	Jimmy going *blow* the whole gig.	to fail, to lose a chance
1	brother	That *brother* got it together.	black male
2	come from	Dig where that dude *come from.*	indicating one's intent or position
1	cop	I going *cop* some shut-eye.	to steal or get

Age Range	Key Word/Phrase	Sentence	Definition
2	cut loose	They *cut loose* from that scene.	to leave or disassociate.
3	dead	They all *dead*, man.	square, boring
1	dig	They got it all together, *dig?*	to understand
2	dig on	He *dig on* them wheels.	to admire
1	down	She got *down* on him.	to criticize
2	fall on by	Joe got to *fall on by.*	to stop in or visit
1	folks	All them good *folks* lives there.	black people
3	'fro	She got a *'fro.*	natural hair style
2	get down	She could really get *down.*	to go to the essentials
1	get it	They going to *get it.*	to succeed
2	get it on	They *get it on* today.	to start
2	get next to	*Get next to* the truck.	to get close enough to cause damage
3	get ready for	Did you *get ready for* that?	to believe
2	gig	He quit that *gig,* man.	job
2	upside the head	He hit him *upside the head*	(to hit someone) on the head
2	groove on	They *groove on* that.	to enjoy
3	half stepping	They always *half stepping* down there.	to act reluctantly, without great effort
2	halfway	She's *halfway* together.	mostly, usually
2	hat up	Kenny already *hat up.*	to leave
3	heart	Do he got the *heart* for that?	courage, determination
2	heavy	That's a *heavy* one.	convincing, powerful
1	hip	She's a *hip* sister.	in the know, aware
2	hustle	They going to *hustle* some fixings.	to find a way to get something
1	jive	He talking about Jimmy and all that *jive.*	unbelievable talk
1	lame	That a *lame* idea.	out of date, stupid
3	lay dead	You just do like I say and just *lay dead.*	to do nothing, don't act
2	lay down	*Lay* that sister idea *down.*	to present, explain
2	lighten up	*Lighten up*, Joe, we got to rap.	to slow down, to relax
1	main man	He the *main man* around here.	the one in charge, boss
2	mean	Them *mean* wheels.	valuable, good quality

Age Range	Key Word/Phrase	Sentence	Definition
3	nappy	His rags ain't *nappy.*	coarse, rough
1	pad	He just got a new *pad.*	home, apartment
3	punch out	He just *punched out* on his job.	to fail
2	push out of shape	I going to *push him out of shape.*	to make angry
1	rags	She got mighty fine *rags.*	good clothing
2	raise on	*Raise on* that stompin round.	stop, cease
3	rank back	Johnny was *ranking* him *back.*	to put down, belittle
1	rap	We got to *rap* about that.	to talk over
3	ride	He come down with his *ride.*	car
1	scarf	You got to *scarf* your dinner.	to eat
3	scoop	You *scooping* enough bread for the trip?	to earn, make
1	sister	See that *sister* over there?	black female
2	slave	He *slaving* away this week.	work
1	slick	That a *slick* trick.	clever, crafty
2	smarts	He got lots of *smarts.*	cleverness, intelligence
2	smoke over	We got to *smoke* it *over.*	to talk over
1	something else	That idea is *something else.*	exceptional, effective
1	soul	Hear that *soul* music.	reflecting black culture
1	spaced out	He sitting back there all *spaced out.*	daydreaming
1	split	He *split* yesterday.	to leave, check out
1	square	She real *square,* man.	old-fashioned
2	step fast	We got to *step fast.*	to move rapidly
2	stone	We got nothing but *stone* runners.	the best, unbeatable
1	straight	That the *straight* truth.	correct, trustworthy
1	sweat	Don't *sweat* it now.	to worry about, be concerned
3	terrible	Your suit *terrible.*	stylish, good quality
2	threads	Them good-looking *threads.*	clothes
2	together	You got it all *together* now?	well organized

Age Range	Key Word/Phrase	Sentence	Definition
2	trip out	He was *tripping out.*	to enjoy something
1	up tight	Johnny got *up tight* about it.	worried, tense
3	vibes	I get bad *vibes* off of him.	feeling, impression
3	wheels	You got your *wheels* today?	car
3	whip it on	You got to *whip it on,* man.	to explain, clarify
2	wrapped too tight	That whole scene is *wrapped too tight.*	unstable

GENERATIVE LANGUAGE SKILLS TEST

A child's ability to generate language that is appropriate to a given situation is central to the skills utilized in reading. Measures of generative language skills include: (1) the number of words used, (2) the sentence structures associated with the words used, and (3) the appropriateness of the words and structures.

It is frequently found that the larger the number of words and expression patterns available to the child in oral speaking, the larger the child's reading vocabulary. A variety of expressions contributes not only to accuracy in the child's use of oral language but to his or her ability to comprehend written language as it grows more sophisticated. The child's flexibility with language can be measured, for example, by the number of synonyms utilized in the description of particular stimulus pictures.

Three subtests of generative language skills included here are: Accuracy of Oral Language, Part A; Quantity of Language, Part B; and Variety of Language, Part C. In the Accuracy of Oral Language Test, the child is asked to use as many words as he can that tell about a particular object or scene pictured. An appropriate score sheet is provided. In Quantity of Oral Language Test, the child is given another set of pictures and is asked to tell what is happening. In this instance, the number of words used by the child is the teacher's criterion. In the Variety of Oral Language Test, the child is given increasingly complex drawings and is asked to describe them. Description is taken down verbatim, if possible. Sentence length, level of interpretation, and word choice are important factors. Scoring the tests will be easier if they are tape recorded, but with a little practice, it is possible to transcribe the important aspects of the child's description.

GENERATIVE LANGUAGE TEST

Part A: Accuracy of Oral Language (see Appendix II)

Directions to the teacher:

Show the child a picture. Check the words on the tally sheet that the child uses and add new words that the child uses correctly. A tape-recorded session for older or verbally sophisticated children is recommended.

Directions to the child:

Tell me what you see in this picture. Tell me as much as you can about the picture I am pointing to. (The teacher continues to point to each picture until the child stops talking about it.)

Picture 1   **Picture 2**

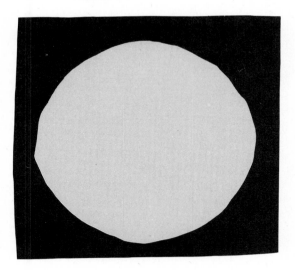   

The use of multiple categories in addition to simple size and variety of vocabulary can be considered in judging a child's language sophistication. The ranges might be: for primary grades, two categories; for middle grades, three categories; for upper grades, four or more.

Categories of language:

Size, materials, use and function, specific features, action, imaginative use, comparisons.

Sentence complexity:

Primary grades: No fragments, but run-on sentences made of individual sentences with few dependent clauses.
Middle grades: Dependent clauses and conjuncted sentences.
Upper grades: Complete use of all grammatical devices, including passive voice.

Picture 3

Picture 4

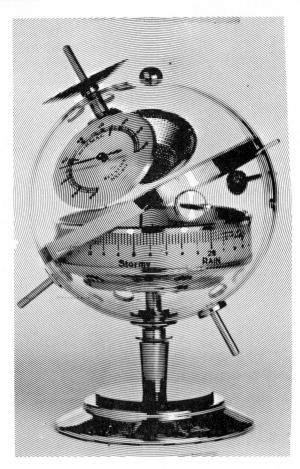

Tally Sheet

PICTURE 1	PICTURE 2	PICTURE 3	PICTURE 4
____ circle	____ parallel	____ angle	____ axis
____ round	____ line	____ line	____ ball
____ line	____ straight	____ straight	____ clock
____ closed	____ side	____ round	____ dial
____ plane	____ angle	____ curved	____ glass
____ center	____ four	____ birds	____ hand
____ equidistant	____ equal	____ mountains	____ handle
____ arc	____ equilateral	____ sun	____ rod
____	____ plane	____ rising	____ screw
____	____ wavy	____ light	____ socket
____	____ pointed	____	____ sphere
____	____ scalloped	____	____ station
____	____	____	____ tube
____	____	____	____ vane
____	____	____	____ weather
____	____	____	____
____	____	____	____
____	____	____	____
____	____	____	____
____	____	____	____

GENERATIVE LANGUAGE TEST
Part B: Quantity of Oral Language (See Appendix II)

Directions to the teacher:

Show the child a picture that depicts action, such as the one shown here. Record the total number of words, including repetitions, the child uses to describe it.

Directions to the child:

What is happening here? (When the child stops talking, the teacher waits 10 seconds and says: "Is there anything else you can say about what is happening here?")

Age Characteristics:

5 years: 25 to 50 words
6 years: 50 to 75 words
7 years: approximately 100 words
Above 8 years: child should be able to use
   200 words or more with a minimum of
   repetitions of content

GENERATIVE LANGUAGE TEST
Part C: Variety of Oral Language

Directions to the teacher:

Show child a simple picture of a boy and girl playing ball. Include other details such as a dog or cat, grass, flowers, sun. (See Appendix II.) Cover with clear contact. Keep notes of content.

Directions to the child:

I want you to tell me a story about this picture.

Level 1: Child merely names objects in picture or doesn't respond. (Preschool)
Level 2: Child describes action, e.g., "The boy is running." Sentences may be fragmented. (Kindergarten)

Level 3: Child verbalizes a relationship between characters and/or objects, e.g., "The boy and girl are playing catch with the ball." (Kindergarten to first grade)

Level 4: The child gives relationships of time, places, cause, and effect, e.g., "It is sunny out so the boy and girl can play outside. The dog is barking because he wants to play ball too." (First to second grade)

Level 5: The child perceives and responds to feelings and emotional reactions. Uses imagination and draws conclusion, e.g., "The children are happy because they like to play outside. It's a new ball they got for their birthday. I think maybe they are twins." (Second grade and up)

SUMMARY

Once these tests are given to a child, the teacher should have a better idea of the oracy base the child already possesses that can be transferred to the printed page. If the child has difficulties performing these skills or following directions, it is possible to plan work that will teach and reinforce the needed skills; such problems will be reflected and probably even heightened when the child attempts to utilize the same processes on the printed page.

Children with meager vocabularies and immature grammatical patterns need a curriculum that is rich in stories, puppets, and creative dramatics. Real experiences, such as walks in the neighborhood and animals in class, will make the language usage meaningful and exciting, regardless of the chronological age of the child. ESL-type games and other materials like those mentioned in Chapter 3 will all prove useful.

It is a waste of time and a tremendous frustration to demand literacy beyond a child's oracy.

SAMPLE CHECK SHEET

Oral Language Tests Check Sheet

	Echoics	Variety of Oral Lang.	Quantity of Oral Lang.	Accuracy of Oral Lang.	Following Directions	Information Recall	Interpretation of Oral Lang.	Inferential Analysis of Oral Lang.	Grammatical Understanding											

H = High Proficiency
M = Medium Proficiency
L = Low Proficiency or # of items correct

STUDENTS

part
III

READING
SKILL
ASSESSMENT

6

Phonics
and
the Decoding Process

A substantial body of research suggests that emphasis on the association of sounds and symbols is a most productive way to teach beginning reading skills. Certainly it is true that most methods of teaching reading include some consideration of phonics.

As we have seen, the child at the outset of language experience acquires a vocabulary and a grammatical style through oral communication. The meanings of words and the associations of these meanings with experience are acquired through listening and speaking. Only after a vocabulary and a style are firmly established can instruction in reading be fruitful. Therefore, a first step in the development of reading skills must be the recall of oral language and its association with written language. As the child encounters the printed word, past experience becomes a guide to the decoding process.

A second step in reading is the recognition of letter-sound relationships. English, like all languages, is based on the understanding of speech sounds which in most instances correspond to the letters we use to represent the sounds of the words they spell. These letter-sound relationships are fundamental to the understanding of English in print.

Linguists have used the term *phoneme* to represent the significant speech sounds in language. The term *grapheme* is used to denote the written symbol associated with a particular speech sound. Phoneme-grapheme correspondence is quite orderly and predictable in most cases. The mastery and internalization of these relationships represents a significant step in the development of the child's reading skills.

The analysis of words is necessarily a part of a higher-order reading process since it adds concept recognition to the task, both separately and in the reading context.

The term *morpheme* refers to the smallest unit of meaning in language. An individual word such as "toy" is one unit of meaning but the word "toys" is two because the *s* adds the meaning of plural. Thus affixes, compounds, and root words can be studied as another aspect of the decoding process.

The child's ability to pronounce a particular word is enhanced by the ability to understand word structure. If we think of the decoding process as a set of problem-solving strategies, we can see that the pairing of oral language with the meaningful interpretation of symbols requires a high level of skill. This process involves a relatively complex structure of thought that includes recognizing letters and words as such, translating those letters into sounds—either individual sounds or syllables—blending the sounds into a word unit that matches an appropriate oral language pattern, and recognizing that pattern as having meaning within the overall context of what is being read.

Eventually these processes become automatic for the child, and his reading becomes smooth and fluent. But the beginning reader or the reader who needs remedial help often requires very specific training and practice in utilizing decoding skills.

DECODING SKILLS

Discovering which steps in the decoding process are causing a problem poses for the teacher another kind of difficulty. Most programs teach decoding skills in a somewhat hierarchical order. An outline of these skills might be as follows:

I.   Sound-symbol relationships
  A.   Consonant sounds
    1.   Initial position: *b*at, *r*ug
    2.   Ending position: ba*t,* ru*g*
  B.   Blends and digraphs in similar positions
  C.   Vowel sounds
    1.   Short sounds in medial positions
    2.   Long sounds in medial positions, and silent *e*
    3.   Multiple spellings for vowel sounds
    4.   Beginning and ending vowels
    5.   Diphthongs
  D.   Irregular spellings
II.   Blending
  A.   Single letters to words: *c-a-t*
  B.   Blends to words: *sl-ee-t*
  C.   Sound units: n*ight, light*
III.   Syllabication
  A.   Oral identification of number of parts in a word
  B.   Rules for division of words
IV.   Structural analysis
  A.   Affixes
    1.   Inflectional endings
      a.   Plurals
      b.   Verb endings: *ed, -ing, -s*
      c.   comparisons: tall, tall*er*
    2.   Prefixes: *un*happy
    3.   Suffixes: announce*ment*
  B.   Compounds
  C.   Irregular plurals and tenses
  D.   Root words
    1.   As an unchanged or little-changed part of longer words: *vary,* in*var*iably

2.   As a derivative from other languages: *tele*-: *tele*vision, *tele*phone, *tele*graph
V.   Context
  1.   As a clue to a distorted blend of sounds: phone is recognized as *fone.*
  2.   As a clue to unfamiliar words/concepts.

Naturally the teacher may be working on several of these skills simultaneously. For example, the beginning reader may be learning to recognize the letters and associate their sounds, and, at the same time, to blend single letters into words. Most children start with the lower-level components within each skill, and if they miss a step in the process, the development of higher-level components may be impaired.

However, it is also important to realize that some children learn to read by whole word or syllable recognition and are fluent readers at an early age without a step-by-step progression. To insist that this child master a more elaborate decoding system is to lose sight of the goal of the process—the reading itself. Teaching decoding skills is appropriate only as a tool, not as an end in itself. Children who are reading well may find some of these skills useful for *spelling* and in *writing* but should not be forced into skill lessons that are unnecessary and meaningless.

In addition, most fluent readers skip many words and "figure out" the meaning of new words from the context of the material they are reading. Rarely will these readers stop to use an elaborate decoding system. Reading from context utilizes picture clues, customary language patterns, and stylistic patterns; this skill is explored in Chapter 8.

When reading impairment does occur, the teacher needs to discover what the gaps are. To find the missing steps, it is useful to have tests that will give specific information such as letter names, phomeme-grapheme correspondence, letter sounds, blending, syllabication, and structural analysis.

ALPHABET RECOGNITION AND GENERATION TEST

The first part of this test requires the child to circle the letter the teacher names. Once more we are tapping the "identification" level of recognition from the Montessori hierarchy of matching, identification, and recall.

The child is given a sheet with rows of letters. When the teacher says one of the letters, the child merely circles it. Because no oral response is required, this test can be administered to a group of children. Part A is identification of capitals, Part B is identification of lower-case letters.

In the second test the child is asked to recall orally a particular letter in each row from a field of letters. Again, Part A is identification of capitals and Part B of lower-case letters. Because the response is oral, this test must be given individually.

ALPHABET TEST: IDENTIFICATION LEVEL

Directions to the teacher:

This test may be given to individuals or groups. Each child will need an answer sheet (in Appendix II). Children may need a marker to stay in the correct row. The letters to be read are given in the Teacher Lists below.

Directions to the children:

Listen to the names of the letters I say. Then find that letter and circle it. Let's try one. (1) Find number 1. (2) With your finger, point to the letter I will say. (3) Now find the letter A and circle it. Good! (Repeat, going through the rest of the list.)

Part A (Upper Case)

1.	A	D	C	R	B	C	P
2.	L	M	N	E	M	Q	C
3.	I	T	F	Z	R	B	N
4.	S	G	F	Z	A	L	X
5.	V	Z	T	K	F	L	W
6.	C	N	O	S	P	Q	B

Teacher List: Part A (Upper Case)

1. *A* 2. *E* 3. *T* 4. *S* 5. *L* 6. *O* 7. *U* 8. *C* 9. *F* 10. *J* 11. *W* 12. *M* 13. *G* 14. *P* 15. *B* 16. *X* 17. *D* 18. *Q* 19. *Y* 20. *I* 21. *N* 22. *Z* 23. *V* 24. *R* 25. *H* 26. *K*

Teacher List: Part B (Lower Case)

1. *x* 2. *i* 3. *m* 4. *v* 5. *r* 6. *e* 7. *t* 8. *w* 9. *g* 10. *c* 11. *y* 12. *k* 13. *n* 14. *d* 15. *l* 16. *p* 17. *j* 18. *f* 19. *s* 20. *u* 21. *o* 22. *z* 23. *a* 24. *h* 25. *q* 26. *b*

ALPHABET TEST: RECALL LEVEL

Directions to the teacher:

This test must be administered individually. Record incorrect responses on a separate sheet.

Directions to the child:

Tell me the name of the letter that is underlined in each row.

Part A (Upper Case)

#						#				
1.	<u>A</u>	R	V	N		14.	D	P	Q	<u>J</u>
2.	W	<u>T</u>	C	P		15.	Y	<u>R</u>	N	W
3.	<u>F</u>	L	T	K		16.	L	M	<u>Z</u>	U
4.	W	M	<u>N</u>	D		17.	T	<u>S</u>	C	P
5.	P	D	<u>B</u>	C		18.	V	L	X	<u>K</u>
6.	R	P	<u>Q</u>	<u>O</u>		19.	<u>X</u>	Z	Y	D
7.	<u>O</u>	S	C	G		20.	B	D	<u>C</u>	E
8.	<u>I</u>	X	L	M		21.	N	<u>E</u>	H	M
9.	S	T	U	<u>V</u>		22.	<u>G</u>	C	D	U
10.	V	<u>W</u>	A	X		23.	R	T	<u>P</u>	F
11.	<u>M</u>	A	F	B		24.	H	E	X	<u>L</u>
12.	P	B	C	<u>D</u>		25.	V	<u>U</u>	W	M
13.	G	T	<u>H</u>	D		26.	K	<u>Y</u>	E	Z

Part B (Lower Case)

#						#				
1.	k	<u>y</u>	e	z		14.	g	t	<u>h</u>	d
2.	v	<u>u</u>	w	m		15.	p	b	c	<u>d</u>
3.	h	<u>e</u>	x	<u>l</u>		16.	<u>m</u>	a	f	b
4.	r	t	<u>p</u>	f		17.	v	<u>w</u>	a	x
5.	<u>g</u>	c	d	u		18.	s	t	u	<u>v</u>
6.	n	<u>e</u>	h	m		19.	<u>i</u>	x	l	m
7.	b	d	<u>c</u>	e		20.	<u>q</u>	s	c	g
8.	<u>x</u>	z	y	d		21.	r	p	q	<u>o</u>
9.	<u>v</u>	l	x	<u>k</u>		22.	p	d	<u>b</u>	c
10.	t	<u>s</u>	c	p		23.	w	m	<u>n</u>	d
11.	l	m	<u>z</u>	u		24.	<u>f</u>	l	t	k
12.	y	<u>r</u>	n	w		25.	w	<u>t</u>	c	p
13.	d	p	q	<u>j</u>		26.	<u>a</u>	r	v	n

PHONEME-GRAPHEME CORRESPONDENCE TESTS

The next tests involve phoneme-grapheme correspondence. The child begins by identifying the initial consonant sounds in a list of words. Then, in Part B, single consonants at the ends of words are tested.

The next part deals with the concept that when two or more consonants appear together, they may produce either a blended sound or a digraph. A *blended sound* can be thought of as two consonants slurred together that still retain most of their original sound value, as in *st*ep. A *digraph,* on the other hand, is a completely new sound produced by two consonants, as in *th*in; here, the original consonant sounds are completely lost.

Finally, Part D tests a student's ability to recognize vowel sounds; both long and short single vowel sounds that appear in the middle of a word in the consonant-vowel-consonant configuration are tested.

The Phoneme-Grapheme Correspondence Test is designed to test the child's ability to write the correct letter from a word clue. This test does not necessarily require a knowledge of spelling, but rather an understanding of the letters related to particular sounds in words.

PHONEME-GRAPHEME CORRESPONDENCE TEST

Part A (Beginning Consonants)

Directions to the teacher:

This test can be given to individuals or groups. The child needs a piece of paper and a pencil. Say the words clearly, but do not emphasize sounds artificially.

Directions to the children:

Write the letter at the beginning of the word I say.

1.	dog	7.	sat	13.	win
2.	ham	8.	vine	14.	tall
3.	lamb	9.	kit	15.	gone
4.	pound	10.	run	16.	yellow
5.	band	11.	note	17.	jump
6.	man	12.	fat	18.	zoo

Part B (Ending Consonants)

Directions to the children:

Write the letter at the end of the word I say.

1.	nick	6.	door	11.	new
2.	rig	7.	ham	12.	men
3.	pastel	8.	careless	13.	jazz
4.	drop	9.	set	14.	muff
5.	barb	10.	end	15.	thirty

Part C (Consonant Blends and Digraphs)

Directions to the teacher:

It may be necessary to complete the first two items with the children to make sure that they understand the concept of a blend.

Directions to the children:

Write the two letters that form a blend sound at the beginning of the words I say.

1.	blast	9.	trinket	16.	spice
2.	brown	10.	closet	17.	smart
3.	drop	11.	crock	18.	swarm
4.	fly	12.	price	19.	sky
5.	fragile	13.	slice	20.	sharp
6.	grass	14.	snail	21.	thin
7.	plaster	15.	glance	22.	phone
8.	stare				

Part D (Vowels)

Directions to the teacher:

The child will need an answer sheet for this test. This should consist of rows of vowel letters in order (*a-e-i-o-u*); see the sample below. Long vowels are tested before short vowels because they are more regular in sound and therefore easier to identify. Children may be tested for long and short vowels separately or the two lists can be given at the same time.

Directions to the children:

Circle the vowel sound that is in the middle of the word I say.

Sample Answer Sheet: Part D (Vowels)

Name _____ Grade _____

1. a   e   i   o   u
2. a   e   i   o   u
3. a   e   i   o   u

Teacher List: Part D (Long Vowels)

1. Safe 2. Dime 3. Fume 4. Rice 5. Cope 6. Sleep 7. Cape 8. Cute 9. Heat 10. Coax

Teacher List: Part D (Short Vowels)

1. Kit 2. Cut 3. Peck 4. Fish 5. Watch 6. Cob 7. Sick 8. Stop 9. Bug 10. Sat

OTHER TESTING FORMATS

The letter-sound correspondence tests described so far require that the children use a recall rather than an identification response. They were designed for children with more advanced skills and require that the children write the letter or letters they think are the correct answers. Some suggested formats for less advanced students are also included in this chapter. Because of their limited usefulness, they are not provided in the Appendix but are included here to give you some alternative possibilities at an identification level.

The short samples that follow require only the identification of existing letters. They can be lengthened and elaborated at the teacher's discretion.

BEGINNING CONSONANTS

Directions to the teacher:

This test may be administered to groups or individuals. However, all items must be read to the children slowly; give them ample opportunity to mark answers. Repeat as needed. Each child will need an answer sheet with boxes, similar to the samples later in this section.

Directions to the children:

If the word I say begins with the sound of *b*, put an X in the box beside the number of the word on your answer sheet. Now listen. Number 1, "bat." Put an X in the box beside the 1 if you think bat begins with *b*.

Sample A: 1. bat   2. cat   3. big   4. beautiful

Do you have an X beside number 1? Good! (Repeat for 2, 3, and 4.) You should not have an X beside number 2. Number 3 and number 4 should have an X in the boxes. (Repeat for sample *B*, using the letter *t*.)

Sample B: 5. dog   6. table   7. tunnel   8. mother

r	9.	rattle	10.	rumble	11.	race	12.	where	13.	table
t	14.	funny	15.	upset	16.	tumble	17.	laugh	18.	fumble
p	19.	terrible	20.	parable	21.	tame	22.	careful	23.	tall
f	24.	pancake	25.	fable	26.	done	27.	yell	28.	five
m	29.	fat	30.	elephant	31.	mouse	32.	near	33.	mean
w	34.	water	35.	winter	36.	mind	37.	nobody	38.	wear
s	39.	top	40.	sun	41.	sit	42.	caught	43.	ear

ENDING CONSONANTS

Directions to the teacher:

Each child needs an answer sheet with boxes, as shown. Proceed as in the test above.

Directions to the children:

If the word I say ends with the sound of *t*, put an X in the box beside the number of the word. Now listen. Number 1, "get." Put an X beside the 1 if you think "get" ends with the sound of *t*. Do you have an X beside number 1? Good! (Repeat for 2, 3, and 4.)

Sample A: 1. get   2. come   3. fat   4. forget

(Repeat directions above, using ending *r*.)

Sample B: 5. fun   6. bigger   7. gum   8. roam

s	9.	light	10.	useless	11.	sold	12.	cats
d	13.	rained	14.	dune	15.	rib	16.	had
k	17.	crank	18.	kin	19.	back	20.	kite

BLENDS AND DIGRAPHS

Directions to the children:

If the word I say has a *c-h* sound in it, put an X in the box beside the number of the word. Now listen. Number 1, "catch." Put an X beside the 1 if you think catch has a *c-h* in it. Do you have an X beside number 1? Good! Where is the *ch* sound? (Repeat for 2, 3, and 4. Check to be sure children can complete sample items.)

Sample A: 1. catch   2. break   3. change   4. table

(Repeat directions above, using *s-t*.)

Sample B: 5. stop   6. taller   7. star   8. unstable

(Continue, pronouncing individual letters of blends and digraphs rather than their sounds.)

Some other common blends and digraphs that the teacher may want to test for include:

	Blends	*Digraphs*
	bl, br, cl, cr, dr, fl	sh, ph
	fr, gl, gr, pl, pr, tr	

SAMPLE ANSWER SHEET

Name _____Grade _____

Sample A

1. [   ]   2. [   ]   3. [   ]   4. [   ]

Sample B

5. [   ]   6. [   ]   7. [   ]   8. [   ]
9. [   ]   10. [   ]   11. [   ]   12. [   ]
13. [   ]   14. [   ]   15. [   ]   16. [   ]
17. [   ]   18. [   ]   19. [   ]   20. [   ]
21. [   ]   22. [   ]   23. [   ]   24. [   ]
25. [   ]   26. [   ]   27. [   ]   28. [   ]
29. [   ]   30. [   ]   31. [   ]   32. [   ]
33. [   ]   34. [   ]   35. [   ]   36. [   ]

VOWEL SOUNDS

Directions to the teacher:

This test may be administered to small groups. Say the words clearly, but do not artificially stress the middle vowel. Check all samples to make sure children understand the instructions. Sample answer sheet follows this test.

Directions to the children:

Tell me which words have the same middle sound. Here are three words.

1. bet   2. mess   3. bill

Which ones had the same middle sound? That's right, "bet" and "mess." Now look at *Sample A.*

Sample A: 1. call   2. red

The words are "call" and "red." Which one has the same sound as "bet" and "mess"? Right, "red." Put an X in the box next to "red" because it has the same middle sound. Let's try again. Which of the next three words has the same middle sound?

1. kind   2. gull   3. mice

Right—"kind" and "mice." Now look at *Sample B* on your paper. The words are "milk" and "file." Which one has the same middle sound as "kind" and "mice"? Yes, "file." So put an X in front of the word "file" because it has the same middle sound as "kind" and "mice." Now let's do the rest.

Sample A: bet, mess, bill

   ANSWER: 1. call   2. <u>red</u>   *(Answer is underlined.)*

Sample B: kind, gull, mice

   ANSWER: 1. milk   2. <u>file</u>

1. bale pack safe
   answer: bull <u>make</u>
	6. sole mind tote
	   answer: <u>hole</u> run

2. cup run seem
   answer: feel <u>tug</u>
	7. site set fresh
	   answer: mint <u>mend</u>

3. mut mule yule
   answer: <u>cute</u> but
	8. gap sat pearl
	   answer: girl <u>map</u>

4. grind fin like
   answer: cinder <u>finder</u>
	9. yes bit sit
	   answer: help <u>mill</u>

5. call mop cod
   answer: <u>hot</u> roll
	10. feel peek nice
	   answer: <u>seek</u> fine

SAMPLE ANSWER SHEET

Name _____ Grade _____

Sample A: 1. ☐ call   2. ☐ red

Sample B: 1. ☐ milk   2. ☐ file

1.	1.	☐	bull		2.	☐	make
2.	1.	☐	feel		2.	☐	tug
3.	1.	☐	cute		2.	☐	but
4.	1.	☐	cinder		2.	☐	finder
5.	1.	☐	hot		2.	☐	roll
6.	1.	☐	hole		2.	☐	run
7.	1.	☐	mint		2.	☐	mend
8.	1.	☐	girl		2.	☐	map
9.	1.	☐	help		2.	☐	mill
10.	1.	☐	seek		2.	☐	fine

BLENDING TEST

Blending tests help determine the child's ability to listen to certain sounds and combine them with other sounds to form a new word. The fact that a child can recognize or produce sounds in isolation does not necessarily mean that he or she can then use them together to form a word. In fact, this is often a difficult task, particularly for the older child, who is having reading problems, or the child who has a limited standard English vocabulary. The task is of critical importance, however, in the development of independent word attack skills.

There are two levels to the Blending Test, each of which uses a different format. The first level uses picture clues in a rebus style and is meant for less mature children. The second level requires more reading skill but uses the identification level for answers.

BLENDING TEST: LEVEL I

Directions to the teacher:

Each child will need an answer sheet (in Appendix II). Be careful not to stress words in an artificial way that gives the students clues. After using the first item as a sample, it may be necessary to demonstrate the process on the blackboard.

Directions to the children:

You have a page with twelve boxes on it. Each box has a word puzzle made up of a picture and some letters. I'm going to say a word and a number, and you will find the puzzle that fits the word and write the number I say in it. Let's try one together. Number one is "snail."

Look for a letter-picture combination for snail and put the number 1 in the box. Do it now. (Check to see if everyone found the correct box. If not, do the example on the blackboard for illustration.) Now let's see if you can do the rest. Number 2 is . . .

Teacher List: Level I

1. *snail* 2. *train* 3. *potter* 4. *stop* 5. *design* 6. *panic* 7. *slipper* 8. *road*

Sample Blending Test: Level I

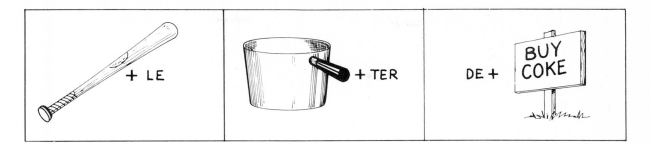

BLENDING TEST: LEVEL II

Directions to the teacher:

Read each word from the teacher list below with normal intonation. You may repeat once. If children are confused, do some hypothetical examples on the board after the first item. Children's copy of the test is in Appendix II.

Directions to the children:

In each row on this paper there are three words. Notice that the words are slightly different either in the way they are divided or the way they are spelled or both. I'm going to say one of the three words and you are going to circle the one you think I am saying. Let's try number 1 together.

Teacher List: Level II

1. *stride*	2. *stringent*	3. *pitcher*	4. *nitrate*
5. *decode*	6. *directions*	7. *silently*	8. *bandana*

Sample Blending Test: Level II

1. str + ite	str + ide	str + eed
2. strin + gent	string + ent	sti + dent

SYLLABICATION TEST

The use of syllables to "sound" words either for reading or spelling is a fairly sophisticated skill that is based on auditory discrimination and blending. It also requires extensive experience with the peculiarities of English words. Unfortunately, very few of the various rules for dividing words into syllables works consistently. Nevertheless, when moderately good readers attack a new word, they almost always begin by sounding the syllables. Testing for syllabication, then, can provide information concerning a reader's use of this strategy and also show areas where direct teaching would be suitable. In our opinion, only the six rules listed below are worth specific teaching.

Syllable rules that are moderately useful are:

1. The number of vowel sounds in each word indicates the number of syllables. For example, shook, cur/tain, prob/a/bly.

2. When double consonants occur between two vowels, the word is usually divided between the two consonants. For example, but/ter, hur/ry, let/ter.

3. Two different consonants are also divided if they occur between two vowels. For example, for/ward, pic/nic, cor/ner.

4. A consonant before an "-le" ending usually goes with the ending to form a syllable. For example, ta/ble, lit/tle, ap/ple.

5. A blend or digraph is treated as one letter.

6. A word with a suffix will be divided before the suffix.

Both parts of the syllabication test use the same set of words. Part A tests for the ability to divide the written form of the words into syllables.

SYLLABICATION TEST

Part A

Directions to the teacher:

This test may be given to groups. Children will need a paper and pencil. You will use the words that appear in Part B and say them orally to the group. Do not artifically stress the syllables in the words. Do a sample with the children to make sure they understand the concept.

Directions to the children:

I'm going to say some words out loud. I'll repeat the word twice. Listen carefully and notice how many parts the word seems to have. You will write on your paper the number of parts you hear. Let's try one.

Part B

Directions to the teacher:

Child's copy of the test is in Appendix II. The teacher reads the directions aloud while the children read them silently.

Directions to the children:

Read each word below and divide it into syllables by drawing a line between each syllable. For example, "undelivered" must be divided into four syllables like this: un/de/liv/ered. Divide each word below in the same way.

Word List for Parts A and B

1. de/vel/op
2. whole/some
3. speed/om/e/ter
4. round/ed
5. light/er
6. float/ing
7. un/shrink/a/ble
8. re/charged
9. in/no/cent
10. bat/tle
11. in/ter/pret
12. un/sus/pect/ing

STRUCTURAL ANALYSIS OF WORDS

In this test we are attempting to discover the child's knowledge of both root words and affixes as an aid to pronunciation and analysis of meaning.

Affixes carry meaning even though they cannot function independently. For example, the "ly" on the end of "quickly" adds the meaning of "like" or "in that manner." These are termed *bound morphemes*. Words that carry meaning by themselves are *unbound*.

Inflectional endings are the first aspect of structural analysis developed since the children have become very familiar with such things as plurals, past tense, and comparison through their regular oral language usage (though they may have no labels for those concepts). Compound words also enter the reading picture quickly. A child may know about "cowboys" long before he or she is conscious of the separate words and how they lend meaning to each other. The recognition of irregular plurals and tenses develops more slowly as children are exposed to them in oral language.

The awareness of root words as aids to meaning comes much later and often needs to be directly taught. The child must develop a working definition of the nature of a root word and be able to identify examples. This implies that the child has decoding and comprehension skills that support each other in the problem-solving process of pronouncing a particular word. Once the root has been identified and labeled, the child learns to use roots and affixes together to see how each contributes to the word's meaning. Again, the recognition of the affixes constitutes a significant clue to the pronunciation of the word as well as to its meaning. For example, *dis*-oriented can be distinguished from *re*-oriented on the basis of configuration, and the definitions of the two words change according to the meaning of the affix, not of the root word.

The first level of the structural analysis test deals with the earliest sets of regular and irregular inflectional endings within context and is suitable for children with some reading skill.

Sample

The boy was_____the horse.

              ride   rided   riding

Level II deals with a series of affixes and requires identification of words according to the meaning of the affix.

Sample

Circle the words in each row that indicate more than one (plural).

a. baby   babies   baby's   babied
b. cries   cried   criers   crying

The third level deals with the child's ability to identify roots within words. The test has rows of four words each. Three words have a common root. The child must underline these roots. The fourth word looks as if the root could be the same, but the meaning and/or pronunciation identify it as being different from the others. The child must cross out the word that does not belong to the group.

Sample

re<u>count</u>   <u>count</u>less   un<u>count</u>ed

STRUCTURAL ANALYSIS TEST: LEVEL I
(Inflectional Endings and Irregulars)

Directions to the teacher:

Each child will need an answer sheet (in Appendix II). Circulate while the children work, so you can answer questions and supply words to those who need help. Test is in the Appendix.

Directions to the children:

Today you are going to read some sentences in which there is a word missing. Under the space are three words, but only one is the right one for that sentence. Let's do sample A together. (Go over sample in Appendix II.) Now do the other sentences in the same way.

STRUCTURAL ANALYSIS TEST: LEVEL II (Affixes)

Directions to the teacher:

Read these directions aloud while the children read them silently. Note that there may be more than one answer in a line. Full test is in Appendix II.

Directions to the children:

1. Circle the word or words in each row that indicate more than one (plural).

a.	baby	babies	baby's	babied
b.	cries	cried	criers	crying
c.	thoughtlessness	rethought	thoughts	thoughtful
d.	ruler's	ruling	rulers	unruled

(Continue with the rest of the test.)

STRUCTURAL ANALYSIS TEST: LEVEL III (Root Words)

Directions to the teacher:

Read aloud while the children read silently. Full test is in Appendix II.

Directions to the children:

Underline the root word in each of the following words if the root word is present. Put an X on the word that does not have the root in it. Look at the sample. Notice that recount, countless, and uncounted have the same root and that country does not.

Sample

recount   countless   co🗙try   uncounted

SUMMARY

The tests in this section are designed to give the teacher as much information as possible concerning the various skills the student brings to the decoding process. It may be determined that components of a skill are missing from the repertoire of the child. The teacher will find it easier to teach the necessary specifics of decoding if he or she is aware of the multiple aspects of the process and can pinpoint individual needs accurately.

However, decoding is just one portion of the total reading process and must be approached as a tool. Decoding is a useful method in the "detective work" of reading. Overemphasis on decoding, however, can lead to word callers rather than readers. Children who learn accurate decoding at the expense of meaning will not maintain the interest or motivation to explore the printed word independently.

SAMPLE CHECK SHEETS

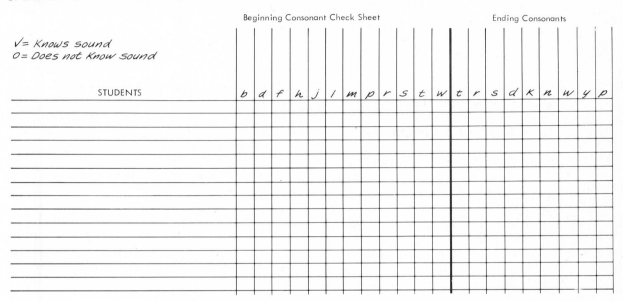

7

The Assessment
of
Oral Reading

Oral reading is a combination of the decoding of words and the attachment of meaning to those words. It can, therefore, be accepted as one evidence that reading is, in fact, taking place. However, the oral pronunciation of words should not be considered as the complete reading act but rather as one of many ways this act may be observed. Oral reading allows us directly to observe the children applying their acquired reading skills, and in this manner it can be utilized as a valuable diagnostic tool.

If the written word is seen both as talk-in-print, as some linguists see it, and as a way of transmitting meaning that may or may not ever be spoken, then oral reading becomes merely one of the many ways to utilize print. For example, the process of oral reading can be viewed as a temporary means of achieving some initial objective in learning to read, such as determining the child's reading level or pronunciation ability. Beyond the classroom, oral reading is of passing interest to many but is seldom required. It has been suggested that only a very small portion of all the words printed are ever actually pronounced aloud, for the value of the printed word lies not in the reader's ability to pronounce but in the ability to comprehend.

Although oral reading may be instructionally useful under some circumstances, it should be quickly passed over in favor of the development of other skills in the regular instructional program. Oral reading does offer a number of advantages to the teacher in the beginning stages of learning to read. It assists the teacher in helping the child associate printed words and the thought units represented by those words. It assists the child by giving her confirmation of her interpretations of the words, and when she is successful it may give her a sense of having accomplished an important task.

Oral reading also provides an opportunity to interpret the printed word through a variation in tone and emphasis. This aspect of reading is more difficult to assess than silent reading. The variation of phrasing and intonation patterns in a given passage can radically change the meaning of what is read, as in this example:

"What are we having for dinner, Stew?"
"What are we having for dinner, stew?"

It is this last aspect that provides both an opportunity and a dilemma for the teacher of reading. On one hand, creative and divergent rendering of an oral passage can be a stimulating and valuable experience for both the reader and the listeners. On the other hand, teaching for a particularly desired or "expected" emphasis pattern can be most frustrating, because often there are few clues to "correct" intonation provided. This intriguing problem accounts for the many variations and interpretations of literature that abound in the theater. These should be kept in mind when children offer different interpretations of materials read.

LIMITATIONS OF ORAL READING

Oral reading is emphasized in many basal reading programs. It provides the teacher with evidence of the child's accomplishment or lack of it. Such skills as word pronunciation and use of punctuation can be verified in this way, thereby giving the teacher information that can be useful in planning instruction. Oral reading in the presence of the teacher and a group of peers, a practice sometimes called round-robin reading, may be advantageous for some children in the early stages of reading training. While the concept of "a word" is being developed and strengthened, reading in a group may help demonstrate the correspondence between the spoken and the written word.

Oral reading may be overused in the classroom, however, consuming an unnecessarily large share of the time allotted to reading instruction. It must also be remembered that the round-robin approach can be a psychological problem for the child. It calls the attention of the entire group to an individual's reading skills or, worse, the lack of them. The learner is "on the spot" a few minutes at a time; the rest of his time he observes his classmates while he supposedly follows along silently. Often this time is spent daydreaming or misbehaving.

Psychologists and learning theorists have generally acknowledged that one of the most important reinforcements in the classroom setting is the relationship of a child to his or her peer group. When any individual is called on to perform to an audience whose opinions and goodwill are important in his life, he does so with a certain amount of anxiety and concern. Acceptance by the group is highly important to him. If he is unsuccessful in his performance, the resulting tension and embarrassment may well have undesirable effects. A child whose skills are less well developed than those of others in his peer group can become virtually paralyzed.

Should this situation continue for some time, the child will in many instances learn to defend himself against his feelings of inadequacy by behaving in a way that clearly tells others that reading is not important. He may well come to believe this himself. For such a child, individual oral reading in a group setting may do more to develop negative attitudes than any other single classroom practice. Oddly enough, frequently the children who comprise the lower half of their class in reading ability are asked to read orally more often than those in the upper half. If positive attitudes toward reading and toward school in general are thought to be important, individual oral reading in a group setting should be minimized.

Excessive use of oral reading can even be a problem for the more capable readers in the classroom. Inattention and boredom are poor reading companions, and certain practices seem to encourage these habits. For example, assigning oral reading to one child after another in order around the reading circle lets the child figure out quickly which part of the text she will be likely to read and reduces her attention to other parts of the lesson. Having each child read the same number of lines or paragraphs usually has the same effect.

Oral reading before silent reading is another practice that can cause the children difficulty, since it ignores the fact that they must perceive and decode the words before they can attack their pronunciation.

The child may develop the habit of reading one word at a time rather than seeing words in blocks or units. The word remains the unit of thought, not the phrase or sentence. Word calling—that is, the correct but labored pronunciation of a long list of words (the sentence) in a relatively meaningless stream—can frequently be found in classes that emphasize oral reading. Teachers may praise clearly and correctly pronounced words, even though such pronunciation reduces the speed of reading material and produces artificial units of thought. Word calling and lack of proper phrasing are habit patterns that can handicap the student. In addition, unwillingness to participate in oral reading and reduced self esteem will be encountered when mistakes in oral reading are used to correct pronunciation errors of a child whose primary language is not standard English. Choral reading, singing, and dramatic presentations are a far more effective means of addressing pronunciation problems than the reading lesson.

It must be remembered that Spanish, Portuguese, German, and many other languages have far more regular phoneme-grapheme relationships than English. It is difficult for a limited English speaker to read orally in front of his peers and potentially embarrass himself in the process; in addition, the phonics rules he is attempting to master simply don't work in a significant number of high-frequency English words. It is difficult to overestimate the frustration engendered by such a situation.

Another serious drawback of the overuse of oral reading circles is that it significantly reduces the potential rate of reading. The oral reading pace becomes the only reading pace. Many children who may be capable of reading more rapidly develop a habit of reading slowly, since this is the only practice they follow in a reinforcing situation, one in which the teacher may praise them. While accuracy in reading is certainly important, careful oral reading may slow down the reading rate.

English and most other languages are highly redundant—that is, their users commonly employ more words, especially such devices as "the" and "a," than are necessary to convey the meaning. In addition, languages have well-used groups of words that are remembered as such—for instance, "quick as a wink." Considerable research suggests that children, when shown an unfamiliar passage from which 20 percent of the words are deleted, can replace more than half the missing words. Anyone who wishes to increase reading flexibility must learn to identify the key words in a paragraph and to recognize the less important words and phrases for what they are. The development of such skills may be impeded by oral reading practice.

Therefore sufficient practice in methods other than oral reading is an important part of the reading program. Particularly in the upper elementary grades, the identification of more and less important words needs to be developed and the reading-learning process streamlined. Individual oral reading in group settings tends to ignore this skill to the point where it ceases to encourage the development of sound and useful reading habits.

USES OF ORAL READING

We do not suggest that oral reading does not have numerous legitimate uses in the classroom. The reading of plays, poetry, and other significant materials that were designed for oral presentation is a most valid and highly useful activity. The expression through voice modulation of intricate shades of meaning is the sole province of the orally read passage and contributes a depth and richness to language that no other form of reading does. These legitimate uses of oral reading, with their limited but very important roles in the acquisition of reading skills, can be highly motivating and meaningful for children.

A teacher can place children in temporary groups for instruction in oral reading with a specific purpose. For example, volunteers who will perform in a play might profitably be asked to read lines orally while instruction focuses on the proper stress, pitch, and juncture of their lines. In the same manner, children who need work in oral reading—of poetry, for instance—might be grouped temporarily for that purpose. The reading of poetry can be greatly enhanced by the choral verse method, and the different uses of the voice can be exemplified in such a way that the child is involved but does not feel the weight of adverse peer group opinion. Small groups or individuals who have rehearsed well and have been urged to use innovative reading styles in poetry not only can share their understanding with others but can encourage them to become similarly involved.

It is useful to have students read orally material they themselves have written. A child who reads a story developed through the Language Experience Approach will obviously be familiar with the story's vocabulary and structure, which will form a useful and familiar bridge toward confidence in oral expression (see Chapter 3).

For children who are shy and have a difficult time expressing themselves even in small groups, the use of puppets and marionettes with a written script can be a valuable instructional tool. In this case, as in the reading of plays, the expressive use of stress, pitch, and juncture can provide the most retiring child with valuable ways to develop oral language skills in conjunction with reading skills.

Finally, the description of the skills related to reading and the affective domain would not be complete without reference to the importance of speaking well in a group, large or small. Certainly, oral reading skill developed through some or all of the methods described here will be beneficial in numerous ways. This means of self-expression can be invaluable in providing opportunities for giving recognition and building self-confidence.

TESTS OF ORAL READING

As a tool for the assessment of reading ability, oral reading inventories can be most useful. Particularly at the outset of the school year, an oral reading test is important to the teacher in gaining first-hand knowledge of the child's skills in this area. The correct pronunciation of words provides evidence of visual perception and decoding skills. The reading of short paragraphs also provides a means of checking the speed of reading and skill in phrasing, recognition of punctuation, and tone. Questions after reading give the teacher important information concerning the child's ability to comprehend what has been read.

Oral reading inventories are generally of two types. The first type, sometimes called a quick assessment, consists of lists of words chosen from graded word lists. The child who can read the lists from the primary level and makes no errors is likely to be able to read primary material. The child is then given successively more difficult lists until he or she misses a predetermined number of words. Then it can be suggested that that child has reached the ceiling or frustration level.

The second type of inventory consists of short paragraphs also graded for difficulty by levels. They furnish information about phrasing, punctuation, and comprehension as well as word recognition.

To gain maximum information on the children's skills, a teacher should administer reading inventories to each child individually and make records of the errors. Usually the quick assessment is given in the first few days of the school year to furnish quick initial information regarding the child's functioning level. Then the oral reading paragraphs can be administered to confirm and extend initial impressions. While information on the child's

reading level will prove helpful, even more valuable is an analysis of the types of errors or miscues the child makes while reading: Does he ignore punctuation? Does she skip words or guess them using only the beginning sound as a clue? Can he determine what a word should be from the context of the passage he is reading? Does she reverse letter order, perhaps reading "not" for "ton"?

A miscue analysis may prove of considerable value at this point. Analysis of the miscue is an attempt to evaluate the oral reader's use of the available array of cue systems. A strategy for the identification of miscues starts with the question, "Does the child's error violate the syntactic (grammatical) or semantic (meaningful) congruence of the sentence?" Only if the answer is "yes" does it become necessary to pursue the nature of the error.

Miscues are evaluated by analyzing the degree to which they disrupt meaning.

Current work suggests that substitutions, insertions, and omissions or variations of these account for most interference in the process of accurate word reproduction (Goodman, 1967; Goodman and Fleming, 1968; Goodman and Burke, 1973). The miscue should be called to the attention of the reader, and then the sentence or phrase should be reread. The repetition of any one or a combination of these miscues calls for a careful analysis of the miscue and possibly further testing.

If the error persists, then the nature of the test results will lead to specific instructional strategies. For example, if the child consistently mixes middle sounds, "mat" for "met" or "nit" for "net," testing for visual acuity or vowel sounding may be in order. A teacher can also gain evidence on attitude and feelings by observing signs of nervousness or insecurity in the child. Children who are fearful of reading will need special kinds of help.

Usually the oral inventory represents a good starting point in the gathering of data on the child's skill development. These tests can also be utilized later to assess the child's progress in oral reading.

It must be emphasized, however, that oral reading tests do not reflect the child's ability to read and comprehend silently. Great gaps can occur between oral and silent reading skills. Oral reading also offers the teacher little indication as to the child's flexibility in rate of reading or the ability to skim, to find particular information, or to utilize headings, illustrations, and graphics to understand the author's meaning. Though some studies have indicated a relatively high correlation between a child's skill in reading aloud and his or her performance in other related reading tasks, it can by no means be assumed that the child who reads well orally can also read well silently.

It is also possible for a child who reads well silently to do a poor job in an oral reading situation. Many children who have become rapid silent readers will skip words or stumble over pronunciation, since their eyes sweep ahead faster than they can actually say the words. This may be especially true of the upper grade child. Silent reading tests will be discussed in the next chapter.

In the San Diego Quick Assessment of Reading Ability and the oral reading passages developed for this book, the following marking system is recommended. The teacher will probably need practice, particularly in the paragraphs, before he or she can mark the errors smoothly. In the paragraphs, omission and substitution of punctuation marks as well as of words should be marked. Naturally other notations may be added as the teacher desires.

Error	How to mark	Sample
Omission	Two lines through word	c̶a̶t̶
Mispronunciation	One line through word	c̶a̶t̶
Hesitation and limited assistance	One x above word	x cat
Refusal (child doesn't say word; teacher supplies word)	Two xs above word	xx cat
Reversal	Arrow	⟵ cat
Insertion	Carat	little the ∧ cat
Substitution	Cross out and write substituted word	ran the cat ~~run~~
Repetition	Wavy line under repeated word	the the cat ran

Research has indicated that there are three reading levels that are valuable to know for choosing appropriate reading materials for a child (Bormuth, 1968). The first is the *independent level*. Here the child recognizes 95 percent of the words in a passage and knows the answers to at least 90 percent of the associated comprehension questions. This is the level the child should be encouraged to use in selecting library books and independent skill exercises. This is the level at which the child will feel most successful. The next is the *instructional level*. Here the child can read 90 percent of the words and answer 75 percent of the comprehension questions. This is the level the teacher utilizes when he or she is working with the child and is available for help with the words the child does not know. Any higher percentage of errors than this is described as the child's *frustration level*, which should be avoided for independent or instructional purposes. Some studies have shown that schools require as many as 50 percent of the children tested to read at their frustration level. Such a practice spells defeat and misery for the child. These three levels will be utilized as guidelines for the oral reading tests in this book.

SAN DIEGO QUICK ASSESSMENT OF READING ABILITY

This test consists of thirteen word lists graded from preprimer through junior high. The words within each list are of about the same difficulty. The first five lists can be considered primary level, the next four lists intermediate level, and the last four lists upper level. Having the words in a column on a 4 by 7 inch index card with the grade level marked on the back is usually the easiest way to prepare the test for administration (See Appendix II)

Because the number of words in each list is limited, zero errors is considered independent level, one error instructional level, and two errors frustration level. The teacher should begin with a list two or three sets below the child's presumed functioning level in school (or lower if there is a possibility the child has reading difficulties) and have her read the words on each list until she makes two errors. Errors are recorded on a separate sheet that can be prepared in multiple copies.

This separate record sheet can be a rough starting point for initial instruction and further investigation. At this point, it would be appropriate to begin a tentative profile on the child's strengths and weaknesses. Formulation of a tentative hypothesis concerning the child's skills can then be supported or contradicted by additional information to be gathered from such techniques as the assessment of oral paragraph reading.

Directions to the teacher:

Each list of ten words should be on an index card. For primary children, begin with a card that is at Level 1; for intermediate, Level 4; and for upper and secondary, Level 6. (See Appendix II.) ask the student to read the words aloud. If he or she misreads any on the list, drop to easier lists until there are no errors made. This indicates the base level.

Directions to the children:

Read each list of words. Say each word carefully. Begin.

Analysis of the test

The list in which a student misses no words is the level at which the child can read independently. One error indicates the instructional level. Two or more errors identify the level at which reading material will be too difficult.

An analysis of a student's errors is useful. Among those that occur with great frequency are the following:

Error	*Examples*
reversal	was for saw
consonant	how for now
consonant clusters	state for straight
short vowel	cane for can
long vowel	wid for wide
prefix	inproved for improved
suffix	improve for improved
miscellaneous	accent, omission of syllables, etc.

As with other reading tasks, the teacher must observe the student's behavior. Such things as posture, facial expression, and voice quality may signal restlessness, lack of assurance, or frustration.

Readiness	1	2	3	4
see	you	road	our	city
play	come	live	please	middle
me	not	thank	myself	moment
at	with	when	town	frightened
run	jump	bigger	early	exclaimed
go	help	how	send	several
and	is	always	wide	lonely
look	work	night	believe	drew
can	are	spring	quietly	since
here	this	today	carefully	straight

5	6	7	8
decided	scanty	bridge	amber
served	certainly	commercial	dominion
amazed	develop	abolish	sundry
silent	considered	trucker	capillary
wrecked	discussed	apparatus	impetuous
improved	behaved	elementary	blight
critical	splendid	comment	wrest
entered	acquainted	necessity	enumerate
realized	escaped	gallery	daunted
interrupted	grim	relativity	condescend

9	10	11	12
capacious	conscientious	zany	galore
limitation	isolation	jerkin	rotunda
pretext	molecule	nausea	capitalism
intrigue	ritual	gratuitous	prevaricate
delusion	momentous	linear	risible
immaculate	vulnerable	inept	exonerate
ascent	kinship	legality	superannuate
acrid	conservatism	aspen	luxuriate
binocular	jaunty	amnesty	piebald
embankment	inventive	barometer	crunch

SAMPLE SCORE SHEET

Reader‗‗‗‗‗‗‗‗‗‗‗‗‗‗‗   Tested by ‗‗‗‗‗‗‗‗‗‗‗

Age ‗‗‗‗‗‗‗Grade ‗‗‗‗‗   Date of Test ‗‗‗‗‗‗‗‗‗

Error Type	*Example*	*Error Type*	*Example*
reversal	was for saw	long vowel	wid for wide
consonant	now for how	prefix	inproved for improved
consonant cluster	state for straight	suffix	improve for improved
short vowel	cane for can	miscellaneous	accent, ommission of syllables, etc.

‗‗‗‗‗‗‗‗‗‗‗‗‗‗‗‗‗‗‗‗‗‗‗‗‗‗‗‗‗‗‗‗‗‗‗‗

Card no. ‗‗‗‗‗	Card no. ‗‗‗‗‗	Card no. ‗‗‗‗‗
Errors	Errors	Errors

‗‗‗‗‗‗‗‗‗‗‗‗‗‗‗‗‗‗‗‗‗‗‗‗‗‗‗‗‗‗‗‗‗‗‗‗

Card no. ‗‗‗‗‗	Card no. ‗‗‗‗‗	Card no. ‗‗‗‗‗
Errors	Errors	Errors

SPANISH WORD LIST

The following word list is designed specifically for children from Spanish-speaking homes. It is especially useful in bilingual programs.

    It is reasonable to expect most first graders to be able to read about 150 of these words by the end of the first school year and all of the words by the end of the second grade, if they are being taught to read in Spanish.

Directions to the child:

Read each word. If you can't pronounce it, please go on to the next word.

Lea cada palabra. Si no puede pronunciarla, por favor continue con la próxima palabra.

a	cuchara	gato	mamá	padre	sol
abajo	cumpleaños	globo	mano	país	solo (alone)
abeja	cuna	grande	manzana	palabra	su
agua		guitarra	mañana	pan	sueño
aire	chico	*gustar	martes	papá	sus
al			más	papel	
ala	*dar	*haber	me	para	también
alto	de	*hablar	mejor	paz	tan
allá	debajo	*hacer	mesa	pelota	tarde
*amar	*decir	hacia	mi (adj.)	pie	taza
amigo	del	hasta	mí (pron.)	por	te (pron.)
amistad	dentro	hermana	mientras	porque	té (tea)
*andar	desde	hermano	miércoles	primavera	tener
antes	después	hija	mío	primero	ti
año	día	hijo	mis	pronto	tía
aquí	dibujo	hoy	muchacha	puerta	tío
árbol	donde		muchacho		tierra
arriba	dos	idea	mucho	¿qué?	tijeras
así	dulces	igual	muñeca	*querer	todo
atrás		invierno	música	queso	*traer
ayer	edad	*ir (form)	muy	¿quién?	traje (dress)
azúcar	el (art.)			quince	tras
azul	él (pron.)				tren
	ella	jardín	nadie		tres
bajo	ellos	juego	naranja	*recordar	tu (adj.)
bandera	en	jueves	ni	recuerdo	tú (pron.)
bebé	encima	juguete	nido	*reir	tuya
bien	entonces		ninguno	reloj	tuyo
blusa	entre	la	niña	respeto	
bonita	esa (adj.)	lado	niño	rojo	
	*escribir	lápiz	no	ropa	último
cada	escuela	las	noche	rosa	un
café	ese (adj.)	le	nombre		una
cama	eso (pron.)	leche	nos	sábado	uno
casa	espejo	*leer	nosotros	*saludar	uña
casi	esta (adj.)	les	nuevo	se (reflex.)	usted
cerca (near)	*estar	letra	nunca	semana	uva
color	este (adj.)	libro		señor	
colorado	estrella	lo	o	señora	vaca
		los	oir	señorita	ventana

como		luna	ojo	*ser	verde
con	fácil	luz	once	si (if)	vida
contento	familia		orquesta	sí (yes)	*vivir
corazón	felicidad	*llegar	oso	siempre	
corto	fiesta	lluvia	otoño	silla	y
cosa	flor			sin	yo
¿cuál?	fruta			sobre (prep.)	
cuando	fuego			sobrino	zapato

*An asterisk in front of a verb means that a form of that verb may be used in place of the infinitive.

Material based on list compiled by Ricardo J. Cornejo and reproduced here with his permission.

ORAL READING PARAGRAPHS

The next step in the diagnostic process is the use of oral reading paragraphs. The child is asked to read aloud each passage carefully. Start two levels below the one indicated as "instructional" on the quick assessment or at the level indicated on the test. The teacher records the errors, omissions, and the like on a separate copy of the same passage and asks the comprehension questions provided for it. A separate card for each passage will prove helpful.

Because paragraphs vary in length, the number of errors for each level are calculated on a percentage basis. Figures are given with the answers for the test. The teacher may wish to make note not only of word-by-word errors, but also of errors in phrasing and punctuation that suggest the child needs specific skill instruction. Since each set of questions inquires into levels of comprehension as discussed in Chapter 2, children with needs in one of these areas can be identified. At this point, the tentative profile of the quick assessment can be strengthened or modified. The same check sheet used for the quick assessment can be used for these paragraphs.

The actual reading paragraphs are printed in the appropriate sizes in Appendix II.

Only the comprehension questions and error scores for each level, plus sample directions for the teacher and for the child, are given here. But first we shall briefly review the comprehension levels described in Chapter 2.

Review of Levels of Comprehension

Level 1	*Memory:* simple recall of information
Level II*	*Translation:* changing material into another form, for example, synonym or art work
Level III	*Inference:* drawing a conclusion from a given fact
Level IV	*Application:* using information or ideas for solving a real-life problem
Level V	*Analysis:* using information given to draw conclusions and analyze possible results
Level VI	*Synthesis:* going beyond the information or story in a creative way
Level VII	*Evaluation:* making a judgment based on logical thinking

*Remember, above Level II, more than one answer is possible if it is logical and fits the story.

ORAL READING TEST

Directions to the teacher:

There are eight levels in this test. The reading paragraphs can be found in Appendix II. Ask each child to read the paragraph aloud. On a separate copy of the paragraph, mark the errors made, as described earlier in this chapter. Children may reread the passage, but no more than one rereading is recommended. When the child has finished reading, ask the comprehension questions for that story. Note the number of correct and incorrect responses.

As a general rule, start with Level I for primary grades, with Level II for intermediate grades, and with Level V for upper grades and secondary school. Stop the test when the child makes errors on more than 25 percent of the words or more than 50 percent of the comprehension questions. At the 95-percent level of accuracy, a paragraph may be considered at a child's independent reading level; the 90-percent level is considered the instructional level of difficulty; below the 85-percent level, a paragraph may be judged a frustration level for a particular child.

Directions to the child:

Read this story out loud. When you are through, I will ask you some questions about what you have read. Ready? Begin.

Preprimer Level

1. What color does Sally get? (memory)
2. What did the man say? (memory)
3. Where was the man? (inference)
4. Where are Jim, Sally, and Dick? (analysis)

Total number of words: 40
Independent level: 2 errors
Instructional level: 4 errors

Primer Level

1. What two colors were on the truck? (memory)
2. Who saw the truck? (inference)
3. Where were Dick and Sally going? (inference)
4. What color does Dick like? (memory)

Total number of words: 60
Independent level: 3 errors
Instructional level: 6 errors

First Level

1. What did Bob see? (memory)
2. Why did Bob say "Yes"? (analysis)
3. What did Bob want to do at the ranch? (inference)
4. Why did Bob lie down? (analysis)
5. What is another word for "ranch"? (translation)

Total number of words: 80
Independent level: 4 errors
Instructional level: 8 errors

Second Level

1. What did Running Deer want to learn about? (memory)
2. What animals were listening to the deer and the wolf? (memory)
3. Where did Gray Wolf want to go? (inference)
4. What will happen to Running Deer? (analysis)

Total number of words: 125
Independent level: 7 errors
Instructional level: 13 errors

Third Level

1. Who is the story about? (memory)
2. Where does a lifeguard sit? (memory)
3. How does the lifeguard know someone needs help? (inference)
4. What might happen if people did not follow the safety rules? (analysis)

Total number of words: 157
Independent level: 8 errors
Instructional level: 16 errors

Fourth Level

1. What are the Indians helping to build? (memory)
2. What did the Indians get tired of? (memory)
3. Why would sailors make good riveters? (analysis)
4. What jobs will the Indians probably get? (inference)

Total number of words: 200
Independent level: 9 errors
Instructional level: 17 errors

Fifth and Sixth Levels

1. Who was angry? Name two reasons for the anger. (memory)
2. Why were the barges left on the lake? (translation)
3. What should be hung on the barges and why? (memory, analysis)
4. What will happen now? (inference)
5. How did Mr. Jones take advantage? (inference)

Total number of words: 230
Independent level: 12 errors
Instructional level: 23 errors

Seventh and Eighth Levels

1. How long are dashes? (memory)
2. What kinds of hurdle fences are there? (memory)
3. How many runners are there on a relay team? (memory)
4. Who is the last man on a relay team? (memory)
5. How would you describe a track meet? (translation)
6. Describe the place where track meets are held. (translation)
7. What is usually used to start a race? (inference)
8. Why do people enjoy watching track meets? (analysis)

Total number of words: 230
Independent level: 12 errors
Instructional level: 23 errors

SPANISH ORAL READING PARAGRAPHS

Direction to the teacher:

Pretests and posttests are provided for preprimer through third grade. The reading paragraphs can be found in Appendix II. Ask each child to read the paragraph aloud. On a separate copy of the paragraph, mark the errors made. Children may reread the passage, but no more than one rereading is recommended. When the child has finished reading, ask the comprehension questions for that story. Note the number of correct and incorrect responses.

Directions to the child:

Lea el párrafo en silencio, luego en voz alta como si estuviera hablando. (First read the paragraph silently, then read it aloud as if you were speaking.) Cuando termina, voy a preguntarle acerca de la historia. (When you finish, I will ask you some questions about what you read.)

Pretests

Easy First Level (Preprimer)

1. ¿Quiénes están en el Zoológico? (analysis)
2. ¿Cuáles son los dos animales? (memory)
3. ¿Cuál de ellos vive en el zoológico? (analysis)

Total number of words: 26
Independent level: 1 error
Instructional level: 3 errors

Hard First Level

1. ¿Qué van a hacer? (memory)
2. ¿Qué cosas esperan sobre la mesa? (memory)
3. ¿Qué comen ellos? (memory)
4. ¿Qué asó el papá? (memory)

Total number of words: 28
Independent level: 1 error
Instructional level: 3 errors

Second Level

1. ¿De qué se trata la historia? (analysis)
2. ¿Quién va a la escuela? (memory)
3. ¿Cómo se sintió Pinocho? (memory)
4. ¿Para quién es la manzana? (memory)

Total number of words: 73
Independent level: 4 errors
Instructional level: 7 errors

Third Level

1. ¿Qué hicieron los niños todas las tardes después de la escuela? (memory)
2. ¿Cómo era el jardín del gigante? (memory)
3. ¿Cómo se sentían los niños en el jardín del gigante? (inference)
4. ¿Por qué se tuvieron que ir del jardín? (analysis)

Total number of words: 79
Independent level: 4 errors
Instructional level: 8 errors

Posttests

Easy First Level (Preprimer)

1. ¿En qué toman el té? (memory)
2. ¿Quién no toma té? (memory)
3. ¿Tita puede hacer algo que Tona no puede, ¿qué es? (analysis)
4. ¿Por qué Tona no toma té? (analysis)

Total number of words: 22
Independent level: 1 error
Instructional level: 2 errors

Hard First Level

1. ¿Qué hace la niña todas las mañanas? (memory)
2. ¿Qué come ella? (memory)
3. ¿En qué toma la leche? (memory)
4. ¿Adónde va la niña? (memory)

Total number of words: 26
Independent level: 1 error
Instructional level: 3 errors

Second Level

1. ¿Por qué es un día especial? (translation)
2. ¿Cómo es la nueva casa? (memory)
3. ¿Nombre las personajes que eran mirando la casa? (memory)
4. ¿Cómo se sintieron ellos a ver la casa, y por qué se sintieron asi? (memory, analysis)

Total number of words: 49
Independent level: 3 errors
Instructional level: 5 errors

Third Level

1. ¿Dónde vive el gato Mustafá? (memory)
2. ¿Qué come él? (memory)
3. ¿Por qué se levanta temprano? (memory)
4. ¿Cuándo llega a la escuela, que dice él para saludar a todos? (memory)

Total number of words: 57
Independent level: 3 errors
Instructional level: 6 errors

SUMMARY

Oral reading assessment is one of the central testing areas for the understanding of the reading process. It is especially useful in the primary grades. Oral assessment reveals many clues to the child's reading strengths and weaknesses during this critical early developmental stage. Marking and analyzing the nature of errors using the tests outlined in this chapter will give the teacher vital information on the most effective ways to meet the individual needs of each child. Knowledge of types of decoding errors can lead to further testing and specific skills instruction. Levels of comprehension will alert the teacher as to the type of questions that may need more practice.

SAMPLE CHECK SHEET

Oral Reading Check Sheet – Level Attained and Types of Errors

Comprehension

Check (✓) if error noted.
Leave blank if no error.

STUDENTS

	Independent Level	Instructional Level	Frustration Level	Omission	Mispronunciation	Insertion	Substitution	Reversals	Refusal w/out help	Error in Consonant	Error in Consonant Cluster	Error in Short Vowel	Error in Long Vowel	Error in Prefix	Error in Suffix	Accent Error	Punctuation Error	Memory	Translation	Inference	Analysis

8

The Assessment
of
Silent Reading

From an instructional point of view, oral reading would appear to be a logical means of identifying a child's reading skills. Print, however, must be decoded silently before it can be read orally. Therefore, oral reading can be viewed as simply an extension of silent reading skills.

If reading is considered a communication process, the author of a passage can be thought of as a sender and the reader as a receiver. The print, then, provides a medium from which the receiver selects and interprets material to suit his or her own purposes, and the reading process implies thinking critically and selecting and evaluating as well as decoding words. It is strongly suggested that reading for information forms the core of subject matter teaching.

DECODING AND SILENT READING

Shortly after the child learns to recognize print as representative of language and gains a vocabulary of approximately 100 words, effective and useful silent reading skills begin to develop. When children read silently, they have the opportunity to gain information in a slightly different way from when they are reading orally. The pronunciation task, which

is difficult for some children, does not necessarily interfere with the child's understanding of the words or the ability to decode them as such. How many times has a child behaved as if he understood the word but was unable to pronounce it? Sometimes the pronunciation of the word, the physical making of the sounds appropriate to the printed symbols, obstructs the process of reading for information.

Of equal importance in the silent reading process is the ability to receive messages from the author directly without interference from the immediate environment. Neither the teacher nor other children participate directly in a child's silent reading. This feature of silent reading tends to personalize the relationship between the author and the reader. This personalization can be utilized in the classroom to motivate readers and to encourage children to spend a considerable amount of time living vicariously through the words of other children, animals, and fantasy characters in the worlds of the past and future as well as the present. Perhaps by not requiring the oral reading task we can introduce the child to scenes far beyond the world of the classroom. It may be that this will encourage reading and stimulate imagination and creative thought in countless ways.

SILENT READING
AND FLEXIBILITY OF RATE

Silent reading, unlike oral reading, is not tied to the physical process of producing words and need not be related to any movement of the throat muscles. Readers thus can develop the ability to vary their reading rates selectively.

It is unfortunate that in many classrooms emphasis on oral reading precludes the development of the habits of varying comprehension and rate, which should be learned early in the reading program. The results of this are countless thousands of young people who, even in college, read at the rate of 200 to 250 words per minute regardless of the nature or difficulty of the material. It is important to note that reading rate is only one factor affecting comprehension and appreciation. Print size, number and size of illustrations, writing style, and subject matter also affect rate.

Many children struggle needlessly with difficult material in order to obtain needed information. Most textbooks are written by experts in a given field, who do not always take the reader's level or age into account. Teachers can help children be aware of this by teaching them to vary their reading rate when appropriate. It is worthwhile for the reader to know the fault does not necessarily rest with him or her. Fast reading of easy material and selected skimming can be useful strategies in all types of reading.

SILENT READING
AND THE STUDY SKILLS

The identification of pertinent information in a passage is a vital part of a child's ability to use the printed word as a source of information or solutions to problems. Outlining, summarizing, and identifying key concepts and key words in prose and poetry are often the central focus of classroom instruction no matter what subject is being considered. It is therefore most important for the elementary school teacher to do everything possible from the earliest stages to help the children develop the study skills associated with silent reading.

A student must first have a clear purpose for reading. If she can then find key words or phrases, she may be able to separate that which most concerns her from that which is of little immediate use.

TESTING FOR SILENT READING
COMPREHENSION

There are two major approaches to testing for silent reading comprehension. These are *Graded Silent Reading Paragraphs* with comprehension questions, and *Cloze Reading Tests*, in which words are systematically deleted by the teacher and are then replaced by the student (Bormuth, 1969). Both have particular advantages and disadvantages for the classroom.

Graded reading paragraphs are a series of paragraphs of increasing difficulty similar to the oral reading paragraphs. The child reads a paragraph, then the teacher asks comprehension questions. If the teacher gives the paragraphs to a group of children, answer sheets may be provided. If the test is given individually, the reading may be timed or untimed at the teacher's discretion. Following each of the paragraphs is a set of questions that fall into three types: memory, inference, and analysis. These, once again, are taken from Bloom's seven levels of comprehension, which were discussed in Chapter 2.

The graded reading paragraphs have inherent strengths that have made their use widespread for many years. These include ease of administration, their ability to tap different levels of comprehension, and the information they provide regarding the rate of reading.

Because these tests can be administered to large groups under normal classroom circumstances, they reduce the amount of time and effort associated with individual testing such as the oral paragraphs require. The directions for completing the tests are easily understood, particularly if the answers to the comprehension questions are multiple choice. This format also makes scoring a simple, one-step operation.

The potential for tapping different levels of comprehension can be most beneficial. It is possible for the teacher to add levels of comprehension beyond those included, if it suits the needs of the class. Translation (the ability to use synonyms), evaluation (the ability to make value judgments), and synthesis (the ability to arrive at new solutions) can all be drawn from reading the paragraph. But since evaluation and synthesis are more subjective levels of comprehension and do not imply only one answer, these types of questions must be asked on an individual basis. Assessing the reading rate also requires individual or small group administration since the teacher must keep an accurate record of the time required to finish reading.

In spite of these strengths, some notable weaknesses of using silent reading paragraphs should be kept in mind. The greatest is the teacher's problem in analyzing the causes of incorrect responses. It is frequently difficult to determine from the examination or even by individual questioning whether an incorrect response was caused by failure to comprehend the paragraph or the question. There may be other reasons as well. There is the problem of prior knowledge, for example. How can a teacher be sure that the information is novel for a particular child? After all, if he already knows the material, he may be able to answer the questions without reading the passage at all. Then, too, a child who may be able to comprehend the passage and the questions may get a lower score because she is unfamiliar with the test procedure itself. Young children who are not familiar with the multiple choice format are particularly likely to get lower scores than those who are. Because of these difficulties, information from these tests (as from all testing instruments) should be used to generate hunches or hypotheses regarding a particular child's difficulties rather than accepted as definitive and valid.

The second instrument used to assess silent reading comprehension is the cloze test. This approach, which was developed within the last twenty-five years, has been extensively utilized as a technique in teaching and readability research and as a means of determining a child's ability to comprehend printed material. The test itself is relatively easy to construct and score.

The most commonly used procedure is to select a passage of about 250 words that is novel for the child. Every fifth word is then deleted and replaced by a blank of a standard length. The child is given the passage with directions to fill in as many blanks as he can with the word he thinks the author intended. The child must write in the exact word; a synonym is not considered correct, even if the alternative makes sense. The interpretation of the scores (or percentage of correct answers) obtained has been the subject of considerable research. If 44 percent of the answers are correct, this score appears to be equivalent to a 75 percent score on a conventional multiple choice comprehension test. This score represents the *instructional level* discussed in Chapter 7. The *independent level* of 90 percent on a multiple choice test is equivalent to 55 percent on a cloze test.

Those who have used the cloze test maintain that this technique taps more than comprehension levels. They see the test as defining the reading act by measuring the degree to which the language patterns of the author and the reader coincide. Using this definition of reading, it may be possible to measure how well a child understands any material we wish to use in the curriculum, whether or not we have "grading" information on it.

It is often difficult for a teacher to assess the appropriateness of books and other reading materials. Is it reasonable to expect a child to read and comprehend a certain passage from material written without "grade level" as a criterion? Can a given group really use the regular social studies or science book? Are the other materials such as magazines or supplementary books within the group's range of ability? Can children who speak a particular dialect follow the ideas and sentence patterns of a book written in standard English? Because the child determines the missing words from the context, cultural language patterns, prior information, and the shades of meaning of other words all contribute to the child's performance. If passages are selected directly from material to be read for content and if reading inventories indicate that the difficulty level is not beyond that of the reader, good utilization of the printed material can be reasonably expected.

Most children find cloze tests challenging and fun—a puzzle rather than a test. This makes their frequent use possible without the children becoming frustrated. The advantages of a cloze test are that it is easy to prepare and score. Many factors of reading comprehension beyond the scope of the multiple choice test are considered, and it assesses widely differing materials for classroom use.

The cloze test also has some disadvantages. The student must be oriented to the testing procedure: Poor results may reflect problems with the format rather than reading performance. It does not give the teacher data related to different levels of comprehension. Also, the scoring of a cloze test necessarily involves a judgmental factor. Children's spelling errors may influence the decision on the answer's correctness. Thus a child who has poor spelling skills may receive a lower cloze score than one with equal reading comprehension ability but better spelling skills.

SILENT READING PARAGRAPHS

There are seven graded reading paragraphs included in this test. These range from primary to upper grade levels. The earlier paragraphs cannot usually be successfully administered to primary children until they have acquired sufficient vocabulary and skill to read short passages independently. Note that some rebus techniques are used at this level to supplement vocabulary—for example:

The 🌼 is red.

The actual paragraphs are printed in appropriate sizes in Appendix II. Only the comprehension questions and sample directions are given here. Lower level paragraphs have four questions, and intermediate and upper level paragraphs have more. This feature makes calculation of the 75 percent instructional comprehension level relatively easy. However, if only lower level questions are answered correctly, the teacher will need to follow up with further assessment in comprehension areas. Questions can be presented orally or in written form.

Two minutes are allowed to read each paragraph. If the child cannot complete the paragraph in that time, the reading rate is probably too slow and this should be noted. Once the questions have been scored, one child's score can easily be compared with his or her previous scores or class averages. The latter practice is recommended only under special circumstances, such as when instructional materials or procedures are being evaluated. We do not recommend comparing one child's progress with that of another for evaluation purposes.

SILENT READING PARAGRAPHS

Directions to the teacher:

The paragraphs can be found in Appendix II. Each paragraph should be on a separate page. Questions and answers may be prepared in a multiple choice format, if desired. Suggested beginning levels are as follows: primary, first grade level; intermediate, third grade level; upper, fifth grade level.

Give an individual or a small group of children the paragraphs they are to read. Allow not more than two minutes for reading the selection. Then have the children turn the page face down and answer the questions in writing as you dictate them. For immature boys and girls, individual administration with oral responses to questions may be necessary.

Directions to the children:

Read the story carefully to yourself. When you have finished, you may reread the story if you have time. I will stop you in two minutes and ask you some questions about what you have read. Ready? Begin.

First Grade Level (51 Words, with Rebus Option)

Memory

1. What does Jane like? (Flowers)
2. What colors are the flowers? (Red and blue)

Inference

3. Where are Mother and Jane? (Outside)

Analysis

4. Why does Jane want to help?

Second Grade Level (150 Words)

Memory

1. What did Mary look at in the store? (Books)
2. What happened to Bill? (He was asleep)

Inference

3. Do Bill, Dick, and Mary like animals? (Yes) How do you know?

Analysis

4. How did Mother feel when she found Bill?

Third Grade Level (150 Words)

Memory

1. What is the first thing a waiter gives the people? (Menu)
2. What is on the menu? (The food the restaurant has and the prices)
3. What does the waiter do when the people are through eating? (Clears the table)
4. What does the waiter bring to the table after the people have been served? (Water, milk, coffee)

Inference

5. How does a waiter try to please his customers? (By serving them in many different ways)

Analysis

6. What qualities does a waiter need?

Fourth Grade Level (142 Words)

Memory

1. What do we call a group of cattle together? (Herd)
2. Where are cattle kept until sold? (Stockyard)
3. How do cattle go to the packing plants? (In trains and trucks)
4. What happens to meat that is not kept fresh? (Put in cans)

Inference

5. What do cattle buyers look for in the animals they buy? (Health, good weight)

Analysis

6.   Why are cattle important?

Fifth Grade Level (157 Words)

Memory

1.   What did Muir want to explore? (A glacier)
2.   How did they get to the top of the glacier? (Spiked their way up)
3.   What was in the lake? (Floating ice)
4.   On the return trip, where were they caught? (On an island of ice)

Inference

5.   What is a crevasse? (A deep crack in the ice)

Analysis

6.   Why did they want to explore the glacier?

Sixth Grade Level (180 Words)

Memory

1.   What group decided on the first flag of the colonies? (Continental Congress)
2.   What part of the flag did they fail to prescribe? (Arrangement of the stars)
3.   Who designed the first flag? (No one knows)
4.   Why were red, white, and blue chosen as the colors? (Perhaps because they were used in the British flag)

Inference

5.   How was the flag designed so that it might be changed as states were added? (Stars and stripes could be added)
6.   Why was more than one designer used? (To obtain a variety of ideas for the best final decision)

Analysis

7.   Why did the new country want a flag?

Seventh Grade Level (158 Words)

Memory

1.   What is our impression of animals found in Ethiopia? (They are normally associated with Africa)
2.   What two animals in particular inhabit the lakes and rivers? (Hippopotamuses and crocodiles)
3.   How are leopards and hyenas described? (Leopards are large and hyenas are fierce)
4.   How many people live in Addis Ababa? (Half a million)

Inference

5.   What makes Addis Ababa a desirable place to live? (Cool climate, modern buildings, and transportation)
6.   In what ways has Ethiopia modernized her capital? (Modern buildings, airport, university, etc.)

Analysis

7.   Why do you think Addis Ababa is the capital city?

CLOZE READING PASSAGES

Children below the second grade reading level will probably not be able to utilize the cloze tests in the usual manner because of a lack of both reading and spelling skills. However, at any level, the teacher can construct an oral cloze test based on the material being used in the classroom. In the oral cloze, the child gives the test answers orally and the teacher records them. In written form, the child is given a copy of the paragraph with words deleted.

Practice Paragraph

Directions to the teacher:

Discuss the answers (following the paragraph) with the children and explain how to find clues or exact words in the context. Lessons on function words and their role in grammatical structure will be easily motivated by these exercises. Copy of the test is in Appendix II.

Directions to the children:

Put one word in each blank. Try to find out what word goes in each blank by looking at the other words in the paragraph. If you can't figure out one answer, skip over it and fill in as many blanks as you can. Then go back and fill in the ones you didn't do.

Bill and Sally live in the same house. They are brother and _____. They both go to _____. When they come home _____ school, they sit at _____ table and have milk _____ cookies. Then they have _____ to play outdoors until _____. When it is time _____ dinner, their mother calls _____. They eat dinner with _____ mother and help her _____ the dishes because she _____ very tired from working.

Answers: sister, school, from, the, and, time, dinner, for, them, their, wash, is

Cloze Reading Tests

Directions to the teacher:

Read the instructions to the children aloud while the children read them silently. Allow the children as much time as needed to complete all blanks. All tests are in Appendix II. Answers and scoring are listed below.

Directions to the children:

Write only one word in each blank. Try to fill in every blank. Don't be afraid to guess. Wrong spelling will not count against you if we can tell what you mean. Are there any questions? You may begin.

Second Grade	*Third Grade*	*Fourth Grade*	*Fifth Grade*	*Sixth Grade*
said	a	animals	be	boy
in	would	among	was	to
around	work	have	learn	Roger
like	children	down	out	a
then	keeper	called	used	collecting
out	but	breathe	the	when
was	hard	sides	man	by
its	them	are	larger	left
big	keeper	scales	stick	as
pet	animals	instead	and	years
Bill	than	fish	not	in
milk	a	help	that	the
into	everyone	there	for	he
saw	in	of	they	Indians
get	animals	ocean	not	they
we	same	water	that	shelter
very	works	in	lion	bark
for	cages	salt	ancient	help
for	be	fish	many	for
and	haircuts	color	wild	had
pet	cleaned	rivers	from	for
back	swept	water	afraid	friend
it	a	called	fires	partnership
looked	ask	are	started	wild
oh	want	gray	still	to
get	lions	group	a	displayed
run	what	called	of	capturing
not	others	not	there	foxes
skunk	to	to	all	tamed
	boys	would	so	animals
	to	backbone	animals	Madison
	fun	near	there	Roger
	animals	are	behind	this
		that	run	Roger
			without	his
				his
				to
				the
				of
				like
				foxes

29 words	33 words	34 words	35 words	41 words
44%: 13 words	44%: 15 words	44%: 15 words	44%: 15 words	44%: 18 words
55%: 16 words	55%: 18 words	55%: 19 words	55%: 19 words	55%: 23 words

SUMMARY

Silent reading is a basic skill. For many people it is the most important of the skills acquired in school. The assessment of silent reading through both conventional graded silent reading paragraphs and cloze procedures should provide the teacher with considerable information on the child's ability to read and comprehend silently.

Special attention should be paid to discrepancies between oral and silent comprehension scores. Is oral reading being emphasized at the expense of understanding, for example? Many techniques for improving silent reading are available, ranging from expensive machines such as the tachistoscope to such simple devices as using an index card to cover what has already been read and thus prevent eye regression. Training in silent reading skills pays rich dividends for the student and should be part of every classroom program.

SAMPLE CHECK SHEET

Silent Reading Check Sheet

STUDENTS	Silent Reading Level	Memory	Inference	Analysis	Cloze Reading Level															

part

IV

READING: FUNCTION AND FUN

9

Function:
Study and Reference
Skills

Frequently the terms "learning to read" and "reading to learn" are found together in educational literature because of the realization that the two tasks are central to the learning process in our public school system. From the middle elementary grades through graduate school a major source of information is the printed word. Even in the midst of a technological society the most routine and mechanical tasks usually involve some response to words in print. Our dependence on reading is apparent in our daily living patterns. *Functional reading*, as this type of reading is often called, is a basic necessity in a society that demands literacy. For filling out a job application, reading the daily newspaper, or deciphering the labels at the supermarket, reading skills are constantly utilized.

Often the reading we do requires us to utilize study and reference skills to gain information. Whether we study a map to find a friend's home, look up a business in the telephone book, or study a manual to assemble a child's Christmas toy, we need these essential skills. The ability to read and to retain what is read is vital to success in life as well as in school.

If good study and reference skills are established in the early and middle elementary years, the student will be more effective in utilizing the available study time and printed learning resources. Among the basic processes related to learning and the study skills are:

1. Reading and study skills
   a. Reading for the general idea (or scanning)
   b. Reading for specific information
   c. Locating information
2. Word information skills
3. Literary appreciation and analysis

We will analyze these skills and their usefulness in the reading repertoire of each child.

READING AND STUDY SKILLS

Scanning refers to the process of "reading" a large section of print for a particular purpose in a relatively short period of time while giving little attention to the irrelevant sections of the material. It includes reading for the general idea, and there are several other subskills we can consider here as well. Scanning may be used to find the general structure in reading material. The child can gather this information by rapidly reading the headings and the lead sentences in each paragraph. This can be done a page or two at a time or for an entire chapter, depending on the purpose. Scanning the preface of a book together with the summaries of chapters and sections can provide a general idea of the structure of the book and its level of detail.

The scanning process gives data on which

the student can base further decisions regarding studying. For example, what portions of a book are particularly relevant to his needs? Such an approach presupposes that the student does have a purpose in reading. Often the teacher has to supply careful guidance in regard to purpose. Children do not automatically establish a purpose for reading before they begin. While doing so is not a reading skill per se, it can make the reading process itself more efficient since the student has something to look for as she begins. The teacher who helps children choose purposes, especially when dealing with content material, will also be helping them acquire a valuable habit.

The concept of scanning can also be utilized in locating specific information. This includes searching for key words that can identify the content being sought. The reader can also locate specific information in a more general way by finding the main ideas of the passage and rapidly rereading the relevant portions for this information. Such a process reduces the amount of material to be read and the amount of time necessary to accomplish a given task.

Describing these methods does not imply that all or even most reading for information should be of a narrow and specific nature. Certainly much that an author has to say about a subject cannot be predetermined and isolated, nor should it be. Nevertheless, it is highly desirable to provide students with a variety of skills for seeking information and using printed material so that in the course of their study they can best utilize the resources at their command. An able and flexible reader can use such procedures with great speed and efficiency.

Another subskill in this area involves the reader's organizing his own concept of the material he is reading. A reader has the choice of either following the author's organization and thought or superimposing his own organizational pattern on the material. Oddly enough, it rarely occurs to children that it is possible to read a book in any other order than the author's. Teachers need to help children become aware of the varied possibilities open to them. Discussing and choosing a purpose for reading and scanning for general format and key ideas can help the reader make this kind of judgment.

Analysis of an author's sources is another study skill that can be most helpful to the student. This implies use of such resources in a book as the bibliography, footnotes, and quotations.

If study and reference skills are considered a part of the reading area, it is easy to see the value of the learning experiences that result from inquiring into the nature of the circumstances surrounding the author and his or her point of view at the time the material was written. All these skills can be developed through the scanning technique or can be explored in greater depth depending on the needs and maturity of the class.

This approach to reading material frequently requires skills in using reference works, dictionaries, textbooks, and the like that go beyond the reading process itself. Critical thinking and evaluation are inherent in this approach. The use of such information location tools as the table of contents, chapter headings, and the index of a book can prove to be vital when reading for information.

The skills associated with these portions of a book include alphabetizing, scanning for key words, and the use of guide words and headings of all kinds. Frequently overlooked in this process is the skill of categorizing and identifying synonyms. In using an index, for example, it is often necessary to search for a general category in which specific information can be found rather than look for a certain word. The use of synonyms and alternate forms of a word or the reduction of a phrase to its most important words is of great value in this process. If a student is seeking information on the Wright brothers' first flight, what word would she look for in the index? Perhaps words that don't even appear in the statement would be most useful. In this example such words as "airplane" or "aviation" would probably be the key to the information sought.

Particularly in areas of study that require multiple sources of information for problem-solving purposes, the use of the table of contents and the index must be automatic. Most children should start to become acquainted with these reference tools in the primary years. The teacher can build the utilization of these tools into early reading experiences and make it habitual. By the middle years the differences between the table of contents and the index and the association of these two guides to the contents of the work should be clearly in the mind of the child. The use of such books as an encyclopedia starts in the middle elementary years and continues to grow through secondary school. The use of reference indexes such as the *Readers' Guide to Periodical Literature* and the library's card catalog necessarily involves extension of the skills acquired in the child's first reading experiences.

In approaching resource materials, the ability to scan can be critical. Rapid reading of the lists in the index or table of contents saves time and can help prevent distracting alternatives. We probably do more scanning in these kinds of lists (from the telephone book to the mail order catalog) than in any other single resource.

A useful approach for developing study skills, which has been developed by Frances P. Robinson (1946), is taught as SQ3R:

Survey (scan through material)
Question (ask yourself a question about what you would like or need to know)
Read (read the relevant material)
Review (scan again with question in mind)
Recite (think, talk, or write down the key information)

This approach can be a beneficial method for organizing the process of reading for meaning.

WORD INFORMATION SKILLS

The use of a dictionary to obtain word information can begin early in a child's reading experiences. The efficient and proper use of dictionaries is a basic necessity if reading to learn is to become a part of the repertoire of a student. Encounters with new or unfamiliar words will be a regular occurrence and can be a positive and challenging experience even for the less able reader. But the experience must be closely related to both the needs of the child and the child's ability. When reference to dictionaries is a regular and consistent part of classroom activity, the children will probably master the necessary skills more easily.

The earliest skill utilized will be alphabetization. This leads quickly to the use of guide words and can usually be learned in the early grades. In the middle and upper grades children should be able to demonstrate skill with the phonetic keys in a dictionary. The diacritical markings and the accent marks give a reader much useful information and need to be specifically taught. The use of the definitions themselves, together with synonyms and antonyms, constitutes the heart of the information contained in any dictionary.

The thesaurus, like the dictionary, can be a useful tool in both the reading and writing of words, but it usually comes into use later than the regular dictionary. Synonyms, antonyms, and the shades of meaning that go beyond the literal can be found here. Again, information location skills such as the use of guide words and alphabetizing are very important in the efficient use of this reference work.

Many secondary school students find themselves handicapped in their first attempts to research and write material because of unfamiliarity with these resources and skills. The teacher at the secondary level may assume the student has some proficiency in using the library and the variety of materials available. The sooner the student is exposed to the techniques of efficient reading, the more he or she will internalize and use the process.

LITERARY APPRECIATION AND ANALYSIS

Information-finding methods should carry over from one task to another. Though the goals of a lesson in literary appreciation may be very different from those of a content-oriented social studies lesson, many of the techniques of information location such as alphabetizing, scanning, reading for specific information, and the use of chapter headings and the like can be valuable. We can ask questions concerning the author's purpose and our own purpose in reading the material. We can scan to see if the material is compatible with our goals. (Some people have been known to scan the ending—just in case!) We can research information about the author from other sources or, if we like the material, other books or stories the author may have written. If we are stressing "reading to learn," then our basic study skills will be useful regardless of the particular material we are reading.

SCANNING TEST

The test for scanning is constructed in two parts. In Level I, particular passages are scanned for specific words or phrases. The child counts the number of times the word or phrase appears in the passage and records it on the answer sheet. Each section has a time limit to encourage rapid reading. All passages are selected from content areas, and the words or phrases to be sought are related to key issues in the material. A check question is included with each paragraph.

The second level of the test identifies skills in locating general ideas in a passage. The teacher times the reading, and then the student must identify the main concept or best title for the passage and decide whether it would provide information about a particular topic. A multiple choice format may be used in this level of the test for ease of correction.

Full size paragraphs and the student answer sheet are in Appendix II. Paragraphs can be cut apart for duplication.

TEST FOR SCANNING FOR INFORMATION: LEVEL I

Directions to the teacher:

In this test each child will need copies of the sample paragraph and the five testing paragraphs on separate sheets. (See Appendix II.) Children's paragraphs should not list the important words, ideas, or check questions. Each child will also need an answer sheet. Sheets should be passed out in advance and kept face down on the desk until they are needed. If the last paragraph, E, is passed out first, then D, and so on, they will be in the correct order. The sample sheet will be passed out later, when the directions are given. The reading of each paragraph is timed, so you will need a stop-watch or a watch with a sweep second hand. Give the directions clearly and check the answers to the sample paragraph to make sure everyone understands. Do not allow the children to look back at the paragraph after time is called.

Directions to the children:

Read each paragraph silently in the time limit I give you. As you read it, remember the number of times you see the "important" word or phrase. Read as quickly as you can without missing the word you are looking for or the important idea of the story. Then I will tell you to turn the page over. When I ask you to, you will write the number of times you found the "important" word or idea. Write it on the answer sheet beside the question number. Then I will read the check questions to you and you will mark the correct space on your answer sheet.

Now let's try one. (Distribute sample sheet face down.) This sheet should be kept face down until I tell you to turn it over. The important word is "mother." Remember the number of times you find "mother" in the sample paragraph. You will have 10 seconds to read this paragraph. When I say "begin," turn the sheet over and start reading silently, remembering the number of times you see "mother." When I say "stop," turn the sheet face down and listen for further directions. Are there any questions? Ready? Begin.

(After 10 seconds) Stop! Turn your sheet face down. Look at your answer sheet. Beside the S-1 write the number of times you saw the word "mother" in the sample paragraph. Now for the check question. Beside the S-2, write the color of the moth that fluttered to a landing. (Pause.) How many of you wrote the number 3 and wrote the word "brown"? Good! The word "mother" appeared three times in the paragraph, and the paragraph said the moth was brown. Turn the sheet over and reread the sample to check your answer.

Now we will do sheet A. The important word is "sail." Remember the number of times you find "sail" in the paragraph. You will have 10 seconds to read this paragraph. When I say "begin," turn the sheet over and start reading silently. Begin! (Ten seconds later) Stop! Turn the sheet over. Beside the A-1 on your answer sheet, write the number of times you saw the word "sail." Now for the check question. Beside the A-2, write the place Christopher wanted to sail to.

Answers: A-1: 4; A-2: India

Now we will do sheet B. The important word is "made." Remember the number of times you find "made" in the paragraph. You will have 10 seconds to read this paragraph. When I say "begin," turn the sheet over and start reading silently. Begin! (Ten seconds later) Stop! Turn the paper over. Beside the B-1 on the answer sheet, write the number of times you saw the word "made." Beside the B-2, write the thing that brick is made of.

Answers: B-1: 4; B-2: hard clay

Now turn over sheet C. (Repeat directions as above, using the important phrases or words listed below. Note the check questions as indicated. Repeat the above for sheets D and E.) If a question calls for a yes or no answer, circle the "yes" or "no" on the answer sheet.

Paragraph C

Reading time:	15 seconds.
Important word:	Philosopher.
Important ideas:	(C-2) Does the paragraph tell how the atom was first named?
	(C-3) Does the paragraph tell how Democritus proved his idea?
Check question:	(C-4) How long ago did Democritus live?
Answers:	C-1: 2; C-2: no; C-3: no; C-4: 2,500 years.

Paragraph D

Reading time:	20 seconds.
Important word:	Engineering.
Important ideas:	(D-2) Does the drill-and-blast method require few men?
	(D-3) Does the paragraph tell how long it took to dig the tunnel?
	(D-4) Does the paragraph tell how the tunnel was to be used?
Check question:	(D-5) How long was the tunnel?
Answers:	D-1: 1; D-2: no; D-3: no; D-4: no; D-5: ¼ mile.

Paragraph E

Reading time:	20 seconds.
Important word:	Carton.
Important ideas:	(E-2) Does the paragraph tell how to make a stage?
	(E-3) Does the paragraph tell how wide the frame should be?
	(E-4) Does the paragraph tell how to make a curtain?
Check question:	(E-5) Which part should you cut off?
Answers:	E-1: 5; E-2: yes; E-3: yes; E-4: no; E-5: top.

TEST FOR SCANNING FOR INFORMATION: LEVEL II

Directions to the teacher:

In this test you ask the child to determine the general idea of a passage by scanning it and then to determine if it is related to a prestated study topic. As in part A, all test readings are timed to ensure that scanning is being done. This is not designed as a reading comprehension test per se, though it may be used as such if it suits the purposes of the teacher. The child will need an answer sheet and a copy of each paragraph on separate sheets. State the topic for study *before* the time to begin reading is called. Be sure to check the answers on the sample.

Paragraphs and answer sheet are in Appendix II. Paragraphs may be cut apart for duplication.

Directions to the children:

Read each paragraph as directed. Be careful to read rapidly because the time you have will be short. Then on your answer sheet choose the title that you think best fits the paragraph and circle the number in front. Then I will ask you whether the paragraph you have read will help you to learn more about the subject for study. Write "yes" or "no" to show if it will help or not. Let's try one.

Sample Paragraph

Topic for study: The history of flight.
Reading time: 30 seconds.
Which title is the best for this passage?

1. Flying Past and Present
2. Space Flight and Today's Planes
3. The Jet in War and Peace
4. Improving Our Airports

What is the best title? Number 2 is the best title. The 2 should be circled.
Does this paragraph fit the topic of study? No; there is no relation to history, the key concept in the topic. After this question you should have the word "no."

Paragraph A

Topic for study: Modern health problems in underdeveloped countries.
Reading time: 30 seconds.
Best title for this paragraph:

1. Life in a Poor Country
2. Industrial Pollution
3. The Care of Babies
4. How to Grow Crops for Your Family

(Answer: 1)
Does the paragraph fit the topic of study? *(Yes)*

Paragraph B

Topic for study: Space in the atomic age.
Reading time: 20 seconds.
Best title for this paragraph:

1. Matter Is Made of Empty Space
2. The Relationship of the Atom
3. Picturing the Size of the Atom
4. Enlarging the Atom

(Answer: 3)
Does the paragraph fit the topic of study? *(No)*

WORD INFORMATION TESTS

This section describes a number of different tests for specific skills.

Alphabetizing Skills Test

Alphabetizing skills are tested through the location and insertion of words in an alphabetical list at Level I and the writing of words in alphabetical order at Level II. At Level III, the use of guide words is tested. The children are given sample guide words with page numbers as they would appear in a dictionary; a list of words must be matched to the correct page numbers that the guide words would indicate.

ALPHABETIZING SKILLS TEST: LEVEL I

Directions to the teacher:

Each child will need an answer sheet (Appendix II). Give directions orally and check to make sure the first item in each part is done correctly.

Directions to the children:

Today we're going to see how well you can find words that are in alphabetical order. Look at your paper. The list at the top is in alphabetical order. The words on the bottom are not in the alphabetical list and you must figure out where they belong. The first word on the bottom is "me." Look at the alphabetical list. Between what two words would "me" fit? (Give the children an opportunity to find the answer.) Yes, the word "me" would go between "man" and "mother" because "man" has an "m" and then an "a" while "mother" has an "m" and then an "o." The word "me" has an "m" and then an "e," and "e" is between "a" and "o" in the alphabet. What are the numbers of "man" and "mother"? Right. So we will write 15 and 16 on our answer sheet and then it will read "me: between 15 and 16." Are there any questions? (Do on the board if necessary.) You may begin now.

me:	between _____	and _____	*(15-16)*
pretty:	between _____	and _____	*(18-19)*
be:	between _____	and _____	*(3-4)*
one:	between _____	and _____	*(17-18)*
the:	between _____	and _____	*(22-23)*
his:	between _____	and _____	*(11-12)*
up:	between _____	and _____	*(23-24)*
just:	between _____	and _____	*(13-14)*
did:	between _____	and _____	*(5-6)*
school:	between _____	and _____	*(21-22)*

ALPHABETIZING SKILLS TEST: LEVEL II

Directions to the teacher:

Each child will need a sheet with the groups of words to be alphabetized. The child can rewrite these words in the correct order or put numbers next to them to indicate the correct alphabetical order. The second approach is more difficult but may help the child who has handwriting difficulties. Do the sample group with the children and check to make sure they have done it correctly. Children's sheet is in Appendix II.

Directions to the children:

On the paper that we have just passed out you will see that there are six boxes. In each box there is a group of words that you are to put in alphabetical order. You are to (teacher chooses):

1. Write the words again in the box in the correct order.
2. Put numbers next to the words showing the alphabetical order—a 1 beside the word that would come first, a 2 beside the one that would come next, and so on.

We will do the sample together. Which word should come first? (Do the sample with the group.) Now do the rest of the boxes by yourself.

ALPHABETIZING SKILLS TEST: LEVEL III

Directions to the teacher:

This test has two parts. The first part requires the child to use the guide words to decide whether certain words would be on a sample page. In the second part the child must decide on what page a particular word would be. Each child will need an answer sheet. You may want to put Part A and Part B on separate sheets so that you can give half of the test at one sitting. Read the top section of the student page to the group and answer any questions about guide words before beginning. Do the sample with the class and check to make sure everyone understands Part A. In Part B, you may do the first answer with the group.

The children's sheet is in Appendix II. The sample from Part A and Part B are shown here. Answers for complete tests follow samples in most of the remaining chapter.

Directions to the children:

Today we are going to do some work using guide words. Listen while I read the paragraph at the top of your answer sheet. (Read to the group and answer any questions.) Now let's do the sample. (Do with the group.)

In Part B the only difference is that you must decide which of these pages the words would go on, and write the page number after the word. What page would the word "instrument" go on? Yes, page 615; write it. Now do Parts A and B.

Part A

Guide words are found at the top of each page in the dictionary and in some other reference books. They repeat the first word on the page and the last word on the page. They can help us find words more quickly. They look like this:

Sample

baby	89	ball

Circle the words that would be on this page:

baffle   back   break   baa   banner

Part B

instantaneously	615	insufficient
insufficiently	616	integrator
integrity	617	intensive
knavery	652	knock
knockabout	653	k.o.

The following word would be on what page?

Sample: instrument   _____

Answers (Part A)

Sample: baffle, back

1.   trumpet, trunk, truss, truly
2.   vexed, vial, vibrate
3.   fossil, forward, foster
4.   block, bliss
5.   untrue, untouchable, unwritten

Answers (Part B)

Sample: 615

1.	615		7.	616
2.	652		8.	652
3.	616		9.	615
4.	616		10.	617
5.	615		11.	653
6.	653		12.	617

Phonetic Dictionary Skills Tests

Phonetic keys, diacritical markings, and accents are used in the next test. Since dictionaries differ in some of the symbols or directions for using their keys, the teacher has the option of using the sample key provided with the test, changing the sample key to match the classroom dictionary, or making a copy of the classroom key. It is probably best to change to the classroom key, but that may make it necessary to change some answers also. The question is not which to use but rather whether the child understands how to use a key and translate the markings into real words. We encourage the teacher to use whatever system is most comfortable.

At Level I the child will be asked to match a known word to its phonetic spelling, such as "cat" to "kat" or "does" to "duz." At the next level the child must write the word from a phonetic spelling. For example, the word "sez" is really spelled "says." On Level III is a test for use of accent markings. The child must choose between words that are spelled the same but accented differently.

The escaped _____ was frightened.

con′vict   con ví ct

In the Level IV test, for diacritical markings, the child will choose between two possible answers to a question.

Which do you wear on your foot?

shō   shü

PHONETIC DICTIONARY SKILLS TEST: LEVEL I

Note: The sample pronunciation key that is included is similar to those found at the beginning of any dictionary. It is meant to be used with the first three levels of this test. Since all dictionaries vary slightly in the markings they use, if you use your regular classroom dictionaries for these activities, some answers will be different.

Directions to the teacher:

Each child will need a test and a sample pronunciation key (both in Appendix II). Do the sample with the children to make sure they all understand. The first part of the directions to the children can be used for any of the levels. You may read the directions and words from the sample key if they are unfamiliar or beyond the decoding skills of the group. Also circulate while children are working so you can help them pronounce words in the key and the regularly spelled words in the test. Do not pronounce the phonetically spelled test words.

Directions to the children:

As you know, letters in English can have more than one sound. When you look a word up in the dictionary you often find the word spelled differently in parentheses after the real spelling. That is to help you pronounce a new word. The different symbols for this kind of spelling are always found in a pronunciation key at the beginning of the dictionary. Today you are going to get a sample pronunciation key like one you would find in the dictionary and we will see if you can use it. Everyone look at the "key" for a moment. (Pause.) Now let's look at your work sheet. (The first part of the directions to the children can be used for any of the levels.)

On one edge of the paper are the special phonetic spellings and on the other are the regular spellings. You are going to try matching the two kinds of spellings. At the top of the page is a sample; let's do that together. What word matches the phonetic spelling "k-a-t" (spell out)? Right—"cat." What number should you put after the phonetic spelling, then? "Three" is correct. What about the next one? (Do samples with the group.) Now do the rest of the page on your own. If you are not sure, use your sample pronunciation key to help you.

Answers

Sample:

kăt	3
sĕl	1
rĕk	2

lŭnj	5		dŭz	13		jĕm	1
kŭp	3		prĭns	15		boi	8
kwĭp	9		krŭm	10		glü	4
thrĕd	6		mĭks	7		daut	14
gĕst	12		tŭng	2		kůd	11

PHONETIC DICTIONARY SKILLS TEST: LEVEL II

Directions to the teacher:

The children will each need a sample pronunciation key and a test sheet. If they have not done Level I or if it has been some time since they did, you may want to use the initial section of those directions concerning the key.

Directions to the children:

(Repeat any of the previous directions necessary.) Today you are going to try to figure out the real spelling for a word that is in the special phonetic spelling. You will probably need to refer to your sample pronunciation key to find out what the word should be. Then you will write the correct spelling next to the special one. First there are two samples to try at the top of the page. Let's do them now. Who can pronounce word *a*? How would you spell it? If you are not sure, look under "z" in your pronunciation key. What are two ways to spell that sound? Write says "s-a-y-s" after sample *a*. (Repeat for *b*.) Now try numbers 1 to 10 by yourself.

Sample: a. sĕz _____
              b. klŏk_____

Answers

Sample: a. says
              b. clock

1. fence
2. come
3. flood
4. lamb

5. room
6. noise
7. cough

8. laugh
9. book
10. beige

PHONETIC DICTIONARY SKILLS TEST: LEVEL III

Directions to the teacher:

A test sheet will be needed. The sample pronunciation key is optional, since only the information on accent will be relevant to this test. Complete the samples with the group to make sure they understand the concept.

Directions to the children:

On the work sheet you have today you can see some sentences with a word missing in each one. Below each sentence are two words; they look alike, but they are pronounced differently. The accent mark tells you which part of the word is stressed more, and that information tells you which word is correct for the sentence. You will circle the correct one. Let's work Sample A together. Read the sentence, please. [Pause.] Now look at the two words. How would you say the first word? [Pause.] How would you say the second word? [Pause.] Which one is correct for the sentence? Read it, please. Everyone circle the correct word. Now try Sample B on your own [Pause.] Which word is correct? [Pause.] Read the sentence. Good! You can begin now.

Sample: A. The escaped_____was frightened.
　　　　　　　　　a. con'vict　　　　b. con vict'

　　　　　　B. I know nothing about the_____.
　　　　　　　　　a. sub'ject　　　　b. sub ject'

Answers

Sample: A. a
　　　　　　B. a

1.	a	5.	a	8.	b
2.	a	6.	a	9.	b
3.	b	7.	a	10.	b
4.	a				

PHONETIC DICTIONARY SKILLS TEST: LEVEL IV

Directions to the teacher:

The children will need a sample pronunciation key and a test sheet. The initial directions regarding the key may be used as desired. Complete the samples with the group and check the answers.

Directions to the children:

In the work we are going to do today you will read a sentence and then decide which of the two phonetic spellings represents the word that is underlined in the sentence. You can use your sample pronunciation key to help you. Both the sounds and the accent marks will help you. Circle the spelling that correctly represents the underlined word. Let's try sample A. Who can read the sentence? [Pause.] Which of the two spellings represents the underlined word? Right! The first word would be pronounced "quit" and it's one syllable. The second is two syllables and is pronounced "quiet." Complete Sample B by yourself and then we'll check it together. [Pause.] What is the correct answer to sample B? Good. Are there any questions?

Sample: A. The night was very quiet.
　　　　　　　　　a. kwĭt　　　　b. kwī'ĭt

　　　　　　B. You are very definite about the answer.
　　　　　　　　　a. dĕf' ə nĭt　　　b. dĭ fī' nt　　　c. de' fĭn ĕt

Answers

Sample: A. b
　　　　　　B. a

1.	b	5.	a	8.	b
2.	c	6.	c	9.	c
3.	b	7.	b	10.	b
4.	a				

DICTIONARY DEFINITIONS TEST

Directions to the teacher:

The children will need a copy of the test (Appendix II). A separate answer sheet may be used if desired. Samples are provided for work with the class. You may read material to the children if their reading skills are not sufficient. At the beginning, a classroom dictionary and one or two examples on the blackboard can be a useful transition set for some groups. Definitions of words with multiple meanings are provided, and the child must use the definition that would be appropriate in a particular sentence.

Directions to the children:

Many times when we don't know what a word means, we go to the dictionary to find out. Sometimes when we do that, we find more than one meaning for a word and we have to figure out which meaning fits into the sentence we are reading. Today we are going to work on a paper to see how well you can figure out which meaning of a word should go into a particular sentence. Look at the sample on your paper. Who can read the definitions for the word "block"? [Pause.] Now read sentence I. Which of the meanings fits in this sentence? Right, *b* does; put a *b* on your answer sheet on the line in front of the I. How about sentence II? Yes, *a* is correct. Write *a* in front of the II. Do the next sample in the same way and we'll check it. (Check Sample B with group). Now do the rest.

Sample: A.   block
  a.   A piece of wood or plastic used as a child's toy for building.
  b.   Something used to stop movement or passage.

  _____   I.   The fallen tree was a block to cars on the road.
  _____   II.   I bought my baby sister some blocks for her birthday.

  B.   crane
  a.   A bird.
  b.   Machine for raising and lowering heavy weights.
  c.   To stretch (the neck) as a crane does [hence, to hesitate].

  _____   I.   I had to crane to see over the fence.
  _____   II.   The arm of the crane lifted the automobile.

Answers

Sample: A. I.   b   B. I.   c
  A. II.   a   B. II.   b

1.	b	6.	b	11.	a
2.	a	7.	c	12.	d
3.	b	8.	d	13.	a
4.	a	9.	d	14.	d
5.	a	10.	a	15.	c

INFORMATION LOCATION TESTS

Tests in this section are related to finding information in various typical resources such as tables of contents or indexes. Level I, Part A, consists of finding particular titles in a sample table of contents and listing the beginning pages. In Part B the child must decide which chapter titles in the sample might contain information concerning a stated topic.

At Level II, two sample indexes are given; Part B is for more advanced groups. The child must list all the sections that might contain information concerning a specific topic, first with the page numbers, then with subject titles. At this level the ability to use synonyms will affect performance. Will the child look under aviation and aeronautics for early flights in space?

Level III tests the child's knowledge of other available resources. A list of references such as the thesaurus and encyclopedia is given, and the child must choose which would contain particular information.

INFORMATION LOCATION TEST: LEVEL I
(Table of Contents Test)

Directions to the teacher:

This test contains two parts. For each part the student will need the Table of Contents and a test sheet, both of which are in Appendix II. Answers may be written on a separate answer sheet if desired. Work the sample with the class and check the answers. If a child has an answer not listed but can show you the reasoning that led to the choice, the answer should be accepted.

Directions to the children:

The table of contents is a very useful part of a book. I know you have all used it often. Today we have a sample table of contents and a work sheet with two parts to it. What is the book about that we have the table of contents for? Part A on the work sheet asks us to find the beginning page of the chapter that probably has information about a particular thing. Look at the sample in Part A. What chapter might be about animals of the Indians? Right. What page does that chapter start on? Write the page number in the blank. (Check.) Now look at Part B. Here we have subjects that might be in several chapters. We have to decide which ones might have the information we want. What subject is listed under sample B? Which chapter or chapters might have this information? Put the number of the chapter on the line. Are there any questions? Remember, there can be several chapters that will fit. List all that might be right. Do Part A, then Part B. You may begin now.

Answers (Part A)

Sample		Animals of the Indians	_(16)_
(56)	1.	Indian medicine	_____
(105)	2.	A famous battle	_____
(8)	3.	The earliest Indians	_____
(36)	4.	Pictures by Indians	_____
(75)	5.	Agreements signed with Indians	_____
(112)	6.	How Indians live now	_____
(29)	7.	Games Indians played	_____
(50)	8.	Jobs of an Indian woman	_____
(23)	9.	Ways Indians wrote things down	_____
(42)	10.	How a brave caught meat	_____

Answers (Part B)

Sample		Indian cooking	*(7, 14)*
(2, 6)	1.	Buffalo	_____
(11, 12, 13)	2.	Indian battles	_____
(9, 10, 14)	3.	Influences of the white man	_____
(3, 4, 5)	4.	Activities Indians enjoyed	_____
(6, 7, 8)	5.	Life in Indian village	_____
(1, 3)	6.	Beginnings of Indian civilization	_____
(9, 11)	7.	Wagon trains crossing the plains	_____
(14)	8.	Present-day life	_____
(6, 7, 14)	9.	Raising Indian children	_____
(1, 6, 7, 8, 14)	10.	The clothing Indians wore	_____

INFORMATION LOCATION TEST: LEVEL II
(Index Test)

Directions to the teacher:

Each part of this test has a different index. The index for Part A, which is easier to read and includes only one task, may be appropriate for less mature readers. Part B has two tasks, and you may want to use both at different times. For each part the student will need the sample index and test sheet in Appendix II. The first task in Part B uses the same general directions as Part A. Answers may be written on a separate answer sheet if desired. Work the samples with the class and check the answers. It is not necessary for the student to put down all the possible listings. Answers given in parentheses are indicative of the many possible answers. Other answers may be accepted if the reasoning is logical.

Part A

Directions to the children:

As you know, the index of a book can be very useful in helping us find information about subjects we are studying. (Show an index in a book, if necessary.) Today we have an exercise to do using a sample index. Look over the index for a few minutes. [Pause.] The directions on your work sheet say, "According to Index A, on what pages would you find information about the following subject?" The sample item is "Finding your own pets." Look in Index A and then write on your work sheet the words you would look up in order to read about this subject. What are the words? Does everyone understand why we listed those items? The rest of Part A is the same.

Answers

Sample: Bait; Havahart trap; Live-catch trap; Trapping.
1. Cages; Exercise wheel; Metabolism wheel; Nesting box; Terrariums.
2. Beaks, care of; Claws, care of; Clipping, wings; Cuts; Disinfectant; First aid; Illness and injury; Lice; Mange; Veterinarian; Vitamins.
3. Amphibians; Bullfrog; Frogs; Horned toad; Leopard frog; Newt; Reptiles; Salamanders; Snapping turtle; Spotted salamander; Tadpoles; Toads; Turtles; Turtles. soft shells.

4. Beetle; Butterfly; Caterpillar; Cocoon; Dragonfly, Flies; Insects; Katydid; Moth; Praying mantis; Walking stick.
5. ASPCA; Mail order firms; Pet dealers; Veterinarian; Zoos.

Part B

Directions to the teacher (Task 1):

Follow the same general directions as for Part A and do the sample with the class.

Directions to the children (Task 2):

List all the numbers of the different categories that might have information about the following topics. The sample item is "Ways to view the stars." Write the number of all the categories you think fit there. Remember, don't write the page numbers, just the numbers in front of the names.

Answers (Task 1)

Sample: 30, 31, 48
1. *17, 18*
2. *23*
3. *23, 32, 36*
4. *61-62*
5. *17-19*
6. *5, 20, 21-25, 125*
7. *110-114, 118*
8. *4-8, 62-80, 88, 99*
9. *32, 33-35, 61-63, 65, 71-74, 82-87, 89-93*
10. *106-108*

Answers (Task 2)

Sample: 35, 36, 37, 48
1. *14, 17, 21, 23, 25, 31, 33, 34, 39, 41, 42, 47*
2. *7, 20, 26, 40*
3. *1, 5, 22, 24, 41*
4. *4, 6, 8, 13, 17, 18, 27, 44*
5. *8, 10, 11, 12, 35*
6. *9, 19, 37, 47*
7. *19, 28, 29, 30*
8. *10, 35, 36, 37, 48*
9. *2, 28, 29, 33*
10. *10, 11, 38*

INFORMATION LOCATION TEST: LEVEL III
(Information Resources Test)

Directions to the teacher:

Each child will need a test sheet (Appendix II). References and directions are on the sheet and should be read orally by the teacher to ensure everyone's understanding. If students do not know some of the references listed, the teacher can explain what they are before beginning. Students are not expected to list all ten topics mentioned. A field trip to a local or college library or a visit to the school library can be valuable before or after this test. The same format can be used with a list of references from the school library or as many of the reference books as possible can be brought to class.

Directions to the children:

Today you have a sheet with a list of titles of reference books you can find at most libraries. The directions on your sheet read: "If you needed to make a report on the following topics, which of the books listed might have the information you would want? List the numbers that are beside the book title. You may be able to use more than one. If you don't know what some of the books are, just skip them." Are there any questions? You may go right to work.

Answers

1. 3, 6, 9, 13
2. 3, 9, 10, 13, 14
3. 1, 3, 9, 11, 14
4. 4, 6, 9, 12
5. 3, 5, 9, 11, 14
6. 3, 8, 9, 11, 15
7. 3, 9, 10, 15
8. 3, 4, 7, 9, 13
9. 2, 3, 4, 6, 7, 9, 12
10. 3, 5, 8

SUMMARY

"Learning to read" and "reading to learn" are integral facets of the child's education. A literate society demands a high level of study and reference skills in connection with written material. There are a great many important skills, such as using maps, graphs, and outlines, that tap the fields of mathematics, science, English composition, and other specific areas; these are not included in these chapters. However, similar testing formats can be used to assess these and other related areas and it is hoped the teacher will pursue all those that seem appropriate to the particular class.

A teacher who is aware of the study skills that the student lacks and who teaches to these needs will help the student immeasurably as he or she moves up through the school system.

SAMPLE CHECK SHEET

Study Skills Check Sheet

List levels attained or % correct – whichever is appropriate for section.

Date Tested–

STUDENT'S SKILLS

Scanning:	
Level I - Paragraph Reached	
% Comprehension	
Level II - Paragraph Reached	
% Comprehension	
Alphabetizing:	
Level I - Words in List %	
Level II - Difficulty Level	
Level III - Guide Words %	
Phonetic Dictionary Skills:	
Level I - Matching %	
Level II - Spelling %	
Level III - Accent %	
Level IV - Diacritical Marks %	
Dictionary Definitions %	
Information Location Test	
Level I - Table of Contents - A %	
- B %	
Level II - Index - A %	
- B %	
Level III - Reference Books %	

10

Fun:
Attitudes and Appreciations
in Reading Skills Development

The main thrust of this book so far has been the assessment of particular reading skills. These skills have been divided into components around which tests have been designed to discover the particular strengths and weaknesses of each student. This process is extremely important to promote efficient use of the teacher's time and to develop material appropriate to the actual functioning level of the student. But the components examined by these tests are only part of the total system that we call reading. Along with these particular skills come other, less tangible reading components that are equally important but are much more difficult to define and assess. These additional components are attitudes and appreciations. They are made up of the feelings and experiences related to reading, to school, to home, and to the self that the student brings to the classroom. For all their elusive nature, they can make the difference between success and failure for the child.

From the time of birth, the child is exposed to language. In the beginning this language is oral, and the child gradually learns through imitation and practice how to communicate (Brown and Bellugi, 1966). Research suggests that the years up to age four and a half constitute a most critical period in the development of a child's language. During this period some children learn to enjoy books. Being read to can be a highly reinforcing ex-

perience, since the child receives individual attention and is able to interact in a positive way with parents, older siblings, or other adults. These pleasant experiences stimulate an interest in books and at the same time increase exposure to a variety of language patterns. Children learn new words, new ideas, and new ways of expressing themselves as they hear the time-honored stories. The youngster who responds "It is I" to the question "Who is there?" is probably imitating his favorite *Three Billy Goats Gruff* rather than his family's typical response to such a question. Parents, nursery school teachers, and others can do much to increase the young child's awareness and appreciation of reading by handling the language exposure inherent in these procedures carefully, enthusiastically, and with sensitivity to the child's interest and needs.

Children who have many reading materials in their environment and who are frequently read to can often be found reliving the experiences they associate with the pictures and words in a particular story without anyone's reading the book to them. Some children learn a book practically word for word after a number of readings. They will announce that you are reading a book incorrectly when you skip a word or two accidentally, even though they have no knowledge of reading or the reading process. Instead, they have memorized what they have heard from previous readings. This type of memorization may lead the child to develop many of the skills necessary for beginning the reading process, such as left-to-right progression and visual and auditory discrimination. Some children will even build a beginning sight vocabulary based on their repeated exposure to favorite stories. By the time the child reaches the first grade classroom, she may have acquired some skill in reading through this procedure. Certainly her physical maturity, language maturity, and attitudes toward books will greatly affect the type of program the teacher must provide.

Of course, not all children will have had the exposure to books or the experiences that provide growth toward reading. Children who lack these experiences may have very different attitudes toward reading than children who have enjoyed early reading contacts. The teacher's approach and methods at the beginning will prove most critical to these children's attitudes and appreciations. Success in the child's early exposure to books and reading in the classroom can provide great encouragement to pursue the reading task further. If the kindergarten and first grade teachers are oriented toward this problem, the child stands a good chance of succeeding in reading. He will find, for example, that he can gain independence in reading more quickly when he is able to identify certain words that are printed in the book rather than waiting for someone else to read them to him. And so his interest and independence will be encouraged.

There is a close relationship between the early development of competencies and attitudes in reading and the mastering of the reading process. These attitudes may well affect the child throughout life and certainly through many years of exposure to reading instruction. The old bromide that "nothing succeeds like success" may be more true for the learning of the reading process than for any other school-related subject. Low achievers in reading may be among the most frustrated and confused children in our schools. They recognize that their reading abilities are less than those of their peers and see in a direct or indirect way that the adults around them believe they are not succeeding. Because reading is such a central skill in the learning process, chilren's attitudes toward themselves and toward the school are greatly affected by their feelings of success and failure in this area. And all too often, reading failure does mean school failure. Because the failure syndrome has such profound effects on the child, the teacher must provide experiences that will afford sufficient success.

There are two principal factors that affect a child's attitude toward reading in the school setting. One is the reinforcement the child gets, both intrinsically from reading with enjoyment and extrinsically from the teacher, other adults, or the peer group during the reading process and its associated tasks. Second, the child's interest in the material will determine in part the amount of time and effort he will put into reading it. For example, if he finds that books are available in the classroom that are closely related to his real interests and the interests of those he admires, his reading time will cease to be time taken from something more fun and will become worthwhile in itself. It is well to remember that from the child's point of view the task of reading is secondary to the subject matter he reads. If he really likes the book or magazine, he will attempt to read it even though the material may be too difficult by some grading standards.

As the elementary years progress and the child's confidence in the ability to master reading skills increases, both the pace and the variety of reading tasks required can increase. The critical factor here is not the grade level or the sophistication of the child's reading skills, but her attitude toward learning to read and her sense of competence in acquiring new skills and encountering novel learning experiences. If the child feels successful, if she feels she can do it, and if she is provided with interesting materials that stimulate her curiosity and enthusiasm, she will learn to read. To capitalize on the interests of the child in helping her learn in reading or in any subject seems fairly obvious to the teacher, as does providing experiences at the child's level of functioning so that she can feel successful. But just as her particular strengths and weaknesses may not be immediately evident, so her interests and attitudes take time to determine. Here again testing may help the teacher assess interests and attitudes more quickly, providing information that can be used to choose books and plan stimulating lessons.

TESTING ATTITUDES AND INTERESTS

How does the teacher effectively determine the child's attitudes and interests toward reading and toward the subjects likely to be encountered in reading instruction? First, he or she determines the degree to which the child identifies with the reading process. This is done directly with a simple questionnaire. Questions should be asked about the child's feelings toward books and reading, the kinds of books he likes, and his favorite activities. A large number of topics might be listed from which the child can select his favorites. The child rates each of these areas according to how much he likes or dislikes them. The list starts with such general topics as animals, cars, science fiction, and space and progresses to specific areas like minibikes, horses, dancing, and moon landings. These questions are provided in fill-in, multiple choice, and ranking formats. Additional questions worded slightly differently can be given later to help the teacher clarify the earlier answers or to indicate changes in attitudes and interests.

Attitudes toward the subject apart from the reading task itself are explored in this approach. For example, a child's negative reaction to reading may be counteracted by a positive reaction to drama or arithmetic. This would suggest to the teacher that reading about arithmetic or drama could be a productive approach in activities that develop reading skills.

In cases where children's attitudes are more negative toward reading and books, a more indirect approach is sometimes fruitful. One such approach is an attitude survey in which the child indicates on a scale how well a particular series of adjectives describes her feelings about school, herself, and reading. This format, originally developed by Osgood, (Osgood et al., 1975) is called the *semantic differential*. It helps the teacher gain insight into the children's personality and the attitudes that affect their behavior during reading instruction. Second, the child can be asked to perform a task such as reading a passage. He is then asked to respond to a questionnaire about the amount of information he has gained from the passage, the amount of time he took to gain this information, and how he felt about this particular reading task. The advantage of this approach is that the child is not abstracting from some nonspecific past experience in which he has read numerous passages but instead is responding to a specific, immediate reading task while it is fresh in his memory. An example of the second approach is presented in Part C of the survey.

This test provides information concerning specific kinds of stories the child likes and, more important, direct data on how to approach the task: negative assessments, willingness to identify with male or female characters, whether the child would like to read more of the story, and so on. This information can help the teacher choose material, particularly to capture the reluctant reader.

In any of the above techniques, it is important for the teacher to approach the assessment of reading attitudes without thinking of blaming or punishing the child. Certainly the child who feels that his answers on a test will affect the teacher's or his parents' attitude toward him will be more anxious and inclined to give answers that will make him look good rather than tell how he really feels. Anxiety may affect the test results either positively or negatively, but its presence should be noted by the teacher. The child's feelings about tests as well as reading may be reflected in his behavior. If he appears unduly nervous or anxious, fidgets a great deal, stops and starts, and so on, the teacher should record this information for later examination.

ATTITUDE AND INTEREST SURVEY

This survey is in three parts and may be given whole or in part. It is to be presented to the student as an interest survey rather than a test for attitudes. Generally speaking, the first part is the most direct and the other two parts are less so. It is a good idea to circulate while the students are filling out the survey to answer questions and help with unknown words. Since this is not a test in the usual sense, questions should be answered and discussion allowed as necessary.

Part A

Directions to the teacher:

The child will need the survey sheet (in Appendix II) and a piece of paper on which to write the answers. Give plenty of time to read the items and complete the answers. Help with spelling or punctuation only if requested. Children who have difficulty with reading and spelling should be given the test orally. Tape recording can be helpful here.

Directions to the children:

Today you have an interest survey to fill out. This will help me choose books and activities for the class that we will all enjoy. Read each question and answer it the best you can. Write your answer on the blank paper. If you have any questions while you are working, just raise your hand. You may start now.

Part B

Directions to the teacher:

The pupils will need the interest survey sheet only (Appendix II). Since this is not a strict test, questions may be answered and help given as necessary.

Directions to the children:

In this part of the interest survey you are to number the choices according to how well you like them. Look at the top of your sheet and you will see the numbers from 1 to 4. Put the number 1 by the subjects or activities you like the most. Then put the number 2 by all the ones you like quite a bit, and so on. Number 4 is what you dislike the most. You don't have to use all the numbers, only those that seem to express your feelings the best. If you have any questions or need any help while you are working, just raise your hand. You may start now.

1. Like a lot
2. Like a little bit
3. Dislike a little bit
4. Dislike a lot

Part C

Directions to the teacher:

The students will need the interest survey sheet from the Appendix. Give help as needed and answer all questions, since this is not a strict testing situation.

Directions to the children:

The papers that you have today contain some passages from different stories. After you read the stories you will answer some questions about how you felt when you read the story. You are to circle the word or phrase that describes how you felt. Are there any questions? If you have questions as you work, just raise your hand and I will come help you. You may begin now.

BUILDING LITERARY APPRECIATION

Building on the child's interests and attempting to foster positive attitudes toward reading are worthy and important goals in the classroom. It has been found that one of the most effective and enjoyable ways to accomplish this is through the frequent use of literature in the reading and language arts program. Everyone enjoys a good story, regardless of age, and children seem to delight in identifying with their favorite storybook characters. In addition, the richness of language expression greatly increases the child's repertoire of vocabulary and language patterns.

There are at least three principal avenues for building literary appreciation in the classroom, and they should all be included in a well-rounded program. The first is the teacher's frequent oral reading of passages designed to stimulate interest. This should be done regularly at odd moments. Poems, short stories, chapters from a book, or short excerpts are all appropriate. This can be done with small groups of children or the entire class but should be for relatively short periods of time. High-interest, fast-moving material related to the interests and age level of the audience are the best choices. Children can gain great appreciation of books and stories, poetry, and plays in this way. Even children who have read a particular story frequently enjoy hearing it again in oral form. The appreciation of great literature through this method with a teacher who is able to read well aloud is a highly motivating activity. Children who have heard a story will frequently ask for a chance to reread it independently so that they can reexperience it.

Oral reading also stimulates language experiences of all kinds in the classroom. Increasingly, classes include children with such a variety of backgrounds and experiences that the teacher may find it difficult to build common goals and understandings. A shared literary experience offers the unique opportunity to enjoy and explore together. A well-chosen story can enlarge the listening and speaking vocabularies of the total group.

Stories that stimulate the children's imagination can lead to more meaningful creative writing and oral expression. Plays and puppet shows can grow from such stimulation. Art, creative writing, dramatics, debates, and discussions are just a few of the possible spin-offs of story time.

Oral reading can also help the child gain a feeling for an author's style as a means of starting to develop his or her own style of expression. The opportunity to discuss and compare story format and style is of great importance in helping the child become aware of the nuances of language.

A second method of building literary appreciation is through language experience. In this approach the child reads his own stories and those of his friends. These stories may be based on individual or classroom experiences or may be modeled on a favorite story—"The Three Bears" may become "The Three Horses," or "Angus and the Ducks" may become "Skippy and the Chickens." In this way children learn much about the development of generative language. Frequently an individual has high interest in the language of the peer group, and so it has intrinsic attention value and motivation for him. This experience then stimulates an individual's own oral expression. A class newspaper, a chart story, or an individually generated story that is typed and distributed to the class can greatly stimulate the group.

The third method of developing literary appreciation is through frequent exposure to the school or public library. Through frequent and well-planned activities, children develop skill in using the library and an awareness of its vast resources. An early library habit can last the child a lifetime.

TESTS FOR INTERPRETATION AND INFERENTIAL READING SKILLS

Children who have extensive exposure to the language and style of good literature can develop many sophisticated reading skills. Through analogy, simile, metaphor, alliteration, and the like, authors add depth to the reader's understanding. The multiple meanings or the various shades of meaning of a given word or phrase not only add information to the passage from the readers' point of view but help them gain insight into the author's motives. Readers who have become sensitive to such techniques can utilize their own imagination and creative abilities to expand the actions and to generalize from the information provided. The enjoyment of fiction is also greatly enhanced when children are encouraged to anticipate the outcome of a passage and to predict the coming events and the actions of characters. A variety of activities for the extension of stories in time and location can be a great asset in the development of skill in interpretation and drawing inferences. Although these tests tap comprehension skills, they are still sophisticated enough to be used as a basis for classroom discussion and a jumping-off place where there is no "right" answer.

Tests can tap some of these advanced skills and aid the teacher in planning further literary experiences for the class. Interpretation through shades of meaning is the basis of the first test in this area. In Part A the student is asked to choose the best word of several to fit into a particular sentence. The basis for the best selection is alliteration, rhyme, and mood.

While the sentences may seem similar to those testing comprehension skills, the choices are more complex and related to "sensing" the language. A "best choice" is what transforms prose to literature.

In Part B, synonyms and antonyms are explored. The child is given a word and must decide what word in a sentence or passage it could replace. He must also decide if the meaning would be the same or opposite. Here tone and interesting word choice add depth to the writing.

The second test looks at interpretation and inference based on literary passages. In Part A the students read a passage and pick the best one-sentence interpretation. In Part B, they must decide which event or idea will follow from the passage given. In this test poetry will be used as well as prose, and ideas, moods, and feelings are interpreted as well as actual events.

LITERARY INTERPRETATION: SHADES OF MEANING TEST

Part A

Directions to the teacher:

The student will need a test sheet, which is in Appendix II. A separate answer sheet may be used if desired. Since literary interpretation is often fairly subtle, the "best" response for a given passage is listed as the answer, and only that answer is to be accepted even though there are other possibilities. Complete the samples with the group and check.

Directions to the children:

In the work sheet you have today, there are a number of sentences with words missing. After each sentence there are several possible answers. All the answers may fit into the sentence but only one is the "best" one, the one that makes the sentence sound right. Look at sample A. We'll do it together._____, read the sentence, please. What are our choices? Which one do you think is the "best" choice? Why does the word "mat" fit best? Right! It rhymes and it's something to sit on. Do sample B on your own. [Pause] Which answer did you choose as best? "Buttered" is right because it starts with "B" and has the same pattern as the old "Peter Piper picked a peck of pickled peppers." "Buttered biscuit" is the same pattern as "pickled peppers." Are there any questions? Do the rest on your own.

Sample A: The cat in the hat sat on the_____.
   1. chair
   2. mat
   3. rat
   4. couch

Sample B: Billy Button bought a_____biscuit.
      1. baker's
      2. tasty
      3. buttered
      4. pickled

Answers

Sample: A. 2
            B. 3

1.	2	5.	3	8.	2
2.	4	6.	2	9.	4
3.	1	7.	4	10.	2
4.	2				

Part B

Directions to the teacher:

The students will need the test sheet (Appendix II) and a separate answer sheet, if desired. There will be one "best" answer for each sentence. If some students are unsure of the meaning of "opposite," do some extra explanation, possibly on the blackboard, before the main section of the test is begun. Complete the sample and check.

Directions to the children:

The work sheet you are going to do today is a little tricky. Look at the sample on your page. First you will see a key word. What is that word? [Pause] Right, "furious." Under that is a sentence. Who can read it? [Pause] The next line is a series of numbers, one for each word of the sentence. Now decide: Which word in the sentence could be changed to the key word—1, 2, 3, 4, 5, or 6? Is there a word in the sentence that you could substitute "furious" for? Right, "angry." What is the number above "angry"? Two is correct, so you would circle the number 2 to show that that is the word you would change. Now, the next line asks if the meaning of the sentence with the new word in it would be the same as before or the opposite. What would it be? Yes, since "furious" means the same as "angry" the meaning would be the same. Circle the word "same." Try sample B by yourself and then stop so we can check it. [Pause] All right, what is the key word? Who can read the sentence? Which word can be changed? Right! What is the meaning of the sentence now, the same or the opposite? Very good! Are there any questions? Do the rest of the questions on your own.

Sample A: *Key word:* furious

Sentence: The angry man sat down quickly.

Word to change: 1 2 3 4 5 6

Meaning: same   opposite

Sample B: *Key word:* quiet

Sentence: The dogs next door are very noisy.

Word to change: 1 2 3 4 5 6 7

Meaning: same   opposite

Answers

Sample: A. 2, same
             B. 7, opp.

1. 5, opp.   5. 6, same   8.   4, opp.
2. 4, opp.   6. 2, same   9.   9, opp.
3. 5, same   7. 3, same   10. 7, same
4. 1, opp.

LITERARY INTERPRETATION AND INFERENTIAL MEANINGS TEST

Part A

Directions to the teacher:

The student will need a test sheet (Appendix II). A separate answer sheet may be used if desired. Since this test concerns itself with literary interpretation, there may be more than one logical interpretation or inference from a particular passage.* However, only one "best" answer is indicated. It is up to the individual teacher to decide whether to accept other alternatives. Complete the sample and check with students.

Directions to the children:

Today we have a work sheet that contains portions of stories, poems, and essays from various books. After each passage there are several statements that explain or interpret what the writing is about. Several may appear correct, but only one would be considered the "best" for that passage. Look at the sample and read it to yourself for a moment, then we'll do it together. [Pause] Who would like to read it for us? What are the possible interpretations of this description?_____, read them please. Which do you think is correct? Yes, 2 is the best answer. Why did you choose it? How could you tell that there had been a big storm? On your answer sheet write your name. Then write "sample" and "2." Write the number of the passage and then the number that indicates the best answer for each item on your paper. Are there any questions? You may begin now.

Sample: In a moment, all was again hushed. Dead silence succeeded the bellow of thunder, the roar of the wind, the rush of the waters, the moaning of the beasts, the screaming of the birds.

1. The animals were frightened.
2. A storm had passed.
3. The countryside was quiet.
4. We walked in the rain.

---

*All passages are taken from William H. McGuffey, *McGuffey's Sixth Eclectic Reader* (New York and Cincinnati: Winthrop B. Smith & Co., 1857).

Answers

Sample: 2

1.	3	5.	1	8.	2
2.	4	6.	4	9.	1
3.	2	7.	2	10.	4
4.	3				

Part B

Directions to the teacher:

The student will need a test sheet (Appendix II). A separate answer sheet may be used if desired. As with Part A, there is usually one "best" answer, but others may be accepted if the teacher wishes. Complete the sample and check with students.

Directions to the children:

On our work sheet for today we have some parts of poems, stories, and essays. For each one you will try to decide what will happen next, either in an actual event or in a person's thoughts or feelings. Read the sample on your page and then we will do it together. [Pause] Who can read it for us? What are the possible answers? Which answer is correct? How did you decide they were going to fight? On your answer sheet put your name, then write "sample" and the number of the answer. What number should that be? Good! Do the same for the rest of the items. You may start now.

Sample: They were both unarmed, and, stretching their limbs like men preparing for a desperate struggle, they planted their feet firmly on the ground, compressed their lips, knit their dark brows, and fixing fierce and watchful eyes on each other, stood there, prepared for the onset.

1.   The men will run away.
2.   The men will die.
3.   The men will fight.
4.   The men will turn to stone.

Answers

Sample: 3

1.	1	5.	3	8.	1
2.	3	6.	4	9.	3
3.	2	7.	2	10.	2
4.	4				

SUMMARY

In this chapter we have described those skills in the reading area related to the affective domain. Certainly attitudes, appreciations, and skills in literary works are a significant part of the mature reader's repertoire of skills.

Teachers have the opportunity through shared literary experience to enrich and broaden the child's skills and appreciations. The excitement and just plain fun of rhyme, riddle, and repartee may become the nucleus of a variety of language arts activities in the classroom and in the outside world. Becoming attuned to the subtleties and nuances of language may increase the child's sense of power over both the spoken and written word. Creative reading, like creative living, becomes a "set" by which one can approach the world.

The tests in this section should give the teacher some insight into the extent of the child's exposure to literary form and analysis and the attitudes and interests the child brings to the classroom. These can form the platform on which to build an effective literary skills program.

Providing books appropriate to the interests and abilities of all children in a class is not an easy task. The more information and resources the teacher has, the better. An interest and enjoyment in reading is the best gift a devoted teacher can bequeath to students, from beginning readers to the most sophisticated teenagers.

SAMPLE CHECK SHEETS

Interest Check Sheet – Types of Reading

Check interest areas.

STUDENTS

Adventure | Animal Stories | Hobby Stories | Biography | Auto-biography | Science | Western Stories | Sports | Fairy Tales | Poetry | Mystery | Minibikes | Love and Romance | Science Fiction | Cars | Horse Stories | Humor | Fantasy

Interest check Sheet – Types of Reading

Check interest areas.

STUDENTS

History | Geography | Art + Music | Ghost Stories | Family Stories | Riddles and Jokes | Fables+Myths | Religion | People of Other Lands | Newspaper | Magazines | Comic Books

Interest Check Sheet – Subjects in School

Check interest areas

STUDENTS

	Arithmetic	Spelling	Reading	Writing Stories	Science	Social Studies	Music	Art	Physical Ed.	Health	Book Reports	English								

Interest Check Sheet – Activities out of School

Check interest areas.

STUDENTS

	Television	Movies	Outdoor games	Watching sports	Hiking and camping	Fishing	Riding minibikes and motorcycles	Reading	Cooking	Hobbies	Animals	Trips	Car races	Slot car races	Being with friends					

Check Sheet – Literary Interpretation

% Correct

STUDENTS

	shade of meaning		Interpretation and Inferential meanings												
	A	B	A	B											

appendix

I

SAMPLE
ANSWER SHEETS
AND
RECORDING DEVICES

A. 🙂 🙁

B. 🙂 🙁

1. 🙂 🙁

2. 🙂 🙁

3. 🙂 🙁

4. 🙂 🙁

5. 🙂 🙁

6. 🙂 🙁

7. 🙂 🙁

8. 🙂 🙁

9. 🙂 🙁

10. 🙂 🙁

11. 🙂 🙁

12. 🙂 🙁

13. 🙂 🙁

14. 🙂 🙁

15. 🙂 🙁

$\swarrow$ = has sufficient discrimination at this level

O = needs additional work

Group Check Sheet – Levels

CHILD'S NAME	LEVEL	LEVEL	LEVEL

Group   Check Sheet — Skills

STUDENTS

Individual Check Sheet   Child's Name _____

V = Knows item
O = Does not know item

Dates
Tested-

STUDENT'S SKILLS

P R O F I L E S H E E T

CHILD'S NAME:

BIRTHDATE:

SCHOOL:

POOR

AVERAGE

HIGH

NOTES:

appendix

II

CHILD TESTS
AND
RELATED MATERIALS

VISUAL DISCRIMINATION TEST: LEVEL I

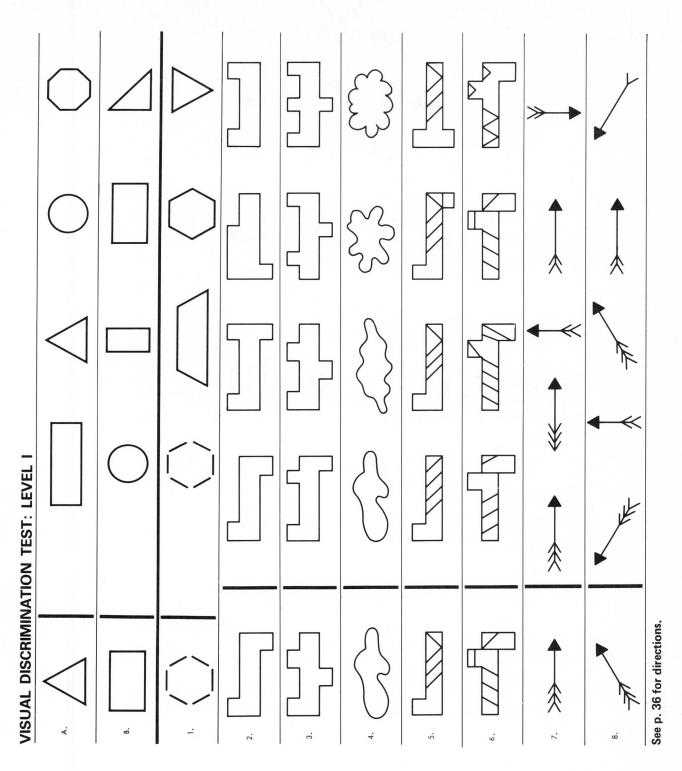

See p. 36 for directions.

9.				
10.	N	V	M	A	N
11.	B	B	D	B	C
12.	J	J	L	J	?
13.	W	W	M	V	A
14.	P	b	B	D	P
15.	c	d	c	C	?
16.	m	n	h	m	n

144

VISUAL DISCRIMINATION TEST: LEVEL III

Name _____

A.	bp	bq	pd	bd	bp
B.	mnn	mnm	nmm	mnn	nnm
1.	gh	gn	ph	bh	gh
2.	sob	sbo	bos	sod	sob
3.	not	ton	not	hot	toh
4.	bad	bab	bad	bob	dad
5.	pot	got	pot	top	tog
6.	pen	gen	pon	nep	pen
7.	awb	baw	amb	awb	awb
8.	still	still	still	still	ztill
9.	today	tobay	tadoy	dayto	today
10.	brwiltz	drwiltz	brwildz	brwiltz	brwiltz
11.	moisten	noisten	moistem	moisten	miosten
12.	running	runing	running	running	running
13.	dentally	dentaly	dentally	bentally	dentally
14.	beautiful	beuatiful	deautiful	becutiful	beautiful
15.	discriminate	disoriminate	discriminate	discrinate	biscriminate
16.	rutherford	rufordther	rudrofther	rutherfora	rutherford
17.	countrified	conutrified	countrified	counfiedtri	countritrified

See p. 37 for directions.

145

VISUAL MEMORY TEST: LEVEL II

Name _____ Grade _____

□　△　○
_____

□　△　○
_____

□　△　○
_____

□　△　○　◊
_____

□　△　○　◊
_____

□　△　○　◊
_____

□　△　○　◊
_____

□　△　○　◊
_____

□　△　○　◊
_____

□　△　○　◊
_____

△　○　▱　◊　□
_____

△　○　▱　◊　□
_____

△　○　▱　◊　□
_____

△　○　▱　◊　□
_____

M　E　L　D　S
_____

M　E　L　D　S
_____

M　E　L　D　S
_____

　　　　　　　　　　　　　　See p. 39 for directions.

AUDITORY MEMORY TEST: LEVEL II

Name _____ Grade _____

A.

1.

2.

3.

4.

5.

6.

7.

8.

9.

10.

LISTENING COMPREHENSION TEST: LEVEL I

Name _____ Grade _____

Sample

    A.   The cat was: (1) little (2) white (3) gray.

    B.   The mouse was: (1) white (2) tiny (3) gray.

1.   The dog was: (1) old (2) gray (3) sleepy (4) soft.
2.   The cowhand was: (1) young (2) sleepy (3) tall (4) old.
3.   The person talking was: (1) eating (2) dreaming (3) yawning (4) hopping.
4.   The time of day is: (1) morning (2) afternoon (3) night (4) summer.
5.   The morning light is: (1) gray (2) white (3) hard (4) soft.
6.   The house was: (1) new (2) dirty (3) old (4) fancy.
7.   The man was: (1) young (2) tall (3) fast (4) jumpy.
8.   The stairs were: (1) steep (2) dusty (3) brick (4) stone.
9.   The children were: (1) quick (2) exhausted (3) happy (4) sitting.
10.   The dogs were: (1) running (2) chasing (3) jumping (4) exhausted.
11.   The ground was covered with: (1) grass (2) leaves (3) flowers (4) dogs.
12.   The room was: (1) deserted (2) lonely (3) intense (4) silent.
13.   The men were: (1) talking (2) staring (3) sitting (4) drinking.
14.   The glasses were: (1) half size (2) half empty (3) completely full (4) completely empty.
15.   The men are going to: (1) sing (2) drink (3) part (4) join.

 See p. 50 for stories and directions.

LISTENING COMPREHENSION TEST: LEVEL II

Name _____ Grade _____

Sample

How would you describe Joe?
(1) lazy (2) careful (3) old (4) cruel

1. The horses were: (1) resting (2) playing (3) working.
2. They felt: (1) cross (2) hot (3) tired.
3. The children were: (1) noisy (2) frightened (3) angry
   (4) happy.
4. The man was: (1) angry (2) calm (3) hurried (4) gentle.
5. The time was: (1) evening (2) summer (3) morning
   (4) afternoon.
6. The cowhand had been: (1) working (2) sleeping
   (3) eating (4) rude.
7. The girl is: (1) sick (2) happy (3) sad (4) crazy.
8. The girl is probably: (1) lonely (2) busy (3) an actress
   (4) his mother.
9. The young man is probably: (1) a soldier (2) a
   photographer (3) her father (4) with the girl.
10. Jane thinks: (1) Jim can read (2) Jim is tall (3) Jim is kind
    (4) Jim is busy.
11. Jane wants Jim to: (1) read to her (2) help her understand
    (3) return her book (4) go to the library.
12. The ship is: (1) old and cracked (2) in a storm (3) on a
    cruise (4) falling apart.
13. The captain is: (1) abandoning the ship (2) radioing for
    help (3) putting the sailors to work (4) going to sleep.
14. The main message of this story is: (1) the coming of
    winter (2) how bugs are different from horses (3) how
    colorful the day was (4) the power and contrast in young
    life.
15. Young animals live: (1) only in pastures and under logs
    (2) in large numbers (3) only if they can run fast (4) in
    many different conditions.

See p. 51 for directions.   **149**

LISTENING COMPREHENSION TEST: LEVEL III

Name _____ Grade _____

1. What does that sentence mean?
   _____ If you save money you will only get pennies.
   _____ If you save money you can be a coin collector.
   _____ If you save money it is as if you had earned it.

2. What should the reader do, according to that statement?
   _____ Live a long time.
   _____ Be careful and save the lives of others.
   _____ Realize that if he is careless he will endanger his life as well as other people's lives.

3. The statement means:
   _____ You should learn to sew.
   _____ Fixing something right away will keep it from getting worse.
   _____ In time things will get better.

4. This probably means:
   _____ Your cuts and bruises will get better.
   _____ We need to learn first aid.
   _____ We will forget about the things that have hurt us after awhile.

5. This tells us:
   _____ If we do something right away it will work out better for us.
   _____ Birds get up early.
   _____ Worms are good to eat.

6. What is likely to happen next?
   _____ ran away.
   _____ hit the tree again.
   _____ sharpened his ax.
   _____ yelled "Timber."

7. What is likely to happen next?
   _____ stopped.
   _____ turned to ice.
   _____ melted.
   _____ caused a flood.

8. Days later he discovered that:
   _____ he had poison oak.
   _____ he had a snake bite.
   _____ he was lost.
   _____ he was hungry.

9. They knew they would soon hear:
   _____ a horn.
   _____ yelling.
   _____ thunder.
   _____ a policeman.

10. All was quiet until Johnny yelled:
    _____ "I caught a fish."
    _____ "I'm sleepy."
    _____ "I want to go to school."
    _____ "I see a pretty cloud."

150

See p. 52 for directions.

Picture 1

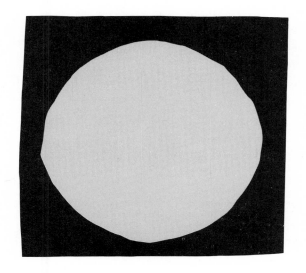

Picture 2

Picture 3

Picture 4

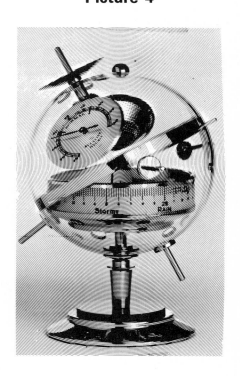

GENERATIVE LANGUAGE TEST: PART B

GENERATIVE LANGUAGE TEST: PART C

See p. 63 for directions.

ALPHABET TEST: IDENTIFICATION LEVEL
PART A: UPPER CASE

Name _____ Grade _____

1.	A	D	C	R	B	C	P
2.	L	M	N	E	M	Q	C
3.	I	T	F	Z	R	B	N
4.	S	G	F	Z	A	L	X
5.	V	Z	T	K	F	L	W
6.	C	N	O	S	P	Q	B
7.	X	V	R	J	N	W	K
8.	C	N	I	M	E	S	F
9.	K	B	H	E	L	F	Z
10.	I	L	J	B	N	K	R
11.	M	W	P	B	Z	N	U
12.	N	W	T	Z	M	L	V
13.	A	B	D	S	G	Z	D
14.	I	P	Q	N	B	G	D
15.	D	K	Q	R	P	B	G
16.	W	X	Z	V	Y	L	W
17.	C	R	H	U	D	Q	O
18.	O	D	N	M	G	R	Q
19.	Y	V	A	W	M	N	X
20.	H	T	I	E	L	B	D
21.	M	N	V	W	H	E	F
22.	V	N	M	U	R	Q	C
23.	V	U	Z	G	B	W	V
24.	R	G	F	M	N	D	H
25.	L	R	A	E	I	H	T
26.	Q	L	B	F	P	V	X

See p. 69 for directions.   153

ALPHABET TEST: IDENTIFICATION LEVEL
PART B: LOWER CASE

Name _____ Grade _____

1.	q	l	b	f	p	v	x
2.	l	r	a	e	i	h	t
3.	r	g	f	m	n	d	h
4.	v	u	z	g	e	w	v
5.	v	n	m	u	r	q	c
6.	m	n	v	w	h	e	f
7.	h	t	i	f	l	b	d
8.	y	v	u	w	m	n	x
9.	o	d	n	m	g	r	q
10.	c	r	h	u	d	a	o
11.	w	x	z	v	y	b	w
12.	d	k	q	r	p	g	g
13.	i	p	q	n	b	z	d
14.	a	b	d	s	g	l	f
15.	n	w	t	z	m	n	v
16.	m	w	p	b	z	k	u
17.	i	l	j	b	n	f	r
18.	k	b	h	e	l	s	z
19.	c	n	i	m	e	w	f
20.	x	v	r	j	n	q	k
21.	c	n	o	s	p	l	b
22.	v	z	t	k	f	l	w
23.	s	g	f	z	a	b	x
24.	i	t	f	z	r	b	n
25.	l	m	n	e	u	q	c
26.	a	d	c	r	b	c	p

 See p. 69 for directions.

ANSWER SHEET: PHONEME-GRAPHEME TEST
PART D: VOWELS

Name _____ Grade _____

1. a   e   i   o   u
2. a   e   i   o   u
3. a   e   i   o   u
4. a   e   i   o   u
5. a   e   i   o   u
6. a   e   i   o   u
7. a   e   i   o   u
8. a   e   i   o   u
9. a   e   i   o   u
10. a   e   i   o   u

1. a   e   i   o   u
2. a   e   i   o   u
3. a   e   i   o   u
4. a   e   i   o   u
5. a   e   i   o   u
6. a   e   i   o   u
7. a   e   i   o   u
8. a   e   i   o   u
9. a   e   i   o   u
10. a   e   i   o   u

See p. 71 for directions.

BLENDING TEST: LEVEL I

Name _____ Grade _____

+ LE	+ TER	DE + BUY COKE
S +	SW +	R +
R + −T	T +	S +
S +	S + + ER	+ ICK

See p. 76 for directions.

BLENDING TEST: LEVEL II

Name _____ Grade _____

1. str + ite   str + ide   str + eed

2. strin + gent   string + ent   stri + dent

3. pit + full   pic + ture   pit + cher

4. ni + trate   night + rate   ni + rat

5. de + code   decc + ode   de + cod

6. dir + ecttions   di + recttons   di + rec + tions

7. sil + ent + ly   si + lente + ly   sil + entl + y

8. ban + dan + a   band + anda   ban + da + na

SYLLABICATION TEST

Name _____ Grade _____

Read each word below and divide it into syllables by drawing a line between each syllable. For example, "undelivered" must be divided into four syllables like this: un/de/liv/ered. Divide each word below in the same way.

1. develop

2. wholesome

3. speedometer

4. rounded

5. lighter

6. floating

7. unshrinkable

8. recharged

9. innocent

10. battle

11. interpret

12. unsuspecting

See pp. 77 and 78 for directions.

STRUCTURAL ANALYSIS TEST: LEVEL I

Name _____ Grade _____

Sample

A. The _____ were crying.
baby   babies   babied

1. The boy was _____ the horse.
ride   rided   riding

2. I see many _____.
toys   toying   toy

3. My balloon is the _____.
big   biggs   biggest

4. The dog _____ over the gate.
jump   jumped   jumping

5. He _____ very fast.
run   running   runs

6. Joe is _____ than Dick.
tallest   taller   talls

7. He is _____ home.
come   comed   coming

8. They will not _____ together.
goes   go   going

9. The _____ are coming soon.
child   childs   children

10. The bird _____ over the house.
flew   flyed   flying

See p. 79 for directions.

STRUCTURAL ANALYSIS TEST: LEVEL II

Name _____ Grade _____

1. Circle the word or words in each row that indicate more than one (plural).

   a. baby   babies   baby's   babied
   b. cries   cried   criers   crying
   c. thoughtlessness   rethought   thoughts   thoughtful
   d. ruler's   ruling   rulers   unruled

2. Circle the word or words in each row that show past.

   a. jumped   run   walks   walked
   b. stopped   flew   is   eating
   c. were   come   listing   brusher

3. Circle the word or words in each row that have a part (affix) meaning "more" or "less than."

   a. bigger   tall   fewer   high
   b. painter   smaller   manly   mixed
   c. paying   happier   frozen   reviews

4. Circle the words with the affix that means "not."

   a. happiness   unhappy   happily   happening
   b. disoriented   reoriented   orienting   orienter
   c. uninterested   interesting   disinterested   reinterest
   d. illegal   legality   leger   legalistic
   e. practical   impractical   practically   practice

5. Circle the words with the affix that means "again."

   a. entering   reenter   unentered
   b. non-negotiable   negotiate   renegotiable

6. Circle the words with the affix that means "against."

   a. freezing   antifreeze   frozen
   b. antisocial   sociability   society

7. Circle the words with the affix that means "with."

   a. educated   coeducate   uneducated
   b. cooperate   operating   inoperable

8. Circle the words with the affix that means "before."

   a. paying   payable   prepaid
   b. viewed   preview   review

STRUCTURAL ANALYSIS TEST: LEVEL III

Name _____ Grade _____

Underline the root word in each of the following words if the root word is present. Put an X on the word that does not have the root in it. Look at the sample. Notice that recount, countless, and uncounted have the same root and that country does not.

Sample:

re<u>count</u>   <u>count</u>less   co̶u̶n̶try   un<u>count</u>ed

Now work the problems below in the same way:

1. unmarked   remark   marking   markproof

2. listen   unlisted   listing   relisted

3. alone   loner   lonely   abalone

4. parental   parentless   transparent   parents

5. refasten   fasten   fastest   unfasten

6. eating   heater   eats   uneaten

7. kindly   unkindly   kindling   kindness

8. famed   famous   famously   famine

9. painful   painless   painstaking   painter

10. reader   reread   ready   reading

SAN DIEGO QUICK ASSESSMENT LISTS

Readiness	1	2	3
see	you	road	our
play	come	live	please
me	not	thank	myself
at	with	when	town
run	jump	bigger	early
go	help	how	send
and	is	always	wide
look	work	night	believe
can	are	spring	quietly
here	this	today	carefully

4	5	6	7
city	decided	scanty	bridge
middle	served	certainly	commercial
moment	amazed	develop	abolish
frightened	silent	considered	trucker
exclaimed	wrecked	discussed	apparatus
several	improved	behaved	elementary
lonely	critical	splendid	comment
drew	entered	acquainted	necessity
since	realized	escaped	gallery
straight	interrupted	grim	relativity

8	9	10	11	12
amber	capacious	conscientious	zany	galore
dominion	limitation	isolation	jerkin	rotunda
sundry	pretext	molecule	nausea	capitalism
capillary	intrigue	ritual	gratuitous	prevaricate
impetuous	delusion	momentous	linear	risible
blight	immaculate	vulnerable	inept	exonerate
wrest	ascent	kinship	legality	superannuate
enumerate	acrid	conservatism	aspen	luxuriate
daunted	binocular	jaunty	amnesty	piebald
condescend	embankment	inventive	barometer	crunch

See p. 87 for directions.

Name _____ Grade _____

Read each word. If you can't pronounce it, please go on to the next word.

Lea cada palabra. Si no puede pronunciarla, por favor continúe con la próxima palabra.

a	cama	edad	*haber	luna
abajo	casa	el (art.)	*hablar	luz
abeja	casi	él (pron.)	*hacer	
agua	cerca (near)	ella	hacia	*llegar
aire	color	ellos	hasta	lluvia
al	colorado	en	hermana	
ala	como	encima	hermano	mamá
alto	con	entonces	hija	mano
allá	contento	entre	hijo	manzana
*amar	corazón	esa (adj.)	hoy	mañana
amigo	corto	*escribir		martes
amistad	cosa	esculea	idea	más
*andar	¿cuál?	ese (adj.)	igual	me
antes	cuando	eso (pron.)	invierno	mejor
año	cuchara	espejo	*ir (form)	mesa
aquí	cumpleaños	esta (adj.)		mi (adj.)
árbol	cuna	*estar	jardín	mí (pron.)
arriba		este (adj.)	juego	mientras
así	chico	estrella	jueves	miércoles
atrás			juguete	mío
ayer	*dar	fácil		mis
azúcar	de	familia	la	muchacha
azul	debajo	felicidad	lado	muchacho
	*decir	fiesta	lápiz	mucho
bajo	del	flor	las	muñeca
bandera	dentro	fruta	le	música
bebé	desde	fuego	leche	muy
bien	después		*leer	
blusa	día	gato	les	nadie
bonita	dibujo	globo	letra	naranja
	donde	grande	libro	ni
cada	dos	guitarra	lo	nido
café	dulces	*gustar	los	ninguno

See p. 89 for directions.

SPANISH WORD LIST (cont.)

niña	papel	rojo	sus	tuyo
niño	para	repa		
no	paz	rosa	también	último
noche	pelota		tan	un
nombre	pie	sábado	tarde	una
nos	por	*saludar	taza	uno
nosotros	porque	se (reflex.)	te (pron.)	uña
nuevo	primavera	semana	té (tea)	usted
nunca	primero	señor	tener	uva
	pronto	señora	ti	
o	puerta	señorita	tía	vaca
oir		*ser	tierra	ventana
ojo	¿qué?	si (if)	tijeras	verde
once	*querer	sí (yes)	tío	vida
orquesta	queso	siempre	todo	*vivir
oso	¿quién?	silla	*traer	
otoño	quince	sin	traje (dress)	y
		sobre (prep.)	tras	yo
padre	*recordar	sobrino	tren	
país	recuerdo	sol	tres	zapato
palabra	*reir	solo (alone)	tu (adj.)	
pan	reloj	su	tú (pron.)	
papá	respeto	sueño	tuya	

*An asterisk in front of a verb means that a form of that verb may be used in place of the infinitive.

ORAL READING PARAGRAPHS

Preprimer Level

The man said, "Can I help you?"
"Yes," said Jim.
"We want to get some balls.
Look over there and you can see them.
I get the blue.
Sally gets the red.
Dick gets the yellow.
We want three balls."

Primer Level

One day Dick said, "Oh, Sally.
Look at the new truck over there.
There is green paint on it.
There is red paint too.
The big new truck is green and red.
I like red paint on trucks and things."

"So do I," said Sally.
"But now we have to walk to school."
And so they went on to school.

First Level

Bob ran for a long way.
Then all at once he saw a ranch.
It was not a very big ranch.
It had a big ranchhouse, a barn, and lots of small animals.
The house was white and red.
Bob lay down near a fence.
He lay there for a long time looking at the ranch.
Then all of a sudden he said, "Yes! This is just the place I want to be.
This ranch will be my new home."

  See p. 90 for directions.

Second Level

"Where is Red Fox?" asked Gray Wolf.

"I don't care about Red Fox," answered Running Deer. "I want to learn about the paths into the woods," he said.

"You are wise. It is good to learn about such things," said the mean Gray Wolf to Running Deer.

"Do you understand where the paths go?" he asked.

"No, I don't," answered Running Deer, "but I would like to find out."

"Both of us want to find out. Let's go deep into the forest and see where the paths go," said Gray Wolf.

"Yes," said Running Deer. "We are wise. We will find out."

Gray Wolf and Running Deer walked away. Some blue birds shook their heads as they watched the deer walking away with the wolf.

Third Level

The lifeguard helps people when they are in the water. He is a good swimmer. He is strong and does not get tired quickly. He can swim fast. He must run into the water if someone needs help.

The lifeguard sits on a tower beside the water. He can see well from there. He must be able to see everyone.

Sometimes the lifeguard blows his whistle. If people do not follow the safety rules, the lifeguard talks to them. He explains what they must do to be safe in the water. The lifeguard makes sure that everyone follows the rules.

If the lifeguard sees someone who needs help, he races to the water and dives in. Soon he is at the side of the person who needs help. The lifeguard takes the person and swims back. He must carry the person in the right way. Otherwise, he could be pulled under the water by the frightened person.

ORAL READING PARAGRAPHS

Fourth Level

In 1886, the lives of the Mohawk Indians changed. The Indians started to work as laborers on a bridge that was being built across the St. Lawrence River. The Mohawks became tired of the hard work of pushing wheelbarrows and moving building materials. They walked out on the bridge when they had time. Others noticed that these Indians had no fear of heights. They would walk a narrow board that was quite high up in the air with only the river below them. It didn't seem to matter to them that they were not walking on solid ground. The Mohawks didn't seem to mind the noise of the riveting high on the bridge, which sometimes makes new construction workers feel dizzy. The Indians were curious about the riveting and kept asking the foremen if they could be allowed to try it. This happens to be the most dangerous work in all construction, and the highest paid. Men who want to do this work are rare and men who can do it are even rarer.

Fifth and Sixth Levels

When Bill repeated one part of the story, he stretched as tall as he could and talked in a low voice. All his friends could imagine Mr. Jones, standing on a barge in the middle of Lake Erie.

"Captain Smith, their barges are floating away from any boat and besides, they are dark and have been clearly abandoned. The law is that abandoned barges can be claimed by anyone who finds them."

Then Bill changed his voice and stood a little less tall, with his hands on his hips, like Captain Smith.

"I don't know what you're saying. These barges were left so we could take a sick girl and her mother to the dock. What makes you think the barges were abandoned?"

Bill talked like Mr. Jones again.

"I know they are abandoned! They didn't put lights on the barges!"

Then, Bill talked in his own voice.

"The captain was mad! He was angry with Mr. Jones for taking advantage of him. He was also upset because he had failed to put on the lights. When the barges are attached directly to the boat, the lights get power from the boat's engines. But when they are not attached, lamps have to be hung on the barges. This rule is very important. They were in such a hurry to help the girl and her mother that nobody thought of lamps!"

ORAL READING PARAGRAPHS

Seventh and Eighth Levels

It's hard to decide what to watch when you attend an outdoor track meet. On a flat, grass-covered field, contestants are involved in jumping and throwing events. On an oval track around the field, runners are competing. To the sports-minded, a track meet is as exciting as a science fiction adventure.

For many, the track events are the most exciting. There is always an abundance of action. If you attend a good-sized track meet, chances are you would see 100-yard and 220-yard dashes, and 440-yard, 880-yard, and 1-mile races.

When ten hurdle fences are put on the track, the hurdle races begin. In the hurdle races, the runners jump over these fences. There are two kinds of hurdle races. In low-hurdle races, the fences are 2½ feet high. Fences 3 or 3½ feet high are used in high-hurdle races. The length of a race determines the distance between the hurdles. They may be anywhere from 10 to 40 feet apart.

In the relay races teams of four runners compete. All racers run the same distance. The first person on all competing teams begins running at the sound of the sharp bang. Each runner carries a small baton or rod. As he completes his lap, he passes the baton to the next runner on his team. Runners who race the final lap are called anchor men. Anchor men are usually the fastest runners.

Easy First Level
(Preprimer)

Mira, mamá.
Mira, un perro.
No, Manolo.
No es un perro.
Es una puma.
¡Mi perro!
¡No, Mupi!
¡No, Mupi, no!
Una puma
y mi perro.

Hard First Level

Vamos a la mesa,
vamos a comer.
Las velas esperan
y el pavo también.
Comen el pavo,
comen el pan, y comen
la batata que asó su papá.

Second Level

¡Qué contento está el señor Gepeto! Hoy es el primer día de clases de Pinocho. Le pone una camisa y le compra algunos lápices y cuadernos.

Pinocho también está muy contento.

Dale esta manzana a tu maestro—dice Gepeto.—Y esta moneda es para ti. Cómprate lo que quieras en el almacén. ¡Pero no olvides! ¡No tes pares a hablar con nadie! Ve derechito a la escuela. Queda al final de la calle.

Third Level

Todas las tardes, a la salida de la escuela, los niños iban a jugar al jardín del gigante. Era un jardín grande y hermoso, cubierto de hierba verde.

¡Cómo nos gusta jugar aquí!—se gritaban unos a otros.

Un día, el gigante regresó . . . Al llegar, vió a los niños jugando en el jardín.

Mi jardín es mi jardín—dijo el gigante. Ya es hora de que lo entiendan. Y no voy a permitir que nadie más juegue en él.

 See p. 93 for directions.

SPANISH ORAL READING PARAGRAPHS: POSTTEST

Easy First Level (Preprimer)

Toman té en la taza.
Tona no toma té.
Tona es una muñeca.
Tita sí toma té.
Toma té en su taza.

Hard First Level

La niña tiene sueño.
Se baña todas las mañanas.
Come piña y toma un vaso de leche.
Va a la escuela con otros niños y niñas.

Second Level

Hoy es día de fiesta en el barrio. Han terminado la nueva casa. Es la más bonita de la calle. ¡Y también la más alto!

Ernesto, Angela, Antonio, y Arturo se sienten muy orgullosos. Ellos vieron crecer la casa, día a día. Saben qué materiales usaron para hacerla.

Third Level

En la ciudad de los gatos vive el gato Mustafá. Muy temprano se levanta, pues le gusta ser puntual. Se baña en la regadera, se piena, ayuda a mamá, y toma su desayuno: jugo, huevos, leche, ye pan. Revisa bien su maleta, nada le debe faltar, y cuado llega a la escuela, saluda a todos: "¡Miau, miau!"

First Grade Level

"Look at these 🌼🌼🌼 , Mother," said Jane.

"I like the red 🌼 . I like the blue 🌼 , too."

"Yes, Jane. They are pretty," said Mother.

"Come in the 🏠 , Jane.

We will look at the 🌼🌼🌼 later."

"Can I help, Mother?" said Jane.

"Yes, you can help. Come in the 🏠 ."

See p. 99 for directions.

SILENT READING PARAGRAPHS

Second Grade Level

Mother looked at the cat and dog. "Come in the house," she said. The black and white dog and the yellow cat came running into the house.

Soon Dick and Mary ran home. School was out. They got in the car with little Bill and Mother. The dog and cat got in the car. Away they went. Soon they came to the big store. All of them went in.

Mother looked at a red coat. Dick looked at some toys. Mary looked at the books. There were many things to look at. No one looked at little Bill.

Soon it came time to go home. "Where is little Bill?" said Mother. "I don't see him." Mother went looking. Dick and Mary went looking.

They walked past the toys and past the books. They came to the beds. "Look!" said Dick. There were little Bill and the dog and cat asleep.

Third Grade Level

A waiter works in a restaurant. He asks people what they want to eat. He brings people many kinds of food.

When people come in he gives them a menu. It tells what food the restaurant has. It also tells how much the food costs. After the people look over the menu, they tell the waiter what they want to eat. The waiter takes their order.

The waiter carries the order to the cook. He gets the food ready, then he gives it to the waiter. The waiter puts it on a tray. He then takes it to the table.

As the people eat, the waiter checks to see that they have the things they need. Sometimes he brings more water, milk, or coffee. When the people have finished eating, the waiter clears the table. He finds out what they want for dessert. The waiter gets the dessert for them.

SILENT READING PARAGRAPHS

Fourth Grade Level

Cattle are raised for their meat and their milk. The meat is called beef. We eat beef more than other meat.

Beef cattle are raised on ranches. A number of cattle are a herd. Herds of cattle feed on grass land. Sometimes they are fed hay. When the cattle are ready they are sent to a stockyard.

A stockyard is where animals are kept until they are sold. In the stockyards the cattle are fattened on corn. Corn-fed cattle give rich quality beef. Buyers visit the stockyards and choose the animals they want. Buyers know how to judge the quality of meat in every animal.

From the stockyards the cattle are sent to a packing plant in trains and trucks. In the packing plant the animals are killed. Some of the meat is put in cans but most is kept fresh.

Fifth Grade Level

Muir wanted to explore a glacier that was between two mountain peaks. He and his partner left their camp on the east side of the mountain. They climbed higher through heaps of fallen logs. They reached the edge of the ice river and spiked their way to the top of the glacier. They crossed to the west side, jumping over each crevasse. On the west side they saw the edge of a forest. They turned north until they came to a huge crevasse. This led into a lake, which was full of floating ice. On the return trip they crossed one crevasse only to face a larger one. They were caught standing on an island in the ice. They crossed the large crevasse by crawling across an ice bridge and from there headed toward camp. They had to spike their way slowly down into one crevasse after another before the two exhausted men finally reached their camp.

SILENT READING PARAGRAPHS

Sixth Grade Level

On June 14 of 1777, the Continental Congress—the governing body of the colonies—decided that the official flag of the colonies should be thirteen stripes alternating red and white, with a blue rectangle at the upper left-hand corner of the flag in which there were thirteen stars, white on a blue field.

The Congress did not prescribe an official arrangement for the stars, so several designs appeared. One designer arranged all thirteen stars in a circle. Another put twelve stars in a circle with the thirteenth in the center.

No one knows who designed the first flag, nor did the Continental Congress leave any record of why it chose red, white, and blues as the colors for the flag. Perhaps it is because the flag grew up around the British flag, which carried those same colors.

The next change in the flag came in 1794 with the admission of two new states. The flag was altered to have fifteen stars and fifteen stripes—a star and stripe for each state.

Seventh Grade Level

Many of the animals we normally associate with Africa are found in Ethiopia. Monkeys and baboons abound in many regions. The elephant and the rhinoceros are seen in widespread areas. Hippopotamuses and crocodiles inhabit lakes and rivers. Snakes are common. Lions are found in parts of the country. Leopards found there are unusually large. Fierce hyenas are everywhere, even in the nation's capital city!

The nation's capital, Addis Ababa, lies eight thousand feet above sea level. The city has a population of half a million people. The high elevation of the city gives its residents a cool climate. Modern buildings, a hospital, a library, a museum, and a university have been built. Three miles from the city a modern airfield links Ethiopia to other countries.

Though developing countries like Ethiopia have many difficulties still to overcome, the progress they have made in recent years gives hope to their people for a better and longer life in the future.

CLOZE READING TESTS

Practice Paragraph

Put one word in each blank. Try to find out what word goes in each blank by looking at the other words in the paragraph. If you can't figure out one answer, skip over it and fill in as many blanks as you can. Then go back and fill in the ones you didn't do.

Bill and Sally live in the same house. They are brother and _____. They both go to _____. When they come home _____ school, they sit at _____ table and have milk _____ cookies. Then they have _____ to play outdoors until _____.

When it is time _____ dinner, their mother calls _____. They eat dinner with _____ mother and help her _____ the dishes because she _____ very tired from working.

   See p. 102 for directions.

CLOZE READING TESTS
Second Grade

Write only one word in each blank. Try to fill in every blank. Don't be afraid to guess. Wrong spelling will not count against you if we can tell what you mean.

"Look in the garden," _____ Bill. "There is something _____ there. Something is walking _____ in there. It looks _____ a little puppy."

Just _____ a little animal came _____ of the garden. It _____ black with white down _____ back. It had a _____ tail. "Let's make a _____ out of it," said _____.

"I'll get it some _____," said Jim. He went _____ the house. His Uncle _____ him come in. "Don't _____ anything now," he said. "_____ are going to eat _____ soon."

"This milk isn't _____ me," said Jim. "It's _____ our new pet. Bill _____ I have a new _____. It's out in the _____ yard. You will like _____. Take a look."

Uncle _____ out the back door. "_____!" he said. "Oh, no. _____ away from it, Bill. _____ away from it. It's _____ a pet. It's a _____!"

Third Grade

The zoo keeper has _____ job that many
children _____ like to have. His _____
seems like play. Most _____ like animals. The
zoo _____ likes many animals, too, _____
he has to work _____ to take care of
_____.

Every day the zoo _____ must feed the
_____. This is more work _____ getting
dinner ready for _____ big family. At home,
_____ eats the same food. _____ the zoo,
all the _____ do not get the _____ thing to
eat.

He _____ hard to keep the _____ clean.
The animals must _____ washed. Some animals
need _____. The cages must be _____. The
floor must be _____.

The zoo keeper knows _____ lot about
animals. Children _____ him many questions.
Some _____ to know all about _____.
Some want to know _____ to feed the bears.
_____ want to know how _____ make a
parrot talk.

The zoo keeper likes _____ and girls to
come _____ the zoo. He has _____
watching them with the _____.

CLOZE EXERCISE
Fourth Grade

Many _____ live in the sea. _____ these are fish. They _____ a bone that goes _____ their backs. It is _____ a backbone. They may _____ through openings in the _____ of their bodies which _____ called gills. Fish have _____ rather than thick skin. _____ of arms and legs, _____ have fins which often _____ them balance and swim.

_____ are two big groups _____ fish. They are the _____ fish and the fresh _____ fish. Fish which live _____ the ocean are called _____-water fish. Often these _____ are blue gray in _____. Fish which come from _____ and lakes where the _____ is without salt are _____ _____ usually brownish-green or _____-green in color.

Another _____ of sea animals is _____ the shellfish. They are _____ really fish at all. _____ be true fish they _____ have to have a _____. Shellfish live in or _____ the water, however, and _____ covered with a shell _____ protects their bodies.

Fifth Grade

Before ancient man could _____ a real

hunter, there _____ something he had to

_____. He had to find _____ how fire could

be _____ as a tool. Without _____ help of

fire, ancient _____ could not eat with

_____ animals. With his pointed _____ he

could spear rabbits _____ mice, but he could

_____ cook them. All animals _____ hunt

have sharp teeth _____ cutting into the meat

_____ kill. Ancient man did _____ have the

sharp teeth _____ a wolf or a _____ or a

dog has. _____ man had seen fire _____

times. Along with the _____ animals, he had

run _____ it. He, too, was _____ of fire.

Many brush _____ and grass fires were

_____ by lightning, as they _____ are

today.

Lightning hits _____ bush or a field

_____ dry grass, and soon _____ is a big

fire. _____ of the animals are _____ afraid

that the hunting _____ forget to hunt. When

_____ is a big fire _____ them, a rabbit

can _____ next to a coyote _____ being

afraid.

Sixth Grade

This is a tale about Roger Jones and his life as an animal tamer. Even as a young _____ Roger showed an ability _____ tame wild creatures. When _____ was twenty, he took _____ job in a circus _____ and taming wild creatures. _____ Roger was badly hurt _____ an Indian elephant, he _____ the circus and worked _____ a mechanic for seventeen _____.

Then Roger traveled West _____ 1877 and headed for _____ valleys of central Oregon. _____ made friends with the _____ who lived there and _____ helped to build _____ out of sticks and _____. In return for their _____, Roger hunted for food _____ their families.

After Roger _____ lived in the valley _____ a long time, his _____ Eddy offered him a _____. Roger wanted to capture _____ animals and send them _____ the South to be _____ in zoos. Roger began _____ wild animals like bears, _____, deer, and antelope. He _____ most of these wild _____. One bear named Dolly _____ was especially attached to _____ as she grew up. _____ bear followed him everywhere. _____ spent the rest of _____ life visiting towns exhibiting animals. People were amazed _____ see him walking down _____ street at the head _____ an assortment of animals _____ bears, deer, elk, and _____.

Sample Paragraph

Possum was warm and snug, riding in the pouch under his mother. But he couldn't see anything in there. Pushing his head through the opening, he peered at the outside world. His mother was up in a tree! Then she saw a big brown moth flutter to a landing. The mother possum snapped it up.

Paragraph A

When Christopher was older, he could sail the little boat himself. "I like to sail a boat," he said. "I would like to learn to be a sailor." "You must learn to be a weaver," his father said. Christopher learned to clean wool and to make the wool into cloth. But more than anything else, he wanted to sail. His dream was to sail to a place called India that he had never seen.

Paragraph B

Have you ever wondered what all the things you see around you are made of? A house may be made of brick, and if you look closely, you can see that the brick is made up of little lumps of hard clay. Each little lump is made up of still smaller ones. How little do you suppose the littlest one is?

Paragraph C

The ancient Greeks liked to talk and argue about all kinds of things. The people who would argue the most were called philosophers. One philosopher thought that if he cut up things into smaller and smaller pieces he would come to pieces that couldn't be cut down any further. These pieces he called atoms. This philosopher was called Democritus. He lived 2,500 years ago. He was considered the father of the atom.

 See p. 110 for directions.

Paragraph D

When the men came to high and rugged mountains, they wondered how they were going to get to the other side. The engineering problems that they faced were very difficult. The mountains were made of hard granite rock and the mountains themselves were very high. The decision was made to dig a tunnel through the mountains. It would have to be almost 1/4 mile long and much of it would have to be drill-and-blast digging through the granite bed rock. This situation called for a large number of workers who would be willing to do very heavy work for long periods of time.

Paragraph E

A cardboard carton makes a good puppet stage. Cut off the top of the carton. Don't cut the sides or the bottom. Trim the sides of the carton to about 14 inches. Cut out the center part of the bottom of the carton in a square. Leave a frame five inches wide. Now put the carton on the table standing on one side and you have a puppet stage.

TEST FOR SCANNING FOR INFORMATION: LEVEL I
ANSWER SHEET

Name_____

Sample Paragraph	**Paragraph B**	**Paragraph D**

Sample Paragraph

S-1 _____
S-2 _____

Paragraph A

A-1 _____
A-2 _____

Paragraph B

B-1 _____
B-2 _____

Paragraph C

C-1 _____
C-2   yes   no
C-3   yes   no
C-4 _____

Paragraph D

D-1 _____
D-2   yes   no
D-3   yes   no
D-4   yes   no
D-5 _____

Paragraph E

E-1 _____
E-2   yes   no
E-3   yes   no
E-4   yes   no
E-5 _____

Sample Paragraph

On a bright day in June, the large Boeing 747 lifted off the runway at the airport. There were over 300 passengers and crew aboard. It is seldom that the passengers on these flights are disturbed by the fact that they are flying at incredibly high altitudes or that their very lives depend on thousands of mechanical parts working exactly as they should. The future of flight, particularly space flight, is even more difficult to understand; yet it is coming, and the time is not too far in the future when we will think it as commonplace as the modern jet ride of today.

Paragraph A

Many of the industrialized countries of the world have problems that are difficult for their leaders to solve. But in the countries that have little or no knowledge of the modern factory or farm, the problems of the survival of the people themselves is almost beyond the imagination. For example, in some countries, where the climate is not ideal for living, there is one baby who dies for every two babies born. The problems of feeding and clothing the people in some countries even with the simplest kinds of goods is beyond the means available, and the result is starvation and death by disease of large numbers of the people. The people who do survive are so busy just providing for themselves and their families that they have little time and energy to help their countries solve the large problems that they face.

Paragraph B

Can we get an idea of the size of the atom and its nucleus? If we could make the whole atom a million times bigger it would be about as big as a pinhead. If we wanted to see the nucleus, we would have to enlarge the atom twenty thousand million times. The atom would be as big as a large trailer but we would just barely be able to see the nucleus itself. Mostly we would see vast empty spaces between the nucleus and its electrons because the greatest part of all matter is empty space.

**TEST FOR SCANNING FOR INFORMATION: LEVEL II
ANSWER SHEET**

Sample Paragraph

Topic for study: The history of flight.
Reading time: 30 seconds.
Which title is the best for this passage?

1. Flying Past and Present
2. Space Flight and Today's Planes
3. The Jet in War and Peace
4. Improving Our Airports

Does the paragraph fit the topic of study?

Paragraph A

Topic for study: Modern health problems in under-developed countries.
Reading time: 30 seconds.
Best title for this paragraph:

1. Life in a Poor Country
2. Industrial Pollution
3. The Care of Babies
4. How to Grow Crops for Your Family

Does the paragraph fit the topic of study?

Paragraph B

Topic for study: Space in the atomic age.
Reading time: 20 seconds.
Best title for this paragraph:

1. Matter Is Made of Empty Space
2. The Relationship of the Atom
3. Picturing the Size of the Atom
4. Enlarging the Atom

Does the paragraph fit the topic of study?

ALPHABETIZING SKILLS TEST: LEVEL I

Name _____ Grade _____

Alphabetical List

1. apple
2. are
3. baby
4. birthday
5. come
6. doll
7. eat
8. girl
9. go
10. has
11. here
12. house

13. is
14. like
15. man
16. mother
17. name
18. play
19. put
20. run
21. saw
22. that
23. them
24. want

The words below are not on the list. Where should they go?

me: between_____and_____

pretty: between_____and_____

be: between_____and_____

one: between_____and_____

the: between_____and_____

his: between_____and_____

up: between_____and_____

just: between_____and_____

did: between_____and_____

school: between_____and_____

See p. 113 for directions.

Sample Paragraph

Topic for study: The history of flight.
Reading time: 30 seconds.
Which title is the best for this passage?

1. Flying Past and Present
2. Space Flight and Today's Planes
3. The Jet in War and Peace
4. Improving Our Airports

Does the paragraph fit the topic of study?

Paragraph A

Topic for study: Modern health problems in under-developed countries.
Reading time: 30 seconds.
Best title for this paragraph:

1. Life in a Poor Country
2. Industrial Pollution
3. The Care of Babies
4. How to Grow Crops for Your Family

Does the paragraph fit the topic of study?

Paragraph B

Topic for study: Space in the atomic age.
Reading time: 20 seconds.
Best title for this paragraph:

1. Matter Is Made of Empty Space
2. The Relationship of the Atom
3. Picturing the Size of the Atom
4. Enlarging the Atom

Does the paragraph fit the topic of study?

ALPHABETIZING SKILLS TEST: LEVEL I

Name _____ Grade _____

Alphabetical List

1.	apple	13.	is
2.	are	14.	like
3.	baby	15.	man
4.	birthday	16.	mother
5.	come	17.	name
6.	doll	18.	play
7.	eat	19.	put
8.	girl	20.	run
9.	go	21.	saw
10.	has	22.	that
11.	here	23.	them
12.	house	24.	want

The words below are not on the list. Where should they go?

me: between_____and_____

pretty: between_____and_____

be: between_____and_____

one: between_____and_____

the: between_____and_____

his: between_____and_____

up: between_____and_____

just: between_____and_____

did: between_____and_____

school: between_____and_____

See p. 113 for directions.

ALPHABETIZING SKILLS TEST: LEVEL II

Name_____ Grade_____

SAMPLE

home
ball
please
water
some

A

big
think
because
after
pull

B

head
hand
hug
hope
high

C

blown
bleat
blue
blowing
bluster
black
blustery

D

mental
menial
menu
menthol
mentality
mend
menace
menagerie

E

thermoelectric
thermos
thermograph
thermal
thermonuclear
thermidor
thermostat
thermotherapy
thermionics
thermometry

See p. 114 for directions.

ALPHABETIZING SKILLS TEST: LEVEL III
PART A

Name _____ Grade _____

Guide words are found at the top of each page in the dictionary and in some other reference books. They repeat the first word on the page and the last word on the page. They can help us find words more quickly.

They look like this:

Sample

baby	89	ball

Circle the words that would be on this page:

baffle   back   break   baa   banner

---

1. trump   950   trust

    trumpet   trunk   tree   truss   truly

---

2. veterinarian   1258   vicar

    vexed   vestry   vial   vibrate   victory

---

3. fortune   325   foul

    fortunate   fossil   forward   foster   found

---

4. blind   98   blood

    block   blend   bleed   bliss   blot

---

5. untold   1303   up

    unto   untrue   untangle   untouchable   unwritten

ALPHABETIZING SKILLS TEST: LEVEL III
PART B

Name _____ Grade _____

instantaneously	615	insufficient
insufficiently	616	integrator
integrity	617	intensive
knavery	652	knock
knockabout	653	k.o.

The following word would be on what page?

Sample: instrument

1. intense _____

2. knob _____

3. intact _____

4. integral _____

5. instinct _____

6. knuckle _____

7. insurance _____

8. knell _____

9. insufficiency _____

10. intelligence _____

11. knot _____

12. intended _____

PHONETIC DICTIONARY SKILLS TEST
PRONUNCIATION KEY

Accent Markings

('), as in mother (muṭh'er), is used to mark primary accent or stress; the syllable preceding it is pronounced with greater emphasis than other syllables in the word. Silent letters are not included. Upside-down letters stand for unaccented syllables: ɐ in alone, ə in system.

ă	act, mat	ō	own, no
ā	able, cake	ô	corn, call
ā̆	dare, chair	oi	oil, boy
ä	car, calm	ou	cloud, out
b	back, tub	p	pat, top
ch	choose, beach	r	rake, cry
d	do, Ted	s	saw, hiss
ĕ	shell, set	sh	shoe, push
ē	knee, equal	t	ten, pit
f	fit, farmer	th	thin, path
ġ	beg, get	ṭh	then, breathe
h	hit, hat	ŭ	sun, love
hw	when, why	ū	cute, few
ĭ	chill, if	ū̇	urge, bird
ī	rise, flight	u̇	pull, took
j	just, edge	ü	true, ooze
k	kept, cap	v	voice, live
l	low, all	w	west, way
m	mine, Tim	y	you, yes
n	on, now	z	zeal, those
ŏ	clock, hot	zh	vision, beige

See p. 116 for directions.

PHONETIC DICTIONARY SKILLS TEST: LEVEL I

Name _____ Grade _____

Sample

kăt	_____	1. cell
sĕl	_____	2. wreck
rĕk	_____	3. cat

lŭnj	_____	1. gem
kŭp	_____	2. tongue
kwĭp	_____	3. cup
thrĕd	_____	4. glue
gĕst	_____	5. lunge
dŭz	_____	6. thread
prĭns	_____	7. mix
krŭm	_____	8. boy
mĭks	_____	9. quip
tŭng	_____	10. crumb
jĕm	_____	11. could
boi	_____	12. guest
glü	_____	13. does
daừt	_____	14. doubt
kừd	_____	15. prince

PHONETIC DICTIONARY SKILLS TEST: LEVEL II

Name _____ Grade _____

Sample

| a. sĕz | _____ |
| b. klŏk | _____ |

1. fĕns	_____
2. kŭm	_____
3. flŭd	_____
4. lăm	_____
5. rüm	_____
6. nŏiz	_____
7. kôf	_____
8. lăf	_____
9. bừk	_____
10. bāzh	_____

See p. 116-17 for directions.   189

PHONETIC DICTIONARY SKILLS TEST: LEVEL III

Name _____ Grade _____

Sample A

The escaped _____ was frightened.
   a. con' vict   b. con vict'

Sample B

I know nothing about the _____.
   a. sub' ject   b. sub ject'

1. We made good _____ in arithmetic.
   a. prog' ress   b. pro gress'

2. The men were lost in the _____.
   a. dez' ert   b. de zurt'

3. I bought a new _____ today.
   a. re kord'   b. rek' erd

4. There was a large pile of _____ by the curb.
   a. ref' us   b. re fuz'

5. I received a watch for a _____.
   a. prez' ent   b. pre sent'

6. He got a _____ to sell candy.
   a. per' mit   b. per mit'

7. You must give me a _____.
   a. re' fund   b. re fund'

8. Many _____ fought against the government.
   a. re bels'   b. reb' elz

9. I am _____ to stay here.
   a. kon' tent   b. kon tent'

10. Will you _____ me home?
   a. kon' duct   b. ken duct'

PHONETIC DICTIONARY SKILLS TEST: LEVEL IV

Name _____ Grade _____

Circle the phonetic spelling that stands for the underlined word.

Sample A

The night was very quiet.
a. kwĭt   b. kwī′ ĭt

Sample B

You are very definite about the answer.
a. dĕf′ e nĭt   b. dĭ fī′ nt   c. de′ fīn et

1. Whose dog is that?
   a. hōz   b. hüz   c. hĭz

2. A whale is a huge sea animal.
   a. hălb   b. hāwl   c. hwāl

3. I would like to be an ice skater.
   a. skăt r′   b. skat′ r   c. skĕt′ r

4. The blue bird is very pretty.
   a. bũrd   b. brīd   c. bĭd

5. Pour the water from the pitcher.
   a. pĭch′ r   b. pĭk′ chr   c. pĭt′ tĕr

6. The author wrote many books.
   a. ŭth′ er   b. ĕr′ thĕr   c. ô′ ther

7. He has on one black shoe and one brown one.
   a. shō   b. shü   c. shăw

8. Please cancel the order.
   a. kăn sel′   b. kăn′ sl   c. kĕn′ sĕl

9. His job is below hers.
   a. bĕl′ ō   b. be′ lū   c. bĭ lō′

10. Who is the main character?
    a. chăr′ ti   b. kăr′ ĭk tr   c. kĕr′ tr

DICTIONARY DEFINITIONS TEST

Name _____ Grade _____

Sample

A.   block
        a. A piece of wood or plastic used as a child's toy for building.
        b. Something used to stop movement or passage.

_____ I.   The fallen tree was a block to cars on the road.
_____ II. I bought my baby sister some blocks for her birthday.

B.   crane
        a. A bird.
        b. Machine for raising and lowering heavy weights.
        c. To stretch (the neck) as a crane does [hence, to hesitate].

_____ I.   I had to crane to see over the fence.
_____ II. The arm of the crane lifted the automobile.

                 junk
        a. A particular type of boat found in the Far East.
        b. Old iron, glass, paper, etc., which may be used again in some form.

_____ 1. He took a truckload of objects to the junk yard.
_____ 2. The Chinese family lived on a junk.

                 row
        a. A noisy or turbulent quarrel.
        b. To propel with oars along the surface of the water.

_____ 3. I can row the boat quickly.
_____ 4. My neighbors had a real row last night.

                 cape
        a. A sleeveless garment fastened around the neck and falling loosely over the shoulders.
        b. A piece of land jutting into the sea.

_____ 5. I loved my new blue cape.
_____ 6. The cape was very rugged.

 See p. 119 for directions.

Name _____ Grade _____

flicker

a. To burn unsteadily.
b. To wave to and fro.
c. A brief spark.
d. A North American woodpecker.

_____ 7. He felt a small flicker of hope.
_____ 8. The flicker made loud raucous noises.

flight

a. Act, manner, or power of flying.
b. The distance covered by a flying object.
c. A number of beings flying.
d. A journey by air.
e. The series of steps or stairs between two adjacent landings.

_____ 9. Our flight has been cancelled.
_____ 10. The discovery of flight was man's greatest invention.

fret

a. An irritated state of mind.
b. To cause corrosion; gnaw.
c. To become eaten, worn, or corroded.
d. An interlaced, angular design.
e. Any of the ridges of wood, metal, or string set across the finger board of a lute or similar instrument.

_____ 11. She's constantly in a fret about her money problems.
_____ 12. The fretwork on the old church was beautiful.

lock

a. A device for securing a door, gate, or lid.
b. A device to keep a wheel from rotating.
c. The mechanism in a firearm.
d. An enclosed portion of a canal, river, etc., with gates at each end.
e. Any of various grapples or holds in wrestling.
f. To fasten or secure.
g. To exclude.
h. A tress or portion of hair.

_____ 13. He hammered the lock on his door.
_____ 14. The lock was closed and ships could not pass.
_____ 15. The lock on the gun was broken.

INFORMATION LOCATION TEST: LEVEL I

Name _____ Grade _____

Table of Contents

PART A

Write the page number for the chapter that probably tells you about the following things.

Sample: Animals of the Indians _____

1. Indian medicine _____
2. A famous battle _____
3. The earliest Indians _____
4. Pictures by Indians _____
5. Agreements signed with Indians _____
6. How Indians live now _____
7. Games Indians played _____
8. Jobs of an Indian woman _____
9. Ways Indians wrote things down _____
10. How a brave caught meat _____

194

PART B

What chapters might contain information about the following subjects? There may be more than one.

Sample: Indian cooking _____

1. Buffalo _____
2. Indian battles _____
3. Influences of the white man _____
4. Activities Indians enjoyed _____
5. Life in Indian village _____
6. Beginnings of Indian civilization _____
7. Wagon trains crossing the plains _____
8. Present-day life _____
9. Raising Indian children _____
10. The clothing Indians wore _____

See p. 120 for directions.

INFORMATION LOCATION TEST: LEVEL II

Name _____ Grade _____

Index A

ASPCA, 8
Amphibians, 10, 53
Bait, 11-12, 37
Beaks, care of, 74-75
Beetle, 70
Bullfrog, 60
Butterfly, 71
Cages, 19-25
Caterpillar, 71
Chameleon, 65
Chipmunk, 13
Claws, care of, 74-75
Clipping, wings, 40
Cocoon, 71
Crows, 39-42
Cuts, 75
Disinfectant, 25
Dragonfly, 71
Exercise wheel, 36
Field mice, 66-38
First aid, 75
Flies, 70
Flying squirrel, 72
Frogs, 53-60
Handling, 17
Havahart trap, 12
Hibernation, 29, 34-35, 49
Horned toad, 66
Illness and injury, 72-75
Insects, 67-71
Katydid, 71

Leopard frog, 56
Lice, 75
Live-catch trap, 11
Lizards, 10, 46, 64-66
Mail order firms, 78
Mange, 75
Metabolism wheel, 37
Mice, 11, 16, 36-38
Moth, 71
Nesting box, 23
Newt, 63
Pet dealers, 73, 76
Praying mantis, 69-71
Raccoons, 11, 16, 32-35
Reptiles, 10
Salamanders, 61-63
Skunks, 16, 27-31, 72
Snapping turtle, 52
Spiny lizard, 65
Spotted salamander, 62, 63
Squirrels, 15
Tadpoles, 54-55
Terrariums, 15, 43-46
Toads, 53-60
Trapping, 7-13
Turtles, 47-52
Turtles, soft shells, 52
Veterinarian, 18, 74
Vitamins, 51, 74
Walking stick, 76
Zoos, 18

PART A

According to Index A, on what pages would you find information about the following subjects?

Sample: Finding your own pets. _____

1. Making cages. _____

2. Health and first aid for pets. _____

3. Water animals. _____

4. Insect pets. _____

5. Prices of pets. _____

INFORMATION LOCATION TEST: LEVEL II

Name _____ Grade _____

Index B

1. Apparent time, 56, 57
2. Asteroids, 4
3. Astronomical unit, 118
4. Barred spiral galaxies, 92, 93
5. Calendar, 48, 49
6. Celestial sphere, 58
7. Comets, 30, 31
8. Constellations, 32, 33-35
9. Cosmic rays, 53, 60-63
10. Distance measurement, 110-114
11.   parallax method, 110, 111
12.   scale models, 114
13. Dwarf stars, 23, 32, 36
14. Earth, 4-6
15.   age of, 17, 18
16.   motions of, 19, 20
17. Galaxies, 82-87, 89-93
18. Giant stars, 65
19. Gravitational force, 17-19
20. Halley's Comet, 48
21. Jupiter, 63, 65, 82
22. Lunar month, 125
23. Mars, 64, 83
24. Mean solar day, 88
25. Mercury, 62, 83
26. Meteors, 88, 89
27. Milky Way, 71-74
28. Moon, 5, 21-25
29.   motion, 20
30.   tides, 23
31. Neptune, 66, 89
32. Planetarium, 106-108
33. Planets, 62-69
34. Pluto, 67, 90
35. Radio scopes, 115
36. Radio telescope, 110-119
37. Reflecting telescope, 114, 117
38. Relativity, 40-42
39. Saturn, 64, 87
40. Shooting stars, 44
41. Solar day, 99
42. Solar system, 62-80
43. Space, 31
44. Stars, 61-63
45.   brightness, 63
46.   evolution, 61-62
47. Sun, 4-8
48. Telescopes, 99-104

PART B

According to Index B, on what pages would you find information about the following subjects?

Sample: Comets _____

1. Age of the earth _____
2. The tides _____
3. Small stars _____
4. How stars began _____
5. How gravity works _____
6. The moon _____
7. Measuring miles in space _____
8. Sun _____
9. Large stars _____
10. Viewing displays about space _____

List all the numbers of the different categories that might have information about the following topics.

Sample: Ways to view the stars _____

1. Our solar system _____
2. Falling bodies in space _____
3. Keeping time in space _____
4. Star clusters _____
5. Making space charts _____
6. Radiation in space _____
7. Cause of tides _____
8. Instruments for astronomy _____
9. Revolving bodies in space _____
10. The theory of relativity _____

INFORMATION LOCATION TEST: LEVEL III

Name_____ Grade _____

Library Reference Books

1. Atlas
2. Dictionary
3. Encyclopedias
4. Familiar Quotations
5. Fieldbook of Natural History
6. Handbook to Literature
7. International Maritime Dictionary
8. Psychological Review
9. Reader's Guide to Periodical Literature
10. Statesman's Yearbook
11. Statistical Abstract of the United States
12. Thesaurus
13. Who's Who in the United States
14. World Almanac
15. Yearbook on Human Rights

If you needed to make a report on the following topics, which of the books listed might have the information you would want? List the numbers that are beside the book title. You may be able to use more than one. If you don't know what some of the books are, just skip them.

1. Report on a famous living author _____

2. Report on a U.S. senator _____

3. Report on world farming conditions _____

4. English report on poetic language _____

5. Science report on ecology _____

6. Health report on mental illness _____

7. Social studies report on the United Nations _____

8. Social studies report on a famous admiral _____

9. English report on word origins _____

10. A science report on the use of rats in experiments _____

INTEREST SURVEY: PART A

Directions:

Name_____ Grade _____

Write the answers to these questions on your own paper.

1. Do you like to read? Why?

2. Do you have a favorite book? What is it?

3. Have you ever read a book more than once? Name one or two. How many times did you read it (them)?

4. Have you ever read a book one of your friends said was good?

5. Do you have a library card?

6. How often do you take books from the library?

7. Do you ever ask the teacher or librarian for help if you are looking for a book?

8. Do you ever read a book instead of watching television?

9. Do you read a book if you have seen the movie or television program based on it? Name some.

10. Write the name of a book you didn't like and tell why.

INTEREST SURVEY: PART B

Name _____ Grade _____

Fill in every blank with one of the four numbers below.

1. Like a lot
2. Like a little bit
3. Dislike a little bit
4. Dislike a lot

1. Subjects in school

_____ Arithmetic	_____ Music
_____ Spelling	_____ Art
_____ Reading	_____ Physical education
_____ Writing stories	_____ Health
_____ Science	_____ Book reports
_____ Social studies	_____ English

2. Activities outside of school

_____ Television	_____ Reading
_____ Movies	_____ Cooking
_____ Outdoor games	_____ Hobbies
_____ Watching sports	_____ Animals
_____ Hiking and camping	_____ Trips
_____ Fishing	_____ Car races
_____ Riding horses	_____ Slot car races
_____ Riding minibikes and motorcycles	_____ Being with friends

3. Things to read about

_____ Adventures	_____ Horse stories
_____ Animal stories	_____ Humor
_____ Hobby stories	_____ Fantasy
_____ Biography	_____ History
_____ Autobiography	_____ Geography
_____ Science	_____ Fables and myths
_____ Western stories	_____ Art and music
_____ Sports	_____ Religion
_____ Fairy tales	_____ People of other lands
_____ Poetry books	_____ Newspaper
_____ Mystery	_____ Magazines
_____ Motorcycles and minibikes	_____ Comic books
_____ Love and romance	_____ Ghost stories
_____ Science fiction	_____ Family stories
_____ Car magazines	_____ Riddles and jokes

INTEREST SURVEY: PART C

Name_____ Grade_____

Read the following stories. After you read each story, circle the word or phrase that describes how you felt when you were reading.

Story A

Mike and Jim ran to their horses quickly. They knew they were going to have to ride fast if they were going to beat the storm. The black clouds were piling up faster and faster. "Come on, Jim, hurry up!" Mike yelled. "We'll never make it at this rate." "I'm trying, Mike," Jim shouted back, "but there's something wrong with this cinch. I can't seem to get it tight."

1. This story sounds
   dull   interesting   exciting   scary   silly
2. I would like to
   forget it   burn it   read it   hear it
3. It makes me feel
   good   alive   interested   bored   sorry
4. The author is probably
   dumb   smart   a good writer   a poor writer

Story B

I'd always wanted to be in a taffy pull, and at last I was going to get a chance. Mother had said there would be one at the next Scout meeting and tonight was the night. She was bringing the sugar and a big pan to melt the syrup in. I could hardly wait to rub the butter all over my hands and then pull the soft candy until it turned white and hard. What a mess! And what fun!

1. This story sounds
   dull   interesting   exciting   scary   silly   funny
2. I would like to
   forget it   burn it   read it   hear it
3. It makes me feel
   good   alive   interested   bored   sorry   mad
4. I think reading is
   dumb   smart   fun   dull   boring   good

Story C

Janey peered through the green leaves. She was sure she had heard a sound in the middle of the big bush. The sunlight filtered through the tall trees of the forest, as Janey strained to see what was inside. Then a small movement caught her eye. Yes, there it was, a small fawn curled in a heap in the protection of the green leaves. "Ohh!" said Janey with a sigh, "he's probably waiting for his mother."

1. This story sounds
   dull   interesting   exciting   silly   enjoyable
2. I would like to
   read it   hear it   see it on television   forget it
3. Books are
   hard   easy   good   bad   interesting   boring
4. I am
   a good reader   a poor reader   an average reader   not a reader

LITERARY INTERPRETATION: SHADES OF MEANING TEST
PART A

Name _____

Choose the word that "best" fits into the sentence.

Sample A

The cat in the hat sat on the _____ .
1. chair
2. mat
3. rat
4. couch

Sample B

Billy Button brought a _____ biscuit.
1. baker's
2. tasty
3. buttered
4. pickled

1. I scream, you scream, we all scream for _____ .
   1. pancakes
   2. ice cream
   3. peaches and cream
   4. coffee with cream

2. I hear the groan and moan of a dying man. His time is fleeting _____ .
   1. quickly
   2. furious
   3. soon
   4. fast

3. Come softly, lovely lady, and lay your _____ in mine.
   1. hand
   2. glove
   3. head
   4. heart

4. Soft silent shores and _____ sand gleam sweetly in the summer sun.
   1. white
   2. silver
   3. sea
   4. packed

See p. 130 for directions.

LITERARY INTERPRETATION TEST: PART A (cont.)

5. The _____ sound made me shudder with dread as though the ghosts were warning me.
    1. whining
    2. crying
    3. wailing
    4. witching

6. "How dare you, sir?" the angry voice _____ .
    1. declared
    2. demanded
    3. decried
    4. said

7. Come, lovely child, and lift your lilting face to the light. The world belongs to _____ .
    1. day
    2. you
    3. everyone
    4. loveliness

8. The sun is shooting wide its crimson _____ and still the child dreams.
    1. path
    2. glow
    3. way
    4. color

9. The shy shepherd herded his little _____ along the crooked path.
    1. group
    2. herd
    3. friends
    4. flock

10. Green grows the grass and _____ in the gracious air.
    1. grateful
    2. graceful
    3. flowers
    4. gruesome

LITERARY INTERPRETATION: SHADES OF MEANING
PART B

Name_____ Grade _____

Circle the number of the word in the sentence that could be changed to the key word. Then tell whether the new sentence means the same or the opposite.

Sample A

Key word: furious
Sentence: The angry man sat down quickly.
Word to change: 1 2 3 4 5 6
Meaning: same   opposite

Sample B

Key word: quiet
Sentence: The dogs next door are very noisy.
Word to change: 1 2 3 4 5 6 7
Meaning: same   opposite

1. Key word: ugly
   Sentence: The girl was truly lovely.
   Word to change: 1 2 3 4 5
   Meaning: same   opposite

2. Key word: barely
   Sentence: The food was abundantly spread.
   Word to change: 1 2 3 4 5
   Meaning: same   opposite

3. Key word: asset
   Sentence: Intelligence is definitely an advantage.
   Word to change: 1 2 3 4 5
   Meaning: same   opposite

4. Key word: possibly
   Sentence: Evidently we are going to leave soon.
   Word to change: 1 2 3 4 5 6 7
   Meaning: same   opposite

5. Key word: vigorous
   Sentence: The enormous boxer was very healthy.
   Word to change: 1 2 3 4 5 6
   Meaning: same   opposite

6. Key word: thrilling
   Sentence: The exciting race was almost finished when we arrived.
   Word to change: 1 2 3 4 5 6 7 8 9
   Meaning: same   opposite

7. Key word: chunky
   Sentence: The short stocky man was no match for the huge fighter.
   Word to change: 1 2 3 4 5 6 7 8 9 10 11
   Meaning: same   opposite

8. Key word: calm
   Sentence: She was obviously aggravated as she stood before the judge.
   Word to change: 1 2 3 4 5 6 7 8 9 10
   Meaning: same   opposite

9. Key word: interested
   Sentence: She made reference to the actor in an off-hand sort of way.
   Word to change: 1 2 3 4 5 6 7 8 9 10 11 12
   Meaning: same   opposite

10. Key word: quantity
    Sentence: The young girl passed out a multitude of copies of the song.
    Word to change: 1 2 3 4 5 6 7 8 9 10 11 12
    Meaning: same   opposite

LITERARY INTERPRETATION: INFERENTIAL MEANINGS TEST
PART A

Name_____ Grade _____

On your answer sheet, write the number that best explains or interprets what each passage is about.

Sample

In a moment, all was again hushed. Dead silence succeeded the bellow of thunder, the roar of the wind, the rush of the waters, the moaning of the beasts, the screaming of the birds.
1. The animals were frightened.
2. A storm had passed.
3. The countryside was quiet.
4. We walked in the rain.

1. Success in every art, whatever may be the natural talent, is always the reward of industry and pains.
    1. Artists can be successful.
    2. It is important to have talent.
    3. To succeed one must work hard.
    4. Life is full of pain.

2. Here rests his head upon the lap of earth. A youth to fortune and fame unknown.
    1. The young man is poor.
    2. The young man is sleeping.
    3. The young man is famous.
    4. The young man is dead.

3. The first general direction that should be given to the speaker is that he should stand erect and firm, and in that posture that gives an expanded chest.
    1. You can breathe better if you stand straight.
    2. When giving a speech you should stand straight.
    3. Speakers should not breathe when talking.
    4. Stand on both feet firmly when talking.

4. Below even this spacious grotto, there seemed another cavern, down which I ventured, and descended about fifty paces, by means of a rope.
    1. The fun of mountain climbing.
    2. Exploring a mountain.
    3. Exploring a cave.
    4. Using a climbing rope.

5. Alas! The white man's ax had been there. The tree that he had planted was dead; and the vine, which had leaped so vigourously from branch to branch, now yellow and withering, was falling to the ground. A deep groan burst from the heart of the Indian. For thirty years, he had watched that oak, with its twining tendrils. They were the only things left in the wide world for him to love, and they were gone.
   1. The Indian is lonely and alone.
   2. The white men are cruel.
   3. The time of the Indian has passed.
   4. Trees take a long time to grow.

6. There is a melancholy music in autumn. The leaves float sadly about with a look of peculiar desolation, waving capriciously in the wind, and falling with a just audible sound, that is a very sigh.
   1. Leaves fall in autumn.
   2. The wind blows in autumn.
   3. Leaves make music when they fall.
   4. Autumn is a sad time of year.

7. We will give the names of our fearless race
   To each bright river whose course we trace;
   We will leave our memory with mounts and floods
   For the path of our daring, in boundless woods.
   1. Explorers name rivers.
   2. Pioneers are going to a new land.
   3. They are going on a trip.
   4. The woods are dangerous.

8. On new year's night, an old man stood at his window, and looked, with a glance of fearful despair, up to the immovable, unfading heaven, and down upon the still, pure white earth, on which no one was now so joyless and sleepless as he.
   1. The old man is celebrating.
   2. The old man is unhappy.
   3. The old man can't sleep.
   4. It is snowing.

9. He woke, to die mid flame and smoke,
   And shout, and groan and saber-stroke,
   And death-shots falling thick and fast
   As lightning from the mountain cloud.
   1. The soldier died in battle.
   2. There was a big fire.
   3. There was a storm.
   4. The soldier was asleep.

10. What rebellious thoughts of the cool river and some shady bathing place, kept tempting and urging that sturdy boy, who, with his shirt collar unbuttoned, and flung back as far as it could go, sat fanning his flushed face with a spelling book.
    1. It is a hot day.
    2. The boy doesn't like spelling.
    3. The boy is lazy.
    4. The boy would like to leave school.

LITERARY INTERPRETATION: INFERENTIAL MEANINGS TEST
PART B

Name _____

For each passage, try to decide what will happen next.

Sample

They were both unarmed, and, stretching their limbs like men preparing for a desperate struggle, they planted their feet firmly on the ground, compressed their lips, knit their dark brows, and fixing fierce and watchful eyes on each other, stood there, prepared for the onset.
  1. The men will run away.
  2. The men will die.
  3. The men will fight.
  4. The men will turn to stone.

1. Meanwhile the south wind rose, and with black wings
    Wide hovering: And now, the thickened sky
    Like a dark ceiling stood.
    1. It is going to rain.
    2. It is going to be windy.
    3. Birds are going to fly.
    4. Clouds are gathering.

2. The sale began. After some paintings and engravings had been disposed of, Samuel's was exhibited. "Who bids three dollars? Who bids?" the auctioneer cried. The artist listened eagerly, but none answered. He thought to himself . . .
    1. "My work is no good."
    2. "The people are laughing at me."
    3. "Can I sell my work?"
    4. "No one will buy my picture."

3. "Away, away, o'er the foaming main!"
    This was the free and joyous strain—
    "There are clearer skies than ours afar;
    We will shape our course by a brighter star."
    1. The men will go on a trip.
    2. The people will go on a voyage.
    3. A storm is coming.
    4. The men are having a dream.

4. The tide and wind were so favorable that the ship was able to come at once to the pier. It was thronged with people and there were repeated cheerings interchanged between shore and ship as friends happened to recognize each other.
    1. The mood of the meeting will be sad.
    2. The mood of the meeting will be reserved.
    3. The mood of the meeting will be interested.
    4. The mood of the meeting will be excited.

See p. 132 for directions.

5. After we had landed on the island, we walked about four miles, through the midst of beautiful plains. At length we came to a little hill, on the side of which yawned a most horrid cavern which, by its gloom, at first struck us with terror. Recovering from the first surprise, however, we entered boldly.
   1. The men will find a bear in the cave.
   2. The cave will fall on them.
   3. The men will explore the cave.
   4. The men will become frightened and run away.

6. The few remaining trees, clothed in the fantastic mourning of autumn; the long line of heavy clouds melting away before the evening sun, and the distant mountains, seen through the blue mist of departing twilight, alone remained as he had seen them in his boyhood. All things spoke a sad language to the heart of the desolate Indian. "The paleface may like it, but an Indian cannot die here in peace," he cried.
   1. The Indian will die.
   2. The Indian will kill the white men.
   3. The Indian will put up his tepee.
   4. The Indian will leave this sad place.

7. But there is something in the thunder's voice that makes me tremble like a child. I have tried to overcome this unmanly weakness but at the first low moaning of the distant cloud, my heart shrinks and dies within me. I am . . .
   1. going to die of heart failure.
   2. going to stay in the house till the storm passes.
   3. going to run and hide.
   4. going to put my head under the pillow.

8. Macpherson himself fell backward, his body hanging partly over the rock. A fragment gave way beneath him and he sank further, till catching with a desperate effort at the solid stone above, he . . .
   1. regained his footing.
   2. fell down the canyon.
   3. yelled for help.
   4. gave a sigh of relief.

9. Oh Sailor-boy! Sailor-boy! never again
   Shall home, love, or kindred, thy wishes repay;
   Unbless'd and unhonor'd, down deep in the main,
   Full many a score fathom, thy frame shall decay.
   1. The sailor is going to battle.
   2. The sailor is having a dream.
   3. The sailor is dead.
   4. The sailor is going home.

10. The pleasant rain! The pleasant rain!
    It hath pass'd above the earth.
    I see the smile of the opening cloud,
    Like the parted lips of mirth.
    1. It is going to rain.
    2. The flowers and grass will grow.
    3. The sky will laugh.
    4. We will need umbrellas.

Bibliography

Allen, H. B., and R. N. Campbell. *Teaching English as a Second Language: A Book of Readings.* New York: McGraw-Hill, 1972.

Anderson, R. C., and D. P. Ausubel. *Readings in the Psychology of Cognition.* New York: Grune and Stratton, 1963.

Arnsdorf, V. E. "The Influence of Indefinite Terms of Time and Space on Comprehension of Social Studies Materials." In "Challenge and Experiment in Reading," ed. J. A. Figurel. *Proceedings of the International Reading Association,* 1962, 7, 159-61.

Aulls, M. W. *Development and Remedial Reading in the Middle Grades.* Boston: Allyn & Bacon, 1978.

Ausubel, D. P. *The Psychology of Meaningful Verbal Learning.* New York: Grune and Stratton, 1963.

Balow, I. H. "Reading and Computation Ability as Determinants of Problem Solving." *Arithmetic Teacher,* 1964, II, 18-22.

Baratz, Joan C., and Roger W. Shuy. *Teaching Black Children to Read.* Washington, D.C.: Center for Applied Linguistics, 1969.

Barbe, W. *Educator's Guide to Personalized Reading Instruction.* Englewood Cliffs, N.J.: Prentice-Hall, 1972.

Barrett, C. Patricia, and G. V. Barrett. "Enjoyment of Stories in Terms of Role Identification." *Perceptual and Motor Skills,* 1966, 23, 1164.

Beaver, J. C. "Transformational Grammar and the Teaching of Reading." *Research in the Teaching of English,* 1958, 2(2), 161-71.

Bicknell, John E. "The Importance of Assessment and Behavioral Objectives in Individualizing Instruction." *Summer Workshop in Individualization of Instruction, 1970.* State University College, Fredonia, N.Y.: Teachers Education Research Center.

Bloom, Benjamin S. "Learning for Mastery," UCLA-CSEIP *Evaluation Comment,* No. 2, 1968.

Bloom, B. S., and others. *Taxonomy of Educational Objectives, Handbook I: Cognitive Domain.* New York: David McKay Co., Inc. 1956.

Bond, G. *Reading Difficulties: Their Diagnosis and Correction.* Englewood Cliffs, N.J.: Prentice-Hall, 1979.

Bormuth, John. "The Cloze Readability Procedure." *Elementary English,* April 1968, 45, 429-36.

Bouchard, John B. "Overview and Meaning of Individualized Instruction," *Summer Workshop in Individualization of Instruction, 1970.* State University College, Fredonia, N.Y.: Teachers Educational Research Center.

Braam, L. S., and A. Berger. "Effectiveness of Four Methods of Increasing Reading Rate, Comprehension, and Flexibility." *Journal of Reading,* 1968, 11, 346-52.

Brinton, J. E., and L. H. McKowan. "Effects of Newspaper Reading on Knowledge and Attitude." *Journalism Quarterly,* 1961, 38, 187-95.

Brittain, Mary M., and C. V. Brittain. "A Study at Two Levels of Reading, Cognition, and Convergent Thinking." *Education,* 1968, 88, 321-25.

Brown, R., and O. Bellugi. "Three Processes in the Acquisition of Syntax." In *Language and Learning,* eds. Emig, Fleming, and Popp. New York: Harcourt Brace Jovanovich, 1966.

Brownell, J. A. "The Influence of Training in Reading in the Social Studies on the Ability to Think Critically." *California Journal of Educational Research,* 1953, 4, 28-31.

Bruner, J. S., Jacqueline J. Goodnow, and G. A. Austin. *A Study of Thinking,* New York: John Wiley, 1956.

Burling, Robbins. *English in Black and White.* New York: Holt, Rinehart, & Winston, 1973.

Burmeister, L. E. *Words from Print to Meaning.* Reading, Mass.: Addison-Wesley, 1975.

Burns, P. C., and B. D. Roe. *Teaching Reading in Today's Schools.* Chicago: Rand-McNally, 1977.

Burns, P. C., and J. L. Yonally. "Does the Order of Presentation of Numerical Data in Multi-Step Arithmetic Problems Affect their Difficulty?" *School Science and Mathematics,* 1964, **64,** 267-70.

Burton, R. W. *An Ounce of Prevention Plus a Pound of Cure.* Santa Monica, Calif.: Goodyear, 1977.

Bush, Clifford L., and Mildred H. Huebner. *Strategies for Reading in the Elementary School.* New York: Macmillan, 1970.

Carrillo, L. W. *Teaching Reading, A Handbook.* New York: St. Martins, 1976.

Carter, H. L., and D. J. McGinnis. *Diagnosis and Treatment of the Disabled Reader.* New York: Macmillan, 1970.

Chall, J. *Learning to Read: The Great Debate Readability.* New York: McGraw-Hill, 1967.

Charis, C. P. "The Problem of Bilingualism in Modern Greek Education." *Comparative Education Review,* June 1976, **20,** 216-19.

Chase, Francis S. "Meeting Individual Differences in Reading." In *Meeting Individual Differences in Reading,* ed. H. Alan Robinson. Chicago: University of Chicago Press, December 1964.

Christensen, C. M., and K. E. Stordahl. "The Effect of Organizational Aids on Comprehension and Retention." *Journal of Educational Psychology,* 1955, **46,** 65-74.

Coley, J. D., and L. B. Gambrell. *Programmed Reading Vocabulary for Teachers.* Columbus, Ohio: Merrill, 1977.

Cooper, J. D., L. E. Cooper, N. Rosen, L. A. Harris, and C. B. Smith. *Decision Making for the Diagnostic Teacher.* New York: Holt, Rinehart, & Winston, 1972.

Cooper, J. L. "The Effect of Training in Listening on Reading Achievement." In "Vistas in Reading," ed. J. A. Figurel. *Proceedings of the International Reading Association,* 1966, **11(1),** 431-34.

Corle, C. G., and M. L. Coulter. *The Reading Arithmetic Skills Program—A Research Project in Reading and Arithmetic.* University Park, Penn.: The Pennsylvania School Study Council, 1964.

Crouse, Richard, and Denise Bassett. "Detective Stories: An Aid for Mathematics and Reading." *The Mathematics Teacher,* November 1975.

Dallmun, M., R. L. Rouch, L. Y. C. Char, and J. J. DeBoer. *The Teaching of Reading.* New York: Holt, Rinehart, & Winston, 1978.

Darrow, Helen Fisher, and Virgil Howes. *Approaches to Individualized Reading.* New York: Appleton Century Crofts, 1960.

DeBoer, John J., and Martha Dallman. *The Teaching of Reading.* New York: Holt, Rinehart, & Winston, 1970.

DeBono, Edward. *Children Solve Problems.* London: Penguin Education, 1973.

Dechant, E. *Diagnosis and Remediation of Reading Disability.* Englewood Cliffs, N.J.: Prentice-Hall, 1977.

———.*Improving the Teaching of Reading.* Englewood Cliffs, N.J.: Prentice-Hall, 1964.

DeLancey, R. W. "Awareness of Form Class as a Factor in Reading Comprehension." *University Microfilms* (Ann Arbor) *Dissertation Abstracts,* 1963, 23m 2975. (Abstract)

Della-Piana, G. *Reading Diagnosis and Prescription.* New York: Holt, Rinehart, & Winston, 1968.

Denslow, O. D. "Vocabulary and Sentence Study of Eight First Grade Science Books." *Elementary English,* 1961, **38,** 487-90.

Dreher, B. B., and C. C. Gervese. *Phonetics.* Dubuque, Iowa: Kendall/Hunt, 1976.

Dulin, Kenneth L. "Teaching and Evaluating Reading in the Content Areas." In *Views on Elementary Reading Instruction,* eds. Thomas Barrett and Dale Johnson. Newark, Del.: International Reading Association, 1973.

Dunne, Hope W. *The Art of Teaching Reading: A Language and Self-Concept Approach.* Columbus, Ohio: Merrill, 1972.

Durkin, Dolores. *Strategies for Identifying Words.* Boston: Allyn & Bacon, 1976.

———.*Teaching Them to Read.* Boston: Allyn & Bacon, 1976.

———.*Teaching Young Children to Read.* Boston: Allyn & Bacon, 1976.

Earle, Richard A. *Teaching Reading and Mathematics.* Newark, Del.: International Reading Association, 1976.

Earp, N. Wesley. "Procedures for Teaching Reading in Mathematics." *Arithmetic Teacher,* 1970, **17,** 575-79.

Ekwall, E. E. *Diagnosis and Remediation of the Disabled Reader.* Boston: Allyn & Bacon, 1976.

———.*Locating and Correcting Reading Difficulties,* 2nd ed. Columbus, Ohio: Merrill, 1977.

Emans, R. "What Do Children in the Inner City Like to Read?" *Elementary English,* 1968, **69,** 118-22.

ERIC. RCS Report. "Content Reading in the Elementary Grades." *Language Arts,* September 1975, pp. 802-7.

Estes T. H., and J. L. Vaughn. *Reading and Learning in the Content Classroom.* Boston: Allyn & Bacon, 1978.

Evans, Dean. "Individualized Reading—Myths and Facts." In *Teaching Reading: Selected Materials,* ed. Walter B. Barbe. New York: Oxford University Press, 1965.

Farr, R. *Measurement and Evaluation of Reading.* New York: Harcourt Brace Jovanovich, 1970.

Fay, L. "Reading Study Skills: Math and Science." In "Reading and Inquiry," ed. J. A. Figurel, *Proceedings of the Tenth Annual Convention of the International Reading Association,* 1965, **10**, 92-94.

Fernald, G. *Remedial Techniques in Basic School Subjects.* New York: McGraw-Hill, 1943.

Fietelson, Dina. *Cross Cultural Perspectives on Reading Research.* Newark, Del.: International Reading Association, 1978.

Figurel, J. A. *Reading Goals for the Disadvantaged.* Newark, Del.: International Reading Association, 1972.

Frankel, J. C. "Reading Skills through Social Studies Content and Student Involvement." *Journal of Reading,* October 1974, pp. 23-26.

Fry, E. *Elementary Reading Instruction.* New York: McGraw-Hill, 1977.

_____."The Readability Principle." *Language Arts,* September 1975, p. 847.

Furth, H. *Piaget for Teachers.* Englewood Cliffs, N.J.: Prentice-Hall, 1970.

Garland, Colden. *Developing Confidence in Teaching Reading.* Dubuque, Iowa: William C. Brown, 1978.

Gilmary, Sister. "Transfer Effects of Reading Remediation to Arithmetic Computation when Intelligence Is Controlled and All Other School Factors Are Eliminated." *Arithmetic Teacher,* 1967, **14**, 17-20.

Goldsmith, A. O. "Comprehensibility of Initials in Headlines." *Journalism Quarterly,* 1958, **35**, 212-15.

Goodman, K. S. "Reading: A Psycholinguistic Guessing Game. *Journal of the Reading Specialist,* 4 (May 1967), 126-35.

Goodman, K. S., and Fleming, J. T., eds. *Psycholinguistics and the Teaching of Reading.* Newark, Del.: International Reading Association, 1968.

Goodman, Yetta M., and Carolyn Burke. *Reading Miscue Inventory Manual.* New York: Macmillan, 1972. See also Laura A. Smith and Margaret Lindberg, "Building Instructional Materials." In *Miscue Analysis,* ed. Kenneth S. Goodman. Urbana, Ill.: National Council of Teachers of English, 1973, pp. 77-96.

Griese, A. A. *Do You Read Me? Practical Approaches to Teaching Reading Comprehension.* Santa Monica, Calif.: Goodyear, 1977.

Guszak, Fran J. *Diagnostic Reading Instruction in the Elementary School.* New York: Harper & Row, 1972.

_____."Teacher Questioning and Reading." *The Reading Teacher,* 1967, **21**, 227-34.

Hall, Mary Ann. *Teaching Reading as a Language Experience.* Columbus, Ohio: Merrill, 1970.

Harper, R. J. C. "Reading and Arithmetic Reasonings: A Partial Correlation and Multiple Regression Analysis." *Alberta Journal of Educational Research,* 1957, **3**, 87-86.

Harris, Albert J. "Influences of Individual Differences on the Reading Program." In *Meeting Individual Differences in Reading,* ed. H. Alan Robinson. Chicago: University of Chicago Press, December 1964.

Harris, L. A., and C. B. Smith. *Reading Instruction.* New York: Holt, Rinehart, & Winston, 1976.

Haskins, J. B. "Headline-and-Lead Scanning vs. Whole-Item Reading in Newspaper Content Analysis." *Journalism Quarterly,* 1966, **43**, 333-35.

Havighurst, Robert J. "Characteristics and Needs of Students that Affect Learning." In *Meeting Individual Differences in Reading,* ed. H. Alan Robinson. Chicago: University of Chicago Press, December 1964.

Heilman, A. W. *Phonics in Proper Perspective.* Columbus, Ohio: Merrill, 1976.

_____.*Principles and Practices of Teaching Reading.* Columbus, Ohio: Merrill, 1977.

Henderson, Richard L. and Donald Ross Green. *Reading for Meaning in the Elementary School.* Englewood Cliffs, N.J.: Prentice-Hall, 1969.

Herber, H. L. "An Experiment in Teaching Reading through Social Studies Content." In "Changing Concepts of Reading Instruction," ed. J. A. Figurel. *Proceedings of the International Reading Association,* 1961, **6**, 122-24.

_____."Reading Instruction in Content Areas: An Overview." *Research in Reading in Content Areas.* Englewood Cliffs, N.J.: Prentice-Hall, 1970.

_____.*Teaching Reading in Content Areas.* Englewood Cliffs, N.J.: Prentice-Hall, 1970.

Herrick, Virgil. *The Elementary School.* Englewood Cliffs, N.J.: Prentice Hall, 1965.

Hillcrich, R. L. *Reading Fundamentals for Preschool and Primary Children.* Columbus, Ohio: Merrill, 1977.

Holquin, Leonard. *Shuck Loves Chirley.* San Francisco: Golden West Press, 1975.

Holt, John. *What Do I Do Monday?* New York: E. P. Dutton, 1970.

Howes, V. M. *Individualizing Instruction in Reading and Social Studies.* New York: Macmillan, 1970.

Hull, M. A. *Phonics for the Teacher of Reading.* Columbus, Ohio: Merrill, 1976.

Hunter, William A. *Multicultural Education through Competency Based Teacher Education.* Washington, D.C.: American Association of Colleges for Teacher Education, 1974.

Irish, Elizabeth H. "The Readability of Mathematics Books." *Arithmetic Teacher,* 1964, **II**, 169-75.

Jantz, Richard K., and Trudi A. Fulda. "The Role of Moral Education in the Public Elementary School." *Social Education,* January 1975, **39**, 24-28.

Jenkinson, Marion D. "The Roles of Motivation in Reading." In *Meeting Individual Differences in Reading,* ed. H. Alan Robinson. Chicago: University of Chicago Press, 1964.

Jensen, Linda R. "Using Creativity in Elementary School Mathematics." *Arithmetic Teacher,* March 1976, pp. 210-15.

Johnson, D. D., and P. D. Pearson. *Teaching Reading Vocabulary.* New York: Holt, Rinehart, & Winston, 1978.

Johnson, Lois V. "Children's Newspaper Reading." *Elementary English,* 1963, **40**, 428-32, 444.

Jordan, D. R. *Dyslexia in the Classroom.* Columbus, Ohio: Merrill, 1977.

Karlin, Robert. *Perspectives in Elementary Reading.* New York: Harcourt Brace Jovanovich, 1973.

——.*Teaching Elementary Reading: Principles and Strategies.* New York: Harcourt Brace Jovanovich, 1971.

Kennedy, E. C. *Classroom Approaches to Remedial Reading,* 2nd ed. Itasca, Ill.: Peacock, 1977.

Kirk, Samuel A., James J. McCarthy, and Winifred D. Kirk. *Examiner's Manual, Illinois Test of Psycholinguistic Abilities,* rev. ed. Urbana, Ill.: University of Illinois Press, 1968.

Kohl, Herbert. *The Open Classroom.* New York: Random House, 1970.

——.*36 Children.* New York: New American Library, 1968.

Lamb, P. *Linguistics in Proper Perspective,* 2nd ed. Columbus, Ohio: Merrill, 1977.

Lamb, P., and R. Arnold. *Reading: Foundations and Instructional Strategies.* Belmont, Calif.: Wadsworth, 1976.

LaPray, Margaret. *Teaching Children to Become Independent Readers.* New York: Center for Applied Research in Education, 1972.

Lees, Fred. "Mathematics and Reading." *Journal of Reading,* May 1976.

Lefevre, C. *Linguistics and the Teaching of Reading.* New York: McGraw-Hill, 1964.

Levine, Isidore N. "Solving Reading Problems in Vocational Subjects." *High Points,* April 1969, **12**, 10-27.

Lucas, Stephen B., and Andrew A. Burland. "The New Science Methods and Reading." *Language Arts,* 1975, **52**, 769-70.

Lunstrum, John P. "Readings in the Social Studies: A Preliminary Analysis of Recent Research." *Social Education,* January 1976, pp. 10-18.

Mager, Robert F. *Preparing Instructional Objectives.* Palo Alto, Calif.: Fearon, 1962.

Mallinson, G. G., H. E. Sturm, and Lois M. Mallinson. "The Reading Difficulty of Textbooks in Junior High School Science." *School Review,* 1950, **58**, 536-40.

Mallinson, G. G., H. E. Sturm, and R. E. Patton. "The Reading Difficulty of Textbooks in Elementary Science." *Elementary School Journal,* 1950, **50**, 460-63.

Marturano, Arlend. "Reading the Future." *Science and Children,* April 1976, No. **13**, p. 46.

Mazurkiewiez, A. J. *Teaching about Phonics.* New York: St. Martin's, 1976.

McCullough, Barbara, and Gene Towery. "Your Horoscope Predicts: You Can Teach Students to Follow Directions." *Journal of Reading,* May 1976, p. 653.

Miller, W. *The First R, Elementary Reading Today.* New York: Holt, Rinehart, & Winston, 1977.

Mohan, Madan. "Motivational Procedures in the Individualization of Instruction." *Summer Workshop in Individualization of Instruction, 1970.* Fredonia, N.Y.: Teachers Education Research Center, State University College.

Neill, A. S. *Freedom—Not License!* New York: Hart Publishing Co., 1966.

Newport, J. F. "The Readability of Science Textbooks for Elementary Schools." *Elementary School Journal,* 1965, **66**, 40-43.

Odell, Lee. "Teaching Reading: An Alternative Approach." *English Journal,* March 1973, pp. 454-58.

Osgood, Charles E., George S. Suci, and Percy H. Tannenbaum. *The Measurement of Meaning.* Urbana: University of Illinois Press, 1957.

Otto, W., C. W. Peters, and N. Peters. *Reading Problems: A Multidisciplinary Perspective.* Reading, Mass.: Addison-Wesley, 1977.

Palmer, William S. "CONPASS: Social Studies: Suggestions for Improvement." *Journal of Reading,* April 1973, pp. 529-38.

——."Teaching Reading in Content Areas." *Journal of Reading,* October 1975.

Patlak, Sanford. "Physical Education and Reading: Questions and Answers." In *Fusing Reading Skills and Content,* eds. H. Alan Robinson and Ellen Lamar Thomas. Newark, Del.: International Reading Association, 1969, pp. 81-88, 201-4.

Payne, Joseph N. (ed.) *Mathematics Learning in Early Childhood.* Reston, Va.: The National Council of Teachers of Mathematics, 1975.

Peal, E., and W. Lambert. "The Relationship of Bilingualism to Intelligence." *Psychology Monographs: General and Applied,* **76**, 1-23, Washington, D.C.: American Psychological Association, 1962.

Petty, W. T., C. P. Herold, and Earline Stoll. "The State of Knowledge about the Teaching Vocabulary." Champaign, Ill.: National Council of Teachers of English, 1968.

Phillips, Darrell G. "Piagetian Perspectives on Science Teaching." *The Science Teacher,* February 1976, **43**, 30-31.

Piaget, J. "How Children Form Mathematical Concepts." *Scientific American,* 1953, **189**, 74-79.

——.*The Moral Judgment of the Child.* New York: Free Press, 1965.

Piaget, J., and Bärbel Inhelder. *The Psychology of the Child.* New York: Basic Books, 1969.

Piercey, **Dorothy.** *Reading Activities in Content Areas: An Ideabook for Middle and Secondary Schools.* Boston: Allyn & Bacon, 1976.

Popham, **W. J., and T. R. Husek.** "Implications of Criterion Referenced Measurement." *Journal of Educational Measurement,* 6(1969), 1-9.

Popham, **W. J. and E. L. Baker.** *Systematic Instruction.* Englewood Cliffs, N.J.: Prentice-Hall, 1970.

Postman, **Neil.** "The Politics of Reading." In *The Politics of Reading: Point-Counterpoint,* ed. Sister R. Winkeljohann. Newark, Del.: International Reading Association, 1973.

Potter, **T. C.** *Taxonomy of Cloze Research, Part I, Readability and Reading Comprehension.* Inglewood, Calif.: Southwest Regional Laboratory, 1968.

Pulaski, **Mary Ann Spencer.** *Understanding Piaget.* New York: Harper and Row, 1971.

Quandt, **I. J.** *Teaching Reading: A Human Process.* Chicago: Rand-McNally, 1977.

Ransbury, **Molly K.** "An Assessment of Reading Attitude." *Journal of Reading,* October 1973, **17,** 25-38.

Renner, **John W., and others.** "An Evaluation of the Science Curriculum Improvement Study." *School Science and Math,* March 1976, pp. 203-6.

Robinett, **R. R.** "Linguistic Approaches for the Bilingual." *Perspectives in Reading: First Grade Reading Programs.* Newark, Del.: International Reading Association, 1965.

Robinson, **Francis P.** *Effective Study.* New York: Harper and Row, 1946.

Robinson, **H. Alan.** "Reading Skills Employed in Solving Social Studies Problems." *The Reading Teacher,* 1965, **19,** 263-69.

_____.*Teaching Reading and Study Strategies: The Content Areas.* Boston: Allyn & Bacon, 1975.

Robinson, **H. Alan, Ellen Lamar Thomas, and others.** *Fusing Reading Skills and Content.* Newark, Del.: International Reading Association, 1969.

Rosenthal, **R.** *Pygmalion in the Classroom: Teacher Expectations and Pupil Intellectual Development.* New York: Holt, Rinehart, & Winston, 1968.

Ruddell, **R. B.** *Reading-Language Instruction: Innovative Practices.* Englewood Cliffs, N.J.: Prentice-Hall, 1974.

Rupley, **William H.** "Content Reading in the Elementary Grades." *Language Arts,* September 1975.

Russel, **David.** *Children Learn to Read.* New York: Ginnis, 1949.

Russel, **David, and E. E. Karp.** *Reading Aids Through Grades.* New York: Teachers College Press, 1970.

Sacks, **Norman P.** "Some Aspects of the Application of Linguistics to the Teaching of Modern Foreign Language." *Modern Language Journal,* 1964, **48,** 7-17.

Sargent, **Eileen E., Helen Huus, and O. Andersen.** In *How to Read a Book,* ed. C. T. Mangrum. Reading Aid Series. Newark, Del.: International Reading Association, 1970.

Sartain, **Harry W.** "Research on Individualized Reading." *In Teaching Reading: Selected Materials,* ed. Walter B. Barbe. New York: Oxford University Press, 1965.

Savage, **J. F., and J. F. Mooney.** *Teaching Reading to Children with Special Needs.* Boston: Allyn & Bacon, 1978.

Sennet, **T. B.** "The Interpretive Story as an Aid to Understanding News." *Journalism Quarterly,* 1954, **31,** 356-66.

Seymour, **Dorothy.** "Black English in the Classroom." *Today's Education,* February 1973, **62,** 63-64.

Shaver, **James R.** "Reading and Controversial Issues." In *A New Look at Reading in the Social Studies,* ed. Ralph Preston. Newark, Del.: International Reading Association, 1969.

Shepherd, **David.** "Reading in the Subject Areas," *Reading for All.* Newark, Del.: International Reading Association, 1973.

Shores, **J. H.** "Reading of Science for Two Separate Purposes as Perceived by Sixth Grade Students and Able Adult Readers." *Elementary English,* 1960, **37,** 461-68.

Silvaroli, **N. J., and W. H. Wheelock.** *Teaching Reading, A Decision-Making Process.* Dubuque, Iowa: Kendal-Hunt, 1975.

Simons, **H. D.** "Black Dialect & Learning to Read." In *Literacy for Diverse Learners,* ed. J. L. Johns. Newark, Del.: International Reading Association, 1974, 3-13.

Singer, **Harry, and Robert B. Ruddell.** *Theoretical Models and Processes of Reading.* Newark, Del.: International Reading Association, 1970.

Smith, **E. Brocks, Kenneth S. Goodman, and Robert Meredith.** *Language and Thinking in the Elementary School.* New York: Holt, Rinehart, & Winston, 1970.

Smith, **Nila Banton.** "Patterns of Writing in Different Subject Areas." *Journal of Reading,* October 1964.

_____.*Reading Instruction for Today's Children.* Englewood Cliffs, N.J.: Prentice-Hall, 1963.

Sochor, **Elona E.** "Literal and Critical Reading in Social Studies." *Journal of Experimental Education,* 1958, **27,** 46-56.

Spache, **E. B.** *Reading Activities for Child Involvement.* Boston: Allyn & Bacon, 1976.

Spache, **G. D.** *Diagnosing and Correcting Reading Disabilities.* Boston: Allyn & Bacon, 1976.

Spache, **G. D., and E. B. Spache.** *Reading in the Elementary School,* 4th ed. Boston: Allyn & Bacon, 1977.

Stauffer, **Russell G.** *The Language-Experience Approach to the Teaching of Reading.* New York: Harper & Row, 1970.

_____.*Teaching Reading as a Thinking Process.* New York: Harper & Row, 1969.

Stewart, William A. "On the Use of Negro Dialect in the Teaching of Reading." In *Language Society and Education: A Profile of Black English,* ed. Johanna S. De Stefano. Worthington, Ohio: Charles A. Jones, 1973.

Strain, Lucille B. "Children's Literature: An Aid in Mathematics Instruction." *Arithmetic Teacher,* 1969, **16**, 451-55.

Strang, Ruth. *Diagnostic Teaching of Reading.* New York: McGraw-Hill, 1969.

Strang, Ruth, and Dorothy Kendall Bracken. *Making Better Readers.* Boston: D.C. Heath, 1957.

Strickland, Ruth. "The Language of Elementary School Children: Its Relationship to the Language of Reading Textbooks and to the Quality of Reading of Selected Children." *Bulletin of the School of Education,* Indiana University, 1962, **7(4)**.

Thelen, Judith. *Improving Reading in Science.* Newark, Del.: International Reading Association, 1975. Reading Aids Series.

Thomas, Ellen Lamar, and H. Alan Robinson. *Improving Reading in Every Class: A Sourcebook for Teachers.* Boston: Allyn & Bacon, 1972.

Tinker, Miles, and C. M. McCullough. *Teaching Elementary Reading.* New York: Appleton-Century-Crofts, 1968.

Tiro, Frank. "Reading Techniques in the Teaching of Music." In *Fusing Reading Skills and Content,* eds. H. Alan Robinson and Ellen Lamar Thomas. Newark, Del.: International Reading Association, 1969, 23-27.

Turner, Thomas H. "Making the Social Studies Textbooks a More Effective Tool for Less Able Readers." *Social Education,* January 1976, **40**, 38-41.

Wagner, L. D. "Measuring the Map-reading Ability of Sixth Grade Children" *Elementary School Journal,* 1953, **53**, 338-44.

Wallen, Carl Y. *Word Attack Skills in Reading.* Columbus, Ohio: Merrill, 1969.

Wilcox, W. "Numbers and the News: Graph, Table or Text?" *Journalism Quarterly,* 1964, **41**, 38-44.

Williams, D. L. "The Effect of Rewritten Science Textbook Materials on the Reading Ability of Sixth-Grade Pupils." Unpublished doctoral dissertation, University of Illinois, 1964.

Willmon, Betty. "Reading in the Content Area: A 'New Math' Terminology List for the Primary Grades." *Elementary English,* 1971, **48**, 463-71.

Wilson, R. M. *Diagnostic and Remedial Reading for Classroom and Clinic.* Columbus, Ohio: Merrill, 1977.

Wittick, Mildren Letton. "The Effects of Social and Emotional Problems on Reading." In *Meeting Individual Differences in Reading,* ed. H. Alan Robinson. Chicago: University of Chicago Press, December 1964.

Woods, M. L., and A. J. Mae. *Analytical Reading Inventory.* Columbus, Ohio: Merrill, 1977.

Zintz, Miles V. *The Reading Process, the Teacher and the Learner.* Dubuque, Iowa: William C. Brown, 1970.

Index